I0901172

IMAGES
of America

JEWS OF TAMPA

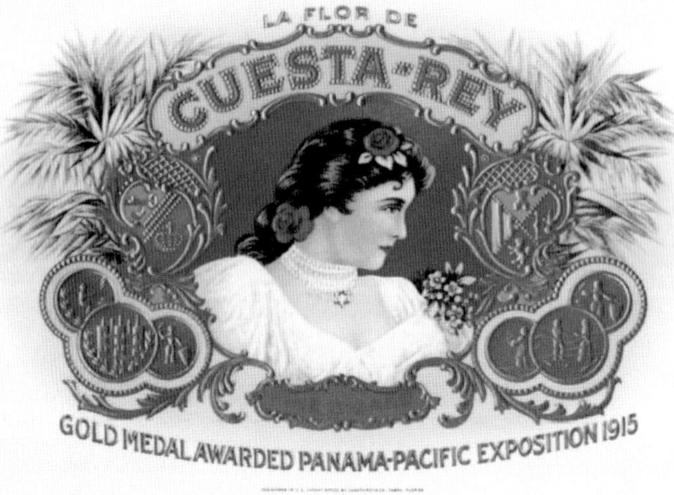

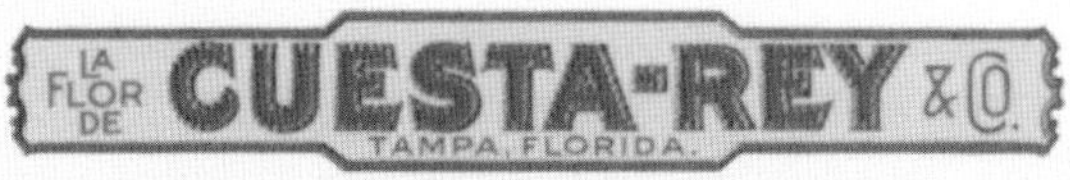

Cuesta-Rey Label from J.C. Newman Cigar Co. Cigar makers helped build Tampa. Between the 1880s and the 1920s, there were more than 300 fully operating cigar factories in Tampa, employing more than 13,000 workers as cigar rollers and tobacco strippers. A century later, following labor strikes, the Great Depression, two world wars, the Cuban embargo, and taxes, only one cigar factory remains. Tampa's celebrated heritage as the Fine Cigar Capital of the World lives on at J.C. Newman Cigar Company, the only surviving cigar factory operating in Ybor City. J.C. Newman, America's oldest family-owned premium cigar makers, began in Cleveland in 1895 and moved to Ybor City in 1954 to be closer to the primary source of tobacco, Cuba. The company moved into the vacated landmark Regensburg factory, built in 1910. The Cuesta-Rey brand, founded in 1884, sells its handmade cigars in 61 countries. The company was purchased by the Newmans in 1959. Note the Mogen David necklace on the woman in the label. (See also page 78.) (Courtesy of the Collections of the Jewish Museum of Florida, originated by Marcia Jo Zerivitz, founding executive director.)

On the Cover: Charter Members of Rodeph Sholom Ladies Auxiliary, August 14, 1917. The group was organized to preserve Jewish traditional values and heritage and to assist the congregation, primarily in raising funds. Shown here are, from left to right, (first row) Mrs. M. Ressler, Mrs. J. Leiter, Mrs. Louis Wohl, Mrs. A. Levine, Mrs. Julius Mairson, Mrs. Ralph Hershon, Paul Losner, Mrs. Max Argintar, Mrs. S. Argintar, Mrs. J. Gordon, and Mrs. L. Ginsburg; (second row) Mrs. Oscar Steinberg, Mrs. Morris Cracowaner, Mrs. A.N. Goldstein, Mrs. Weil, Mrs. Brodie, Mrs. J. Fleischman, Mrs. Elizabeth Lassman, Mrs. Henry Brash, Rabbi Ralph B. Hershon, Mrs. Herman Juster, Mrs. E.H. Steinberg, Mrs. David Kasriel, Mrs. Max Losner, and Mrs. S. Herscovitz. This photograph was featured in the Tishri/Heshvan 5740 (fall 1979) issue of *Women's League Outlook* in an article titled "Reprise . . . Ladies Auxiliary to Sophisticated Sisterhood," by Helene Wagenheim. (Courtesy of the Collections of the Jewish Museum of Florida, originated by Marcia Jo Zerivitz, founding executive director.)

IMAGES
of America

JEWS OF TAMPA

Dr. Rob Norman and Marcia Jo Zerivitz

ARCADIA
PUBLISHING

Copyright © 2013 by Dr. Rob Norman and Marcia Jo Zerivitz
ISBN 978-1-4671-1062-4

Published by Arcadia Publishing
Charleston, South Carolina

Printed in the United States of America

Library of Congress Control Number: 2013947703

For all general information, please contact Arcadia Publishing:
Telephone 843-853-2070
Fax 843-853-0044
E-mail sales@arcadiapublishing.com
For customer service and orders:
Toll-Free 1-888-313-2665

Visit us on the Internet at www.arcadiapublishing.com

This book is dedicated to the Jewish pioneers who contributed to the development of the Tampa community, maintained the traditions of our heritage, and preserved their family photographs, so that we can tell this story. May this be a lesson and an inspiration to the present generations to save and label photographs to continue the history. This documentation of our collective memory helps ensure Jewish continuity.

Contents

Acknowledgments

Jews of Tampa was written to document for present and future generations the stories of people who helped build the community. People *are* history. Their lives are inspirational, especially for young people.

Most of the contents of this book were gathered by Marcia Jo Zerivitz as she trekked around Florida during the 1980s, retrieving material evidence of Jewish life in Florida that had not previously been recorded or organized. As a result of the MOSAIC project, working with volunteers in communities around the state, including Tampa, the story emerged through oral histories, photographs, documents, and artifacts. It was a powerful grassroots effort that resulted in deep pride in this newfound history.

The Tampa Task Force had done a superb job in collecting items. MOSAIC evolved into the Jewish Museum of Florida on Miami Beach, which now has a collections and research center open to the public that documents the more than 250 years of Jewish life in Florida. Local communities, however, wanted more. Marcia Jo Zerivitz and Dr. Rob Norman partnered to continue the story of Jewish life in Tampa, involving yet more people in the process.

Thanks to the following for sharing our passion for telling and perfecting the story and/or for technical assistance: Mary Friedman Kramer, Dorothy "Dolly" Williams, Doris Rosenblatt, Rabbi Lazer Rivkin, Dr. Canter Brown Jr., Dr. Gary Mormino, Bernice Wolf at Rodeph Sholom, Dr. Carl Zielonka, staff at Hillsborough County Public Library System, Ibsen Morales, and Todd Bothel, registrar at the Jewish Museum of Florida.

All photographs are courtesy of the Collections of the Jewish Museum of Florida, originated by Marcia Jo Zerivitz, founding executive director, unless otherwise noted in the caption. The following sources of photographs are indicated by their abbreviations: Tampa-Hillsborough County Public Library System (HCPL); State Library and Archives of Florida, Florida Memory Project (FSA); Tampa Bay History Center (TBHC); and University of Florida George Smathers Library & Digital Archives (UF).

INTRODUCTION

The Spanish explorer Juan Ponce de Leon discovered Florida 500 years ago. He first landed on Florida's east coast in 1513 and named the area La Florida in tribute to the beauty of the lands. In 1521, he sailed again and arrived in Tampa Bay. For 250 years, only Catholics could live in Florida. In the Treaty of Paris (1763), Britain got possession of Florida and people other than Catholics were allowed to settle there, including Jews. The first Jews resided in Florida in 1763, in Pensacola.

Tampa had its origin in 1824, when Fort Brooke was erected to keep watch on the Seminole Indians. Jewish peddlers and merchants came and went as the economic opportunities intermittently opened up and weakened. There were about 100 Jews across Florida at the time of statehood in 1845.

Probably the first permanent Jewish settler in the Tampa area was Emaline Ouentz Miley in 1844. She had 12 children, operated citrus groves, and died there in 1907. It appears that Max and Fishel White were among Tampa's first Jewish merchants. They operated a gentlemen's furnishing store at Washington and Marion Streets in 1858. After the Civil War, Jews arrived in a series of waves. Their entrepreneurial spirit helped to vitalize the area. In many cases, the Jews did not remain but moved on.

With the arrival of Henry Plant and his railroad in 1884 and the relocation of the cigar industry from Key West in 1886, Tampa became a center of growth. Glogowski, Maas, Brash, Oppenheimer, Falk, Wolf, Wohl, and Stein are some of the Jewish families, mostly German, who settled during this boom period. Romanian Isidor Kaunitz was the first Jewish merchant in multiethnic Ybor City, which was so welcoming that at one time there were more than 80 Jewish businesses there.

The Maas family opened its first store in Tampa in 1886, marking the beginning of one of the largest department store chains in Florida, which lasted 105 years. Jewish merchants participated in the economic growth of Tampa, opening many businesses.

Herman Glogowski, a Jew who served four terms as mayor, officiated at the cornerstone ceremony for the Tampa Bay Hotel, which opened in 1891. In 1894, thirty-one men and women met in the home of Moses Henry Cohen to organize Schaarai Zedek as an Orthodox congregation.

The Cuban War of Independence in 1898 brought prosperity to local businessmen. Relatives from Key West, Ocala, and Jacksonville, many of Romanian background, gravitated to Tampa. Max Argintar arrived in Tampa in 1902 and opened his store in 1908 in Ybor City. His son Sammie continued the 96-year-old operation in the same location.

The Orthodox faction of the Congregation Schaarai Zedek brought a lawsuit in 1902, charging "dirty tricks" on the part of the "Reformers" in an attempt to take control of the congregation and the building. As a result, Schaarai Zedek became Reform, and a new Orthodox congregation, Rodeph Sholom, was established.

Like other cities in the New South, after each war, Tampa benefited from the expansion. Also, like other cities, civic-minded Jewish immigrants became successful merchants and continued to play major roles in the development. There was not much evidence of antisemitism or discrimination, as in other areas of Florida. In Tampa, Jews were in the forefront of the economy. The opportunities afforded by the expansion eased resentment of jobs being taken by Jews, as was often experienced in other cities. Jews worked hard, cared about their city and the people, and were respected.

By the end of World War I, Tampa's Jewish community was the second largest in the state. Growth propelled the creation of new synagogues, expansion of religious schools, and inauguration of youth clubs and newspapers. Jews were active in civic affairs and held leadership positions. "Salty" Sol Fleischman, "the Dean of Florida's Sportscasters," broadcast almost every sports event in the area for more than 50 years.

With the advent of World War II, Tampa's shipyards and Air Force base increased activity, and local Jews joined the war effort. The Young Men's Hebrew Association, founded in 1906, became the Jewish Community Center after the war. Hadassah and Jewish fraternities were started in the 1930s. Rabbi David L. Zielonka served Congregation Schaarai Zedek from 1930 to 1970. He and Clarence Darrow joined with other religious leaders in 1931 in an interfaith debate. Post–World War II development and migration from the North spurred growth in the Jewish community.

During the 1950s and 1960s, the civil rights movement led to intense debate within the Jewish community, while Zionism received near-unanimous support. In 1954, the J.C. Newman Cigar Company bought a landmark factory and actively participated in the resurgence in cigar manufacturing. Today, it is the lone survivor of the industry that propelled the growth of Ybor City and Tampa.

Since Charles Slager's appointment as Tampa's postmaster in 1871, Jews have remained in the forefront of political life and have rallied to support civic and cultural causes. Harry Sandler served in the Florida legislature and then the 13th Judicial Circuit Court from 1932 until 1964. Dr. Richard Hodes was elected to the Florida House of Representatives in 1966, where he served for 16 years. Helen Gordon Davis, the first woman from Hillsborough County elected to state office, served in both the Florida House and Senate. Sandra Warshaw Freedman entered politics in 1974 as a city councilwoman and in 1986 was elected the first female mayor of Tampa.

Jerome Waterman played a major part in the growth of aviation in Tampa. The Tampa Jewish Community Council was formed in 1969. By the 1970s, the Jewish community dedicated new congregations, established Hillel Day School, and built facilities for the elderly. The *Jewish Floridian* made its Tampa debut in 1979; the local editor was Judy Rosenkranz. James Shimberg was inducted into the National Housing Hall of Fame in 1985. Native Tampa brothers Martin and Myron Uman have made significant contributions in science. In 1984, Leonard Levy was chair of the Super Bowl XVIII Task Force; in 1991, he served as cochair of Super Bowl XXV. Malcolm Glazer, who owns the NFL's Tampa Bay Buccaneers, in 2005 purchased the world's most popular soccer team, Manchester United, and he attracted the 2009 Super Bowl to Tampa.

In 1995, the Jewish Community Center and the Jewish Federation merged on the 21-acre campus that also houses the Weinberg Village Senior Residences. A second campus in South Tampa is being planned by the JCC-Federation. Karen and Jim Dawkins established the *Jewish Press of Tampa* in 1988. Current area congregations include Schaarai Zedek (Reform), Beth Am (Reform), Rodeph Sholom (Conservative), Kol Ami (Conservative), Chabad Lubavitch (Orthodox), Bais Tefilah (Orthodox), Temple David (Orthodox), Young Israel (Orthodox), Beth Israel of Sun City (Reform), Beth Shalom of Brandon (Reform), and Or Ahavah (Jewish Renewal). Jewish community life is enriched with Hillel at the University of South Florida, a day school, two *mikvaot* (ritual baths), and branches of national Jewish and Zionist organizations.

Many of the families who settled over a century ago are now in their fifth generation in Tampa. Today, the Jewish population is approximately 23,000. The Tampa Jewish community continues to expand its presence and leadership roles internally and throughout the region.

One

JEWISH PIONEERS

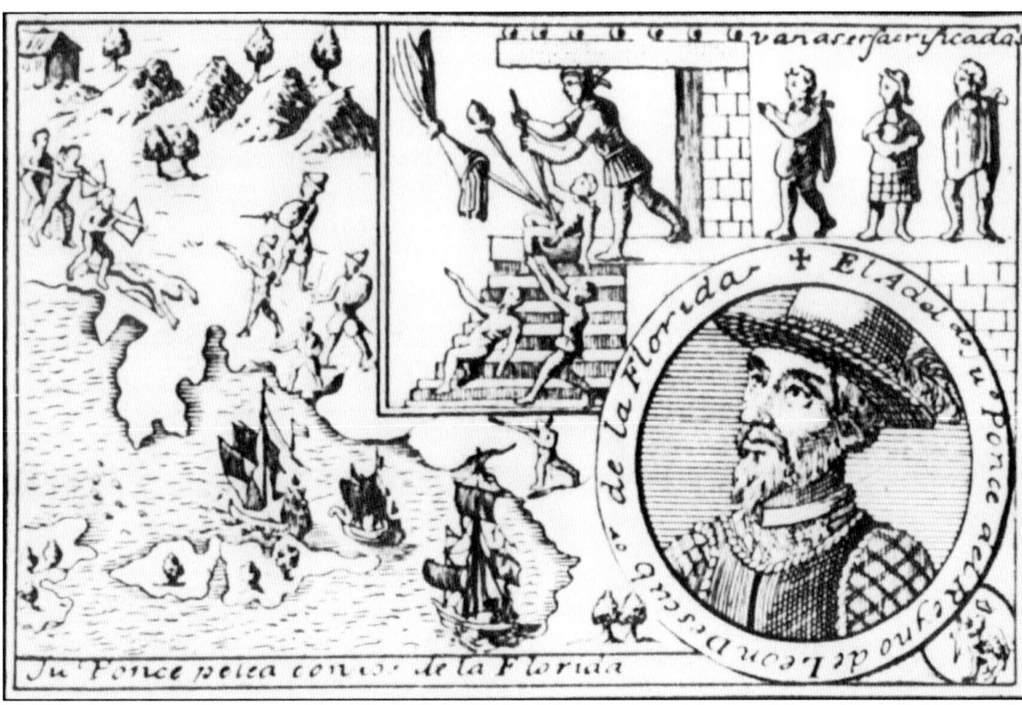

JUAN PONCE DE LEON. Juan Ponce de Leon arrived in Tampa Bay in 1521. He was followed by Panfilo de Narvaez in 1528 and Hernando de Soto in 1539. It is possible that conversos sailed with these Spanish explorers. During the Spanish Inquisition, Jews were required to convert to Catholicism, go into exile, or be killed. In their conversion, some secretly maintained their Jewish traditions and became conversos. For 250 years, only Catholics could live in Florida. (Courtesy of FSA.)

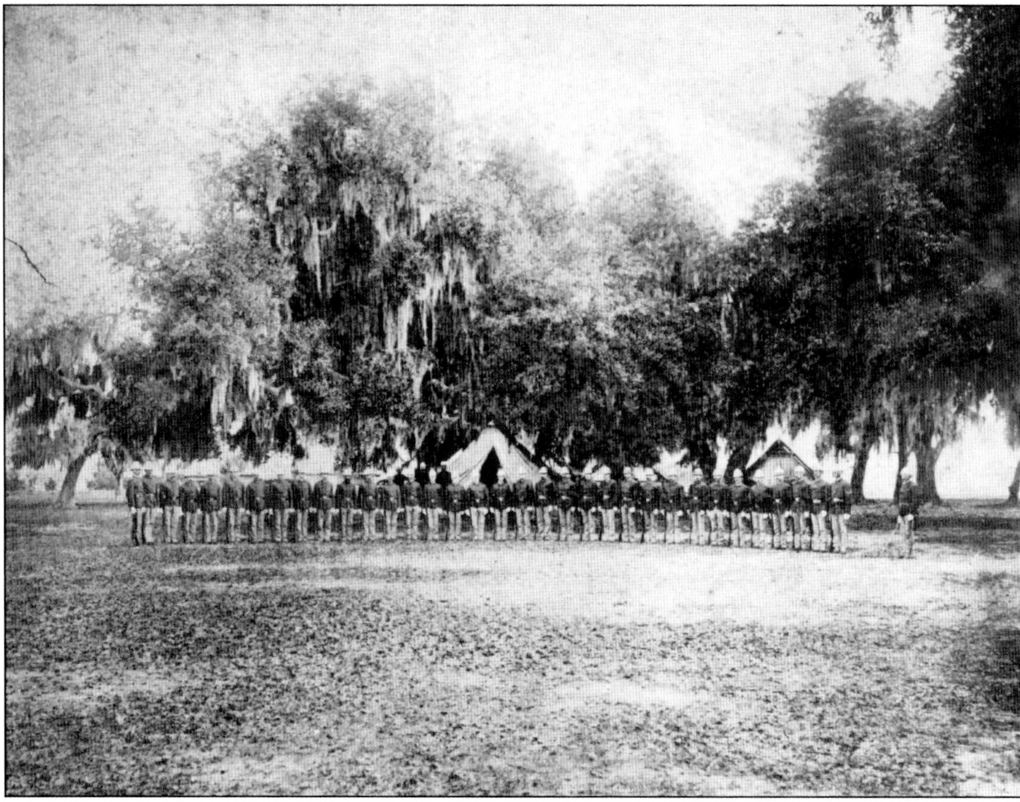

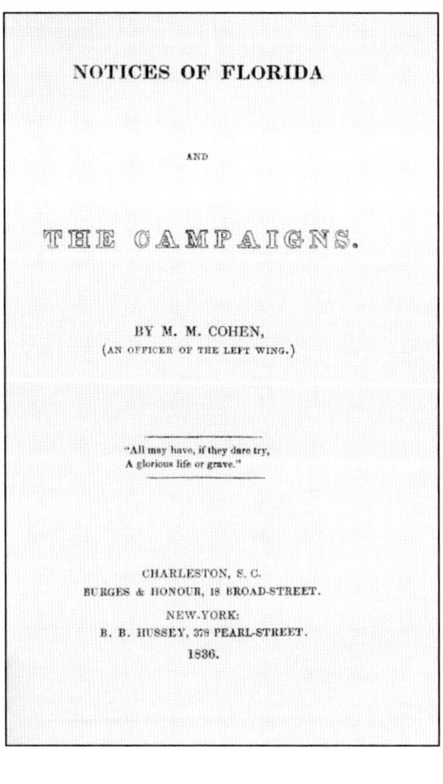

NOTICES OF FLORIDA

AND

THE CAMPAIGNS.

BY M. M. COHEN,
(AN OFFICER OF THE LEFT WING.)

"All may have, if they dare try,
A glorious life or grave."

CHARLESTON, S. C.
BURGES & HONOUR, 18 BROAD-STREET.
NEW-YORK:
B. B. HUSSEY, 378 PEARL-STREET.
1836.

FORT BROOKE, HEADQUARTERS FOR THE SECOND SEMINOLE WAR (1835–1842). This post was built on the Hillsborough River to contain the Indians. One Jew who served there was US Army lieutenant Meyer M. Cohen, who volunteered at the outbreak of the war. For five months, he made detailed notes, which he turned into one of the few books that provided an eyewitness account of the war. (Courtesy of HCPL.)

***NOTICES OF FLORIDA AND THE CAMPAIGNS*, 1836.** Following his service in the Second Seminole War, Meyer M. Cohen wrote a book about the conflict. In it, he described the history of Florida, the Seminole Indians, and the Army's efforts to engage and remove them. While using a liberal, romanticized prose style, the book does provide a detailed, in-depth account of the conflict.

EMALINE OUENTZ MILEY, FIRST KNOWN JEWISH SETTLER. At age 18, immigrant Emaline married William Miley, who was not Jewish, only after he agreed to sell his slaves. They arrived in Thonotosassa in 1844, cleared land, built a log cabin, and planted the area's first orange grove. Emaline survived the Indians, raised 12 children, and, after William's death, expanded the groves. She is buried in Thonotosassa, where there is a Miley Road. (Courtesy of Martha Parr's "Homesteading in Hillsborough County," *Sunland Tribune*, November 1941.)

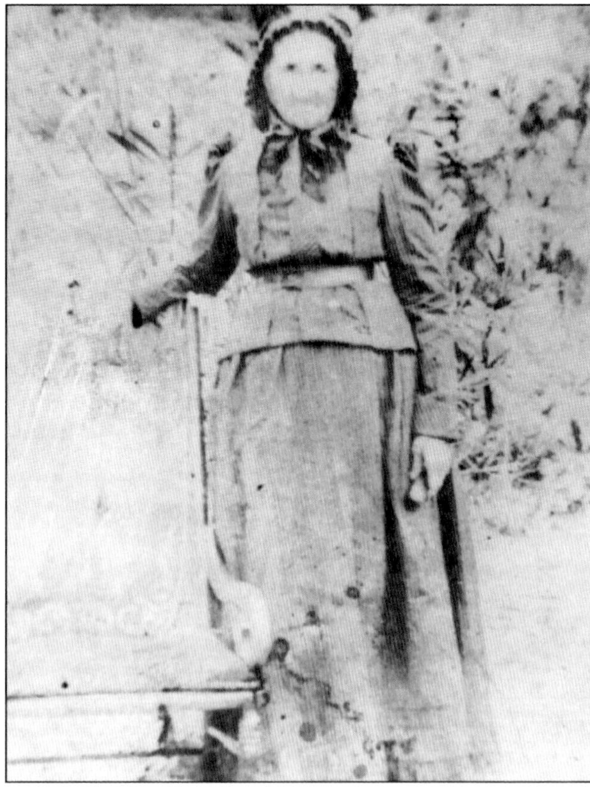

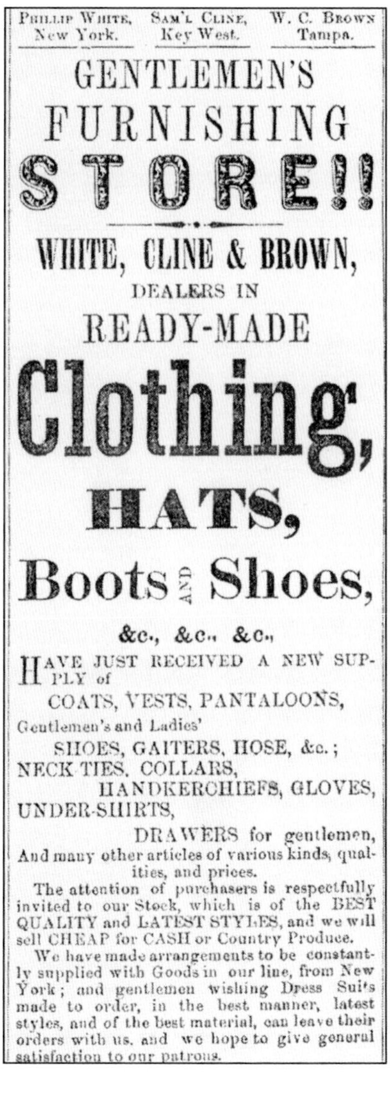

MAX WHITE STORE ADVERTISEMENT, 1860. Jewish merchants arrived before and after the Civil War. Attracted by the Florida frontier, Max White, Marcus Brendt, George Blum, David Kloppenburg, S. Sternberger, Gustave Lewinson, Edward Bettman, and Isidore Blumenthal were among those who came, some with wives, and opened stores. Polish immigrant Avraham Mordechai Weiss (Max White) arrived from Key West in 1858 and was a tailor in his uncle Fishel's business.

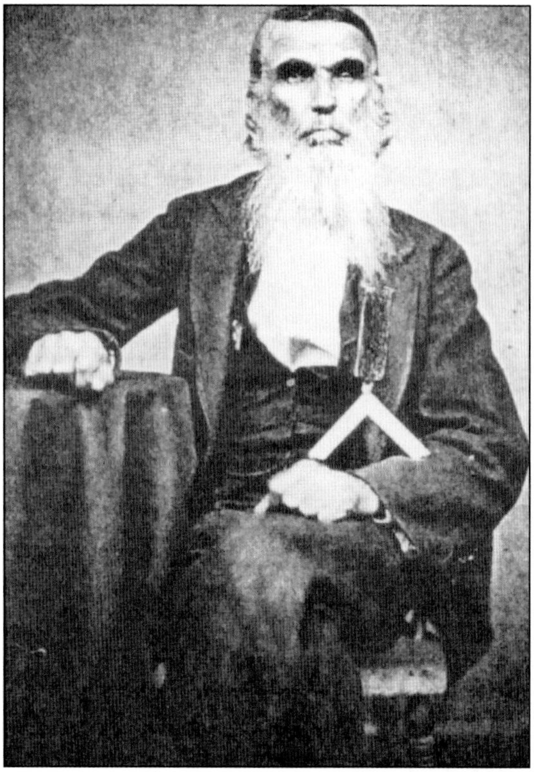

Charles Slager, First Jewish Politician, 1871. German immigrant Slager, who came to Florida in his 30s, was a leading merchant in Jacksonville. As economic conditions changed, Jews moved around the state. He and his wife, Nina, arrived in Tampa in 1870. Charles Slager, a merchant, joined the Masons, accepted appointment as Tampa postmaster, and later served as Hillsborough County sheriff and tax collector as well as serving on the school board.

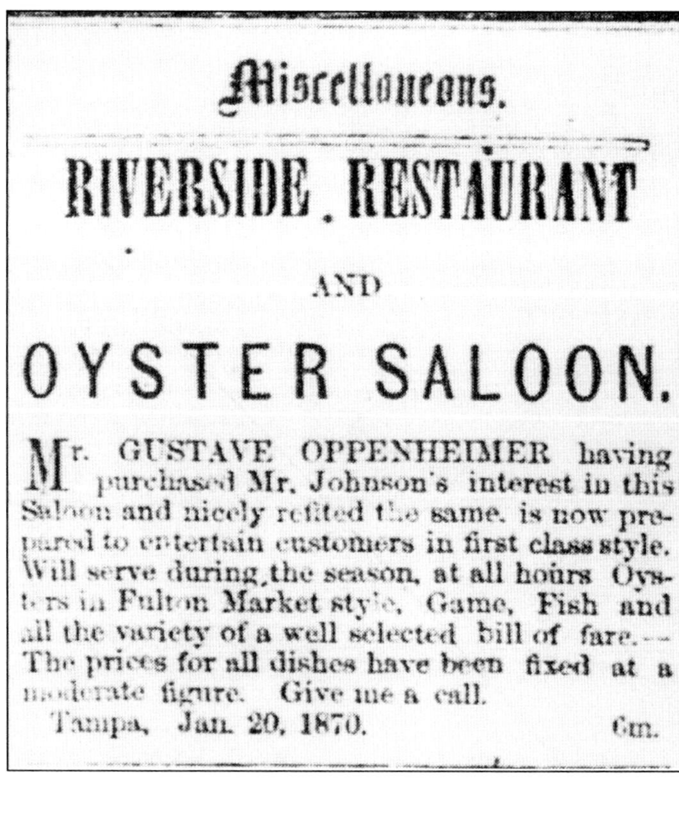

Miscelloneons.

RIVERSIDE RESTAURANT

AND

OYSTER SALOON.

MR. GUSTAVE OPPENHEIMER having purchased Mr. Johnson's interest in this Saloon and nicely refitted the same, is now prepared to entertain customers in first class style. Will serve during the season, at all hours Oysters in Fulton Market style, Game, Fish and all the variety of a well selected bill of fare.— The prices for all dishes have been fixed at a moderate figure. Give me a call.

Tampa, Jan. 20, 1870. 6m.

Riverside Restaurant and Oyster Saloon, 1870. Arriving on a steamer from New York, Gustave Oppenheimer brought vitality and style to the local business environment. According to the *Florida Peninsular,* Tampa's weekly newspaper published from 1855 to 1874, his restaurant was located on Water Street near the Hillsborough River ferry and offered "Fulton Market style" food. (Courtesy of UF.)

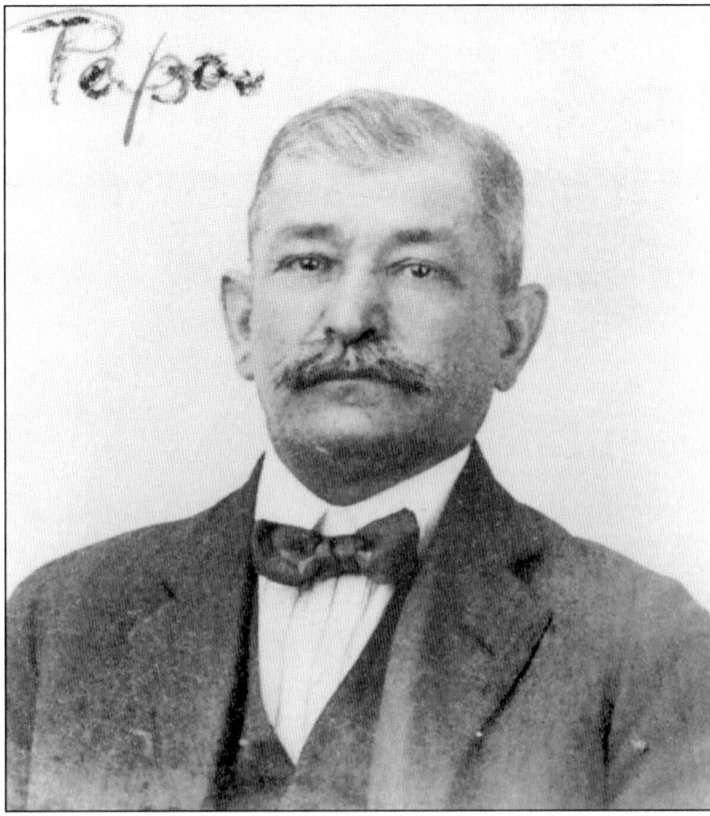

PHILIP DZIALYNSKI (1833–1896). Dzialynski arrived in Jacksonville from Prussia around 1853. He was the first member in what is considered to be the longest continuous Jewish family in Florida. He opened businesses in Madison, Bartow, Fort Meade, and, from 1879 to 1881, in Tampa, at the corner of Washington and Tampa Streets. In 1877, with others, he created the Tampa & Fort Meade Telegraph Company that helped link Tampa to the outside world.

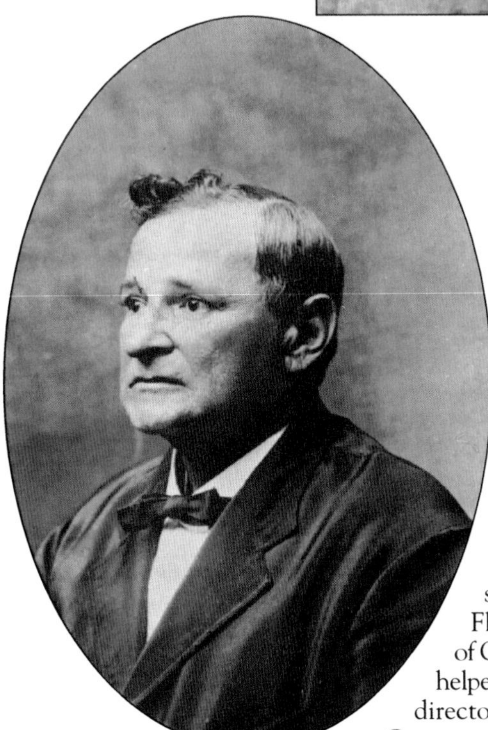

GEORGE DZIALYNSKI (1857–1937). In 1857, Philip Dzialynski and his wife, Ida Ehrlich, produced a son, George, the first-known Jewish boy born in Florida, in Jacksonville. George married Bertha Zadek of Gainesville in 1883. They moved to Tampa, where he helped operate his father's store and is listed in the 1899 city directory as a travel agent at 101 Horatio Street in Tampa. George carried a pocket watch with Hebrew numerals.

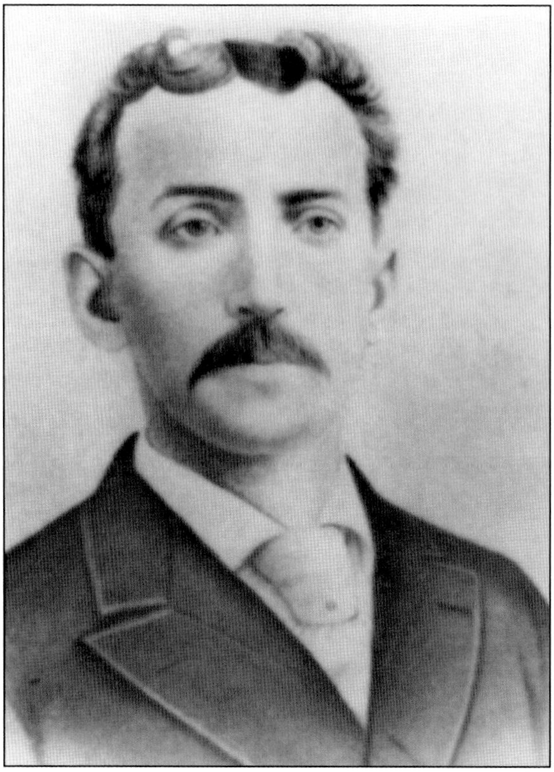

HERMAN GLOGOWSKI (1854–1909). German immigrant Glogowski married Bertha Brown of Gainesville in 1883. They moved to Tampa the next year, and he opened a clothing store. Glogowski had a talent for business and people and contributed to Tampa's civic and Jewish growth. Like other Jews, he became a leader in the Masons and was first president of the German-American Club. Active in the Tampa Board of Trade, he helped develop incentives to bring cigar factories to the area. (Courtesy of TBHC.)

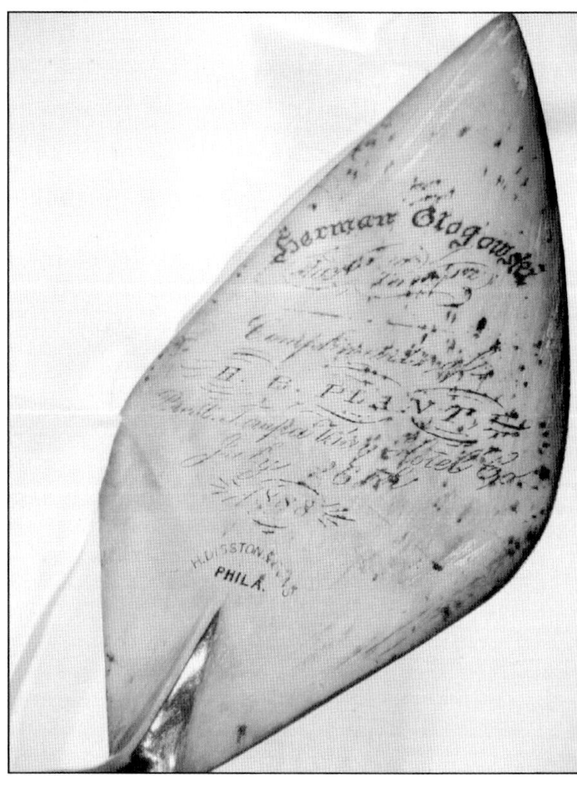

TROWEL USED IN TAMPA BAY HOTEL GROUND BREAKING, 1888. Glogowski served as municipal judge (1880–1886), then was elected mayor for four nonconsecutive terms (1886–1893), during which time he used this trowel in the ground breaking for Henry Plant's hotel. He led Tampa through its transitional and formative period, promoted private investment and development, improved public works and sanitation, and enhanced the fiscal stability of the city. Glogowski—president in 1898–1899 of Tampa's first Jewish congregation, Schaarai Zedek—laid the cornerstone for its building in 1899. (Courtesy of TBHC.)

Abe Maas (1855–1941). Maas, seen here around 1922, was a founding member of many charitable and civic groups in Tampa. He was a longtime leader of the Tampa Board of Trade and, as the founder of the Tampa Elks Lodge No. 708 in 1902, was known as "the father" of the lodge. A founder of Congregation Schaarai Zedek, Maas served as its president for 29 years.

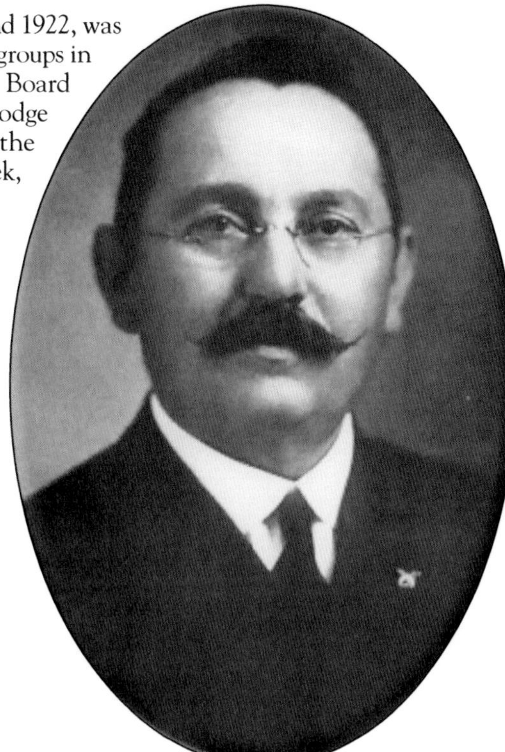

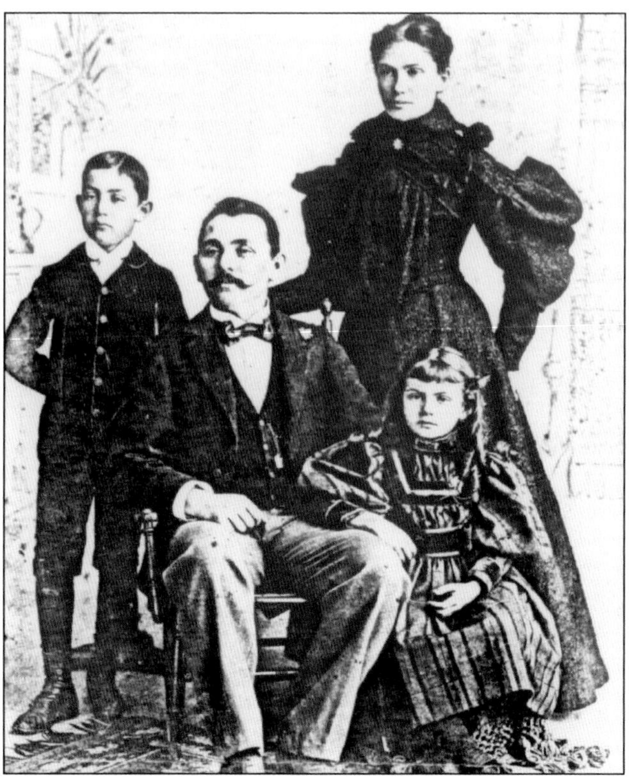

Abe and Bena Wolf Maas and Children, 1895. The Maas family came from Germany in the 1880s, moving first to Georgia and then to Florida. Abe arrived in Tampa in 1886 and opened his first store, marking the beginning of the more than 100-year history of one of the largest department store chains in Florida. As a pioneer for women's rights, Bena Maas was also a civic and Jewish leader. (See page 87.) The couple is seen here with their children, Sol (left) and Jessie.

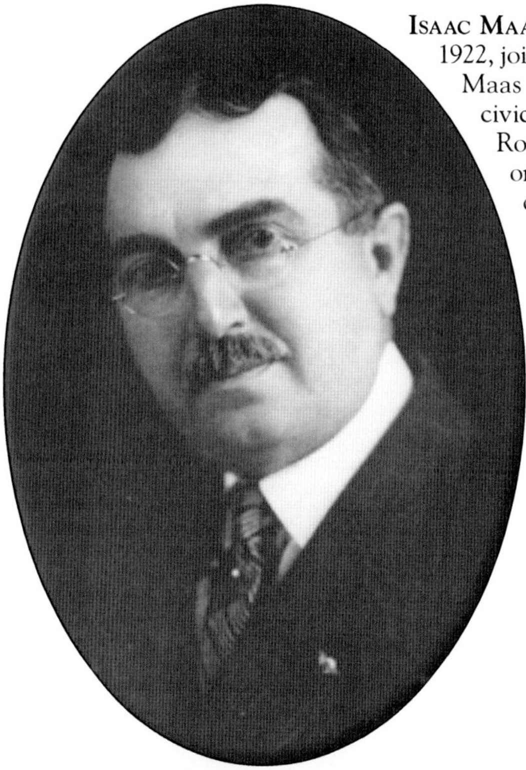

Isaac Maas (1851–1935). Isaac Maas, seen here around 1922, joined his brother Abe in Tampa in 1887, forming Maas Brothers. Isaac, the general manager, was a civic leader involved in the Shriners, Masons, Elks, Rotary, Tampa Yacht and Country Club, and other organizations. He was a leader in selling war bonds during World War I. He and his wife, Fanny, liked to travel and collect art.

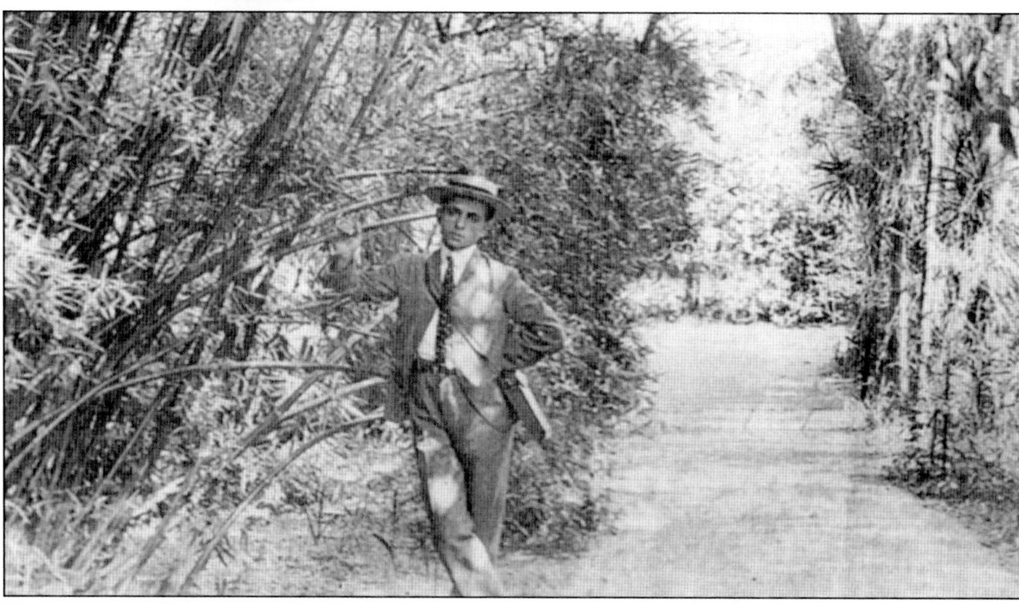

Ernest Maas (1880–1947). Abe and Isaac Maas brought cousin Ernest from Germany to Tampa in 1893 when he was 13 years old. He started as a porter in Maas Brothers. Upon learning to speak English, he became a buyer. Ernest, seen here around 1900, started a women's clothing store and, in 1937, joined other family members at Weil-Maas. He and his wife, Maude, had two children, Ernest Jr. and Audrey. Ernest was a founder of University of Tampa and first president of the Jewish Welfare Federation (1941–1945), which became the Federation.

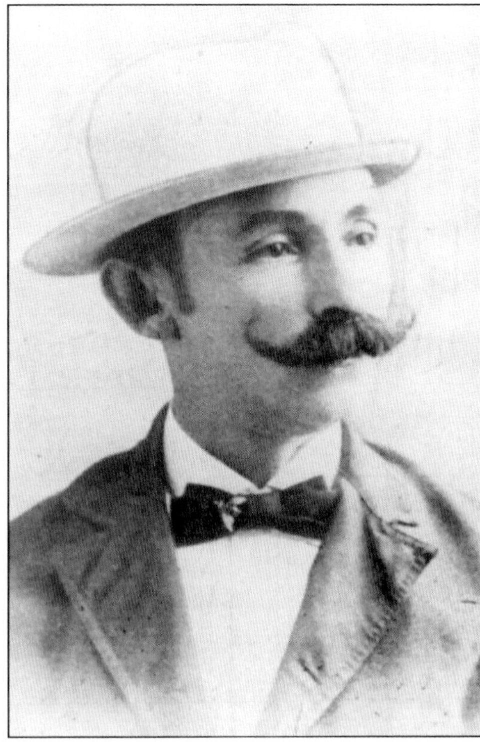

Isidor Kaunitz, 1891. A Romanian immigrant, Kaunitz was known for the white hat that he habitually wore. He named his store El Sombrero Blanco. He was the first Jewish merchant in Ybor City. As other Jewish immigrants arrived, they knew they could get employment from Kaunitz, who empathized with their struggles with antisemitism and knew many of their families from the "old country." (See page 67.)

Brash Family. This undated photograph shows Henry Brash (standing, center) with his unidentified family members. In 1870, German immigrant Henry Brash (1587–1928) came with his parents, Henrietta and Solomon, to Marianna, Florida. In 1879, Henry was elected as Marianna mayor, serving for three terms as Florida's earliest known Jewish mayor. In 1888, he married Sarah Zelnicker. They moved to Tampa in 1894 and raised five children: Alma, Florence, Isaac, Ruth, and Victor. Henry Brash was part of the group that formed Rodeph Sholom.

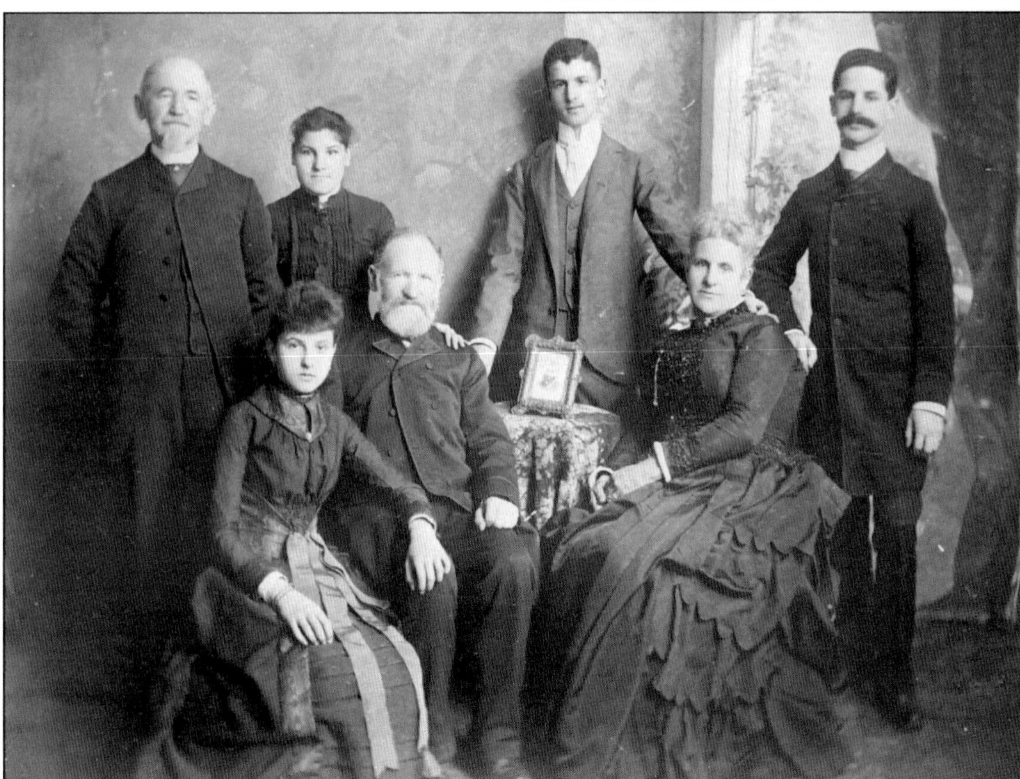

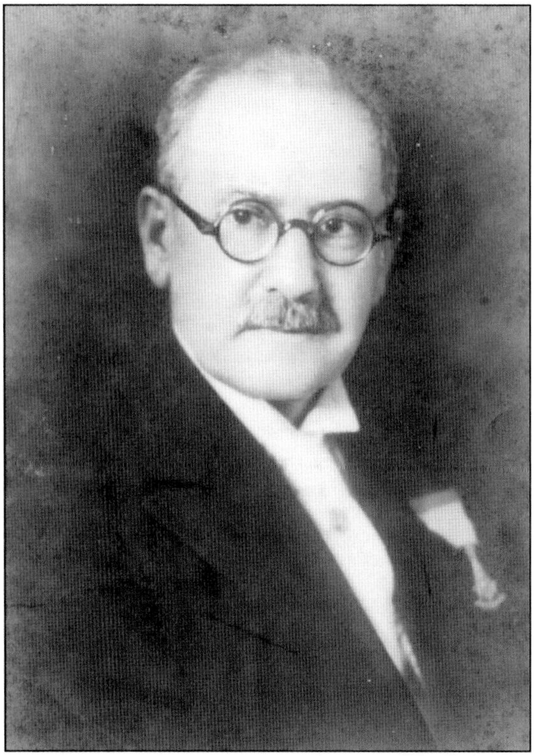

Dr. Louis Oppenheimer (1854–1939). Dr. Oppenheimer came to Tampa in 1895. He served as house physician for the Tampa Bay Hotel and performed operations by lamplight on his kitchen table. He did the city's first abdominal operation and invented many surgical procedures and instruments used today. His brochure touting Tampa as a health resort is considered the deciding factor for troop embarkation during the Spanish-American War. Practicing medicine and surgery in Florida for more than 50 years, he was president of the Hillsborough County Medical Society, which conferred on him its first Honorary Life Membership, as did the state medical association. He and his wife, Alberta, had seven children. His funeral was held on the day of a hurricane, and still, more than 2,000 attended to pay tribute to this man of intellect, musical and medical talent, civic contributions, and humanitarian spirit.

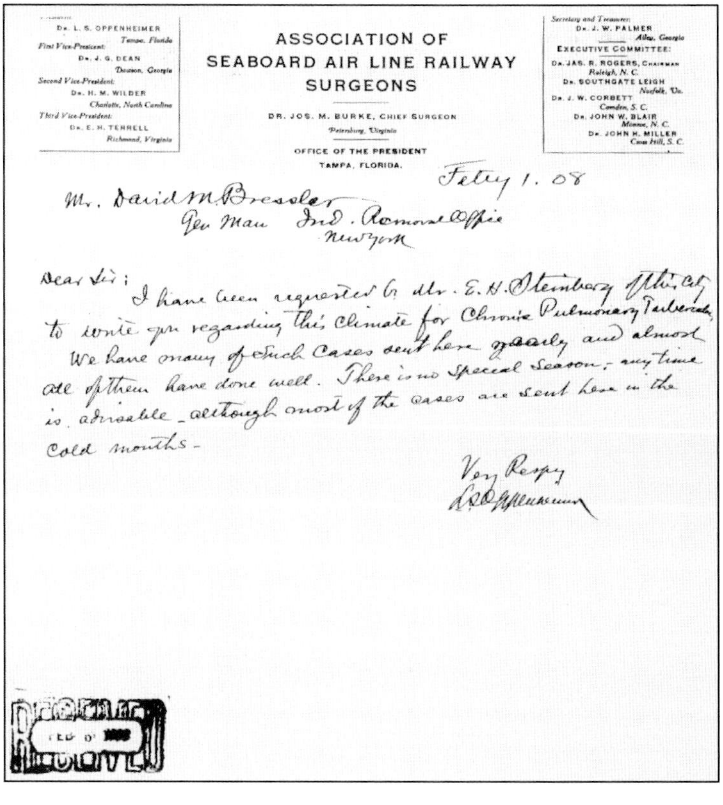

Dr. L. S. Oppenheimer, Tampa, Florida
First Vice-President: Dr. J. G. Dean, Dawson, Georgia
Second Vice-President: Dr. H. M. Wilder, Charlotte, North Carolina
Third Vice-President: Dr. E. H. Terrell, Richmond, Virginia

ASSOCIATION OF SEABOARD AIR LINE RAILWAY SURGEONS

DR. JOS. M. BURKE, CHIEF SURGEON, Petersburg, Virginia

OFFICE OF THE PRESIDENT
TAMPA, FLORIDA.

Secretary and Treasurer: Dr. J. W. Palmer, Ailey, Georgia
Executive Committee: Dr. Jas. R. Rogers, Chairman, Raleigh, N. C.; Dr. Southgate Leigh, Norfolk, Va.; Dr. J. W. Corbett, Camden, S. C.; Dr. John W. Blair, Monroe, N. C.; Dr. John H. Miller, Cross Hill, S. C.

Feby 1. 08

Mr. David M Bressler
Gen Man Ind. Removal Office
New York

Dear Sir;
I have been requested by Mr. E. H. Steinberg of this city to write you regarding this climate for Chronic Pulmonary Tuberculosis.
We have many of such cases sent here yearly and almost all of them have done well. There is no special season - any time is advisable - although most of the cases are sent here in the cold months -

Very Respy
L S Oppenheimer

Letter from Dr. Louis Oppenheimer, 1908. Dr. Oppenheimer expounds on Tampa's climate and its healing qualities for those suffering from chronic pulmonary tuberculosis.

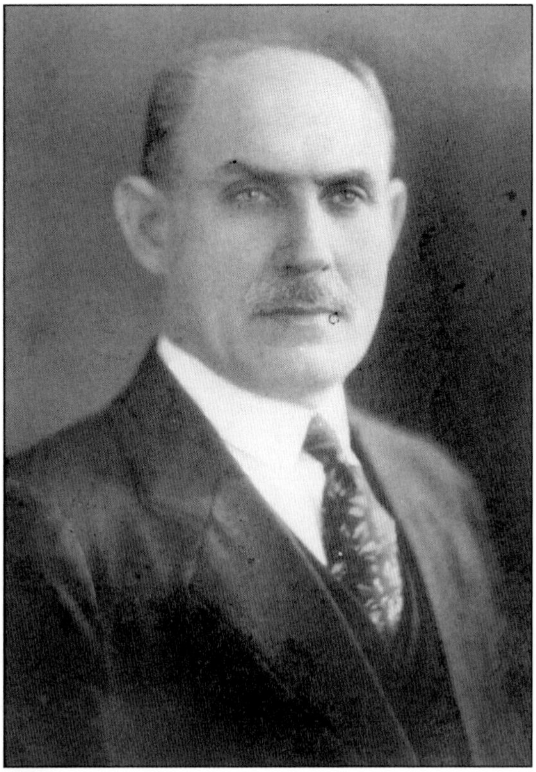

DAVID STEIN (1873–1956). Stein came to Tampa from Lithuania in 1901, worked in sales, and, in 1924, opened the Home Furniture Company in Ybor City. All of his children were in the furniture business. David was a dedicated volunteer in Jewish welfare organizations and in the larger community. Elected in 1925 as president of Congregation Rodeph Sholom, he served until 1947 and was then chosen honorary president for life.

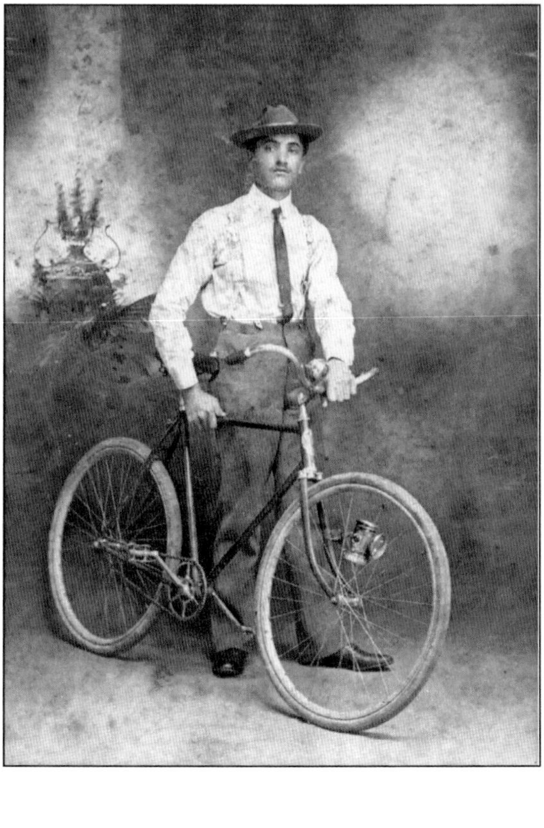

MAX ARGINTAR (1883–1964). In 1904, Romanian immigrant Max Argintar was the first in his family to arrive in Tampa. He got a job with Isidor Kaunitz, who had met him at his home in Romania. Argintar, seen here in 1902, opened his own store in Ybor City. In 1910, he visited *landsman* in Key West, where a *shiddach* was made with Annie Davis. Patriotic and civic-minded, the couple raised six children in Tampa. (See pages 68 and 123.)

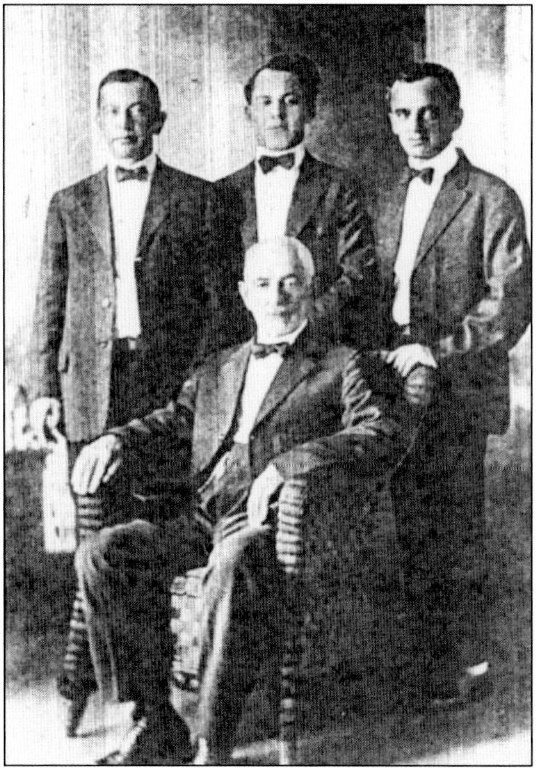

David L. Rippa. Romanian immigrants David Rippa and his wife, Toba, came to Key West in 1888. When the cigar industry declined there, they moved to Tampa. They were the parents of Harry, Della, Joe, Louis, Charlie, and Jack. Born in 1889, Jack was the only of their children born in the United States. At 17, Harry enlisted in the Spanish-American War. Seen here with David (seated) in 1917 are, from left to right, Harry, Joe, and Louis. (See page 66.)

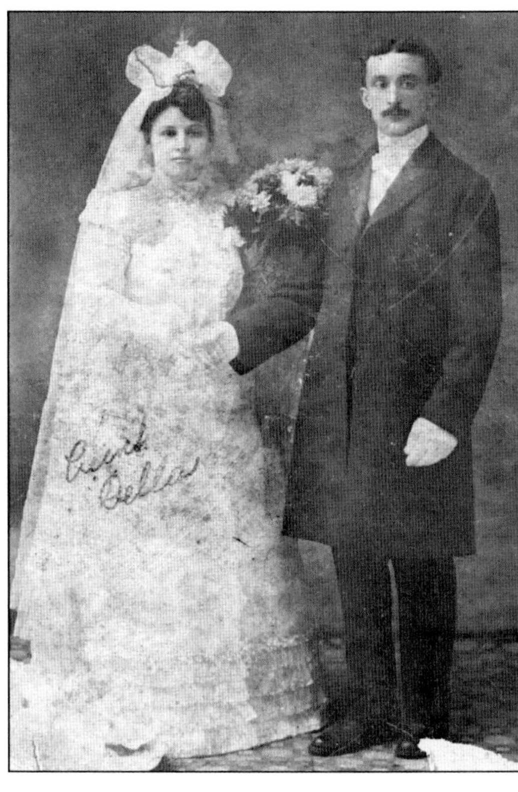

Wedding of Della Rippa, 1910. Della Rippa, the only daughter of Toba and David Rippa, married William Friedman, who was elected mayor of Dade City on December 17, 1926.

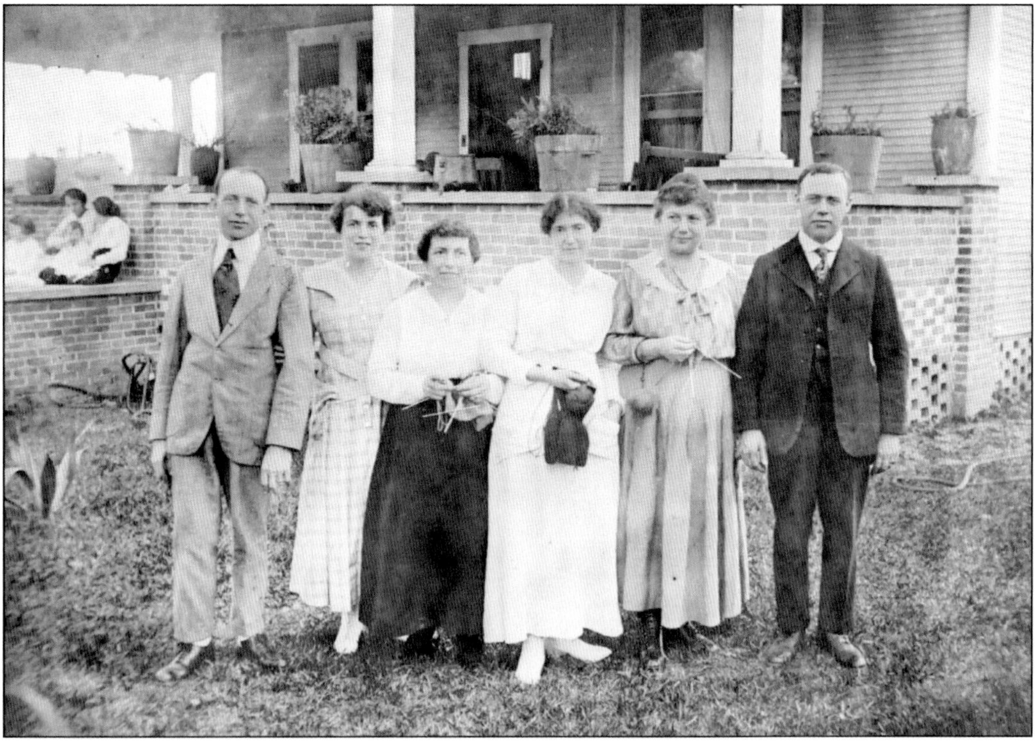

Wolf Siblings, 1917. Joseph and Hannah Wolf came to America from Germany with their family in 1883. Joseph had spent time in Tampa to benefit his health. One son, Fred, settled in Tampa in 1889, and another, Morris, came in 1893, and the two operated Wolf Brothers store and were civically involved. Morris started the Community Chest and brought baseball winter training to Tampa. Shown here are, from left to right, Morris, Martha, Jenny, Julia, Philabena (who married Abe Maas), and Fred.

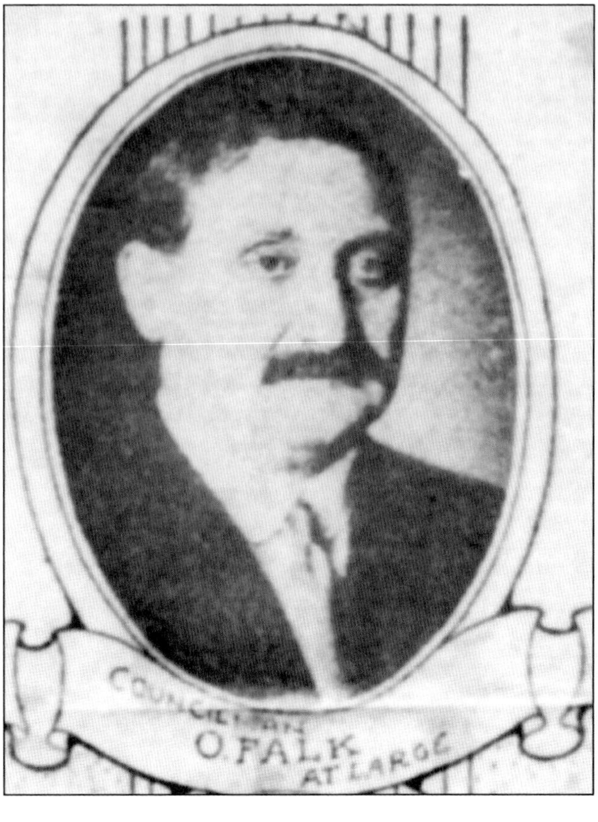

Offim Falk, c. 1910. Lithuanian immigrants Offim and Emma Falk and Morris and Sarah Falk first came to Key West and then settled in Tampa in 1895. The brothers opened O'Falks Department Store in 1899. Offim Falk was elected to the Tampa City Council in 1910, and served for four years.

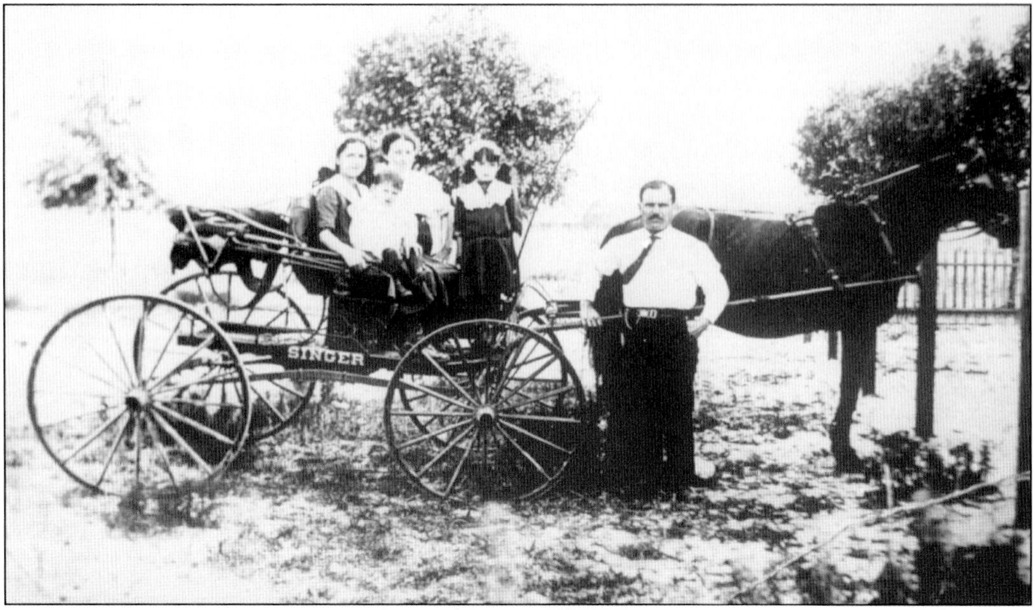

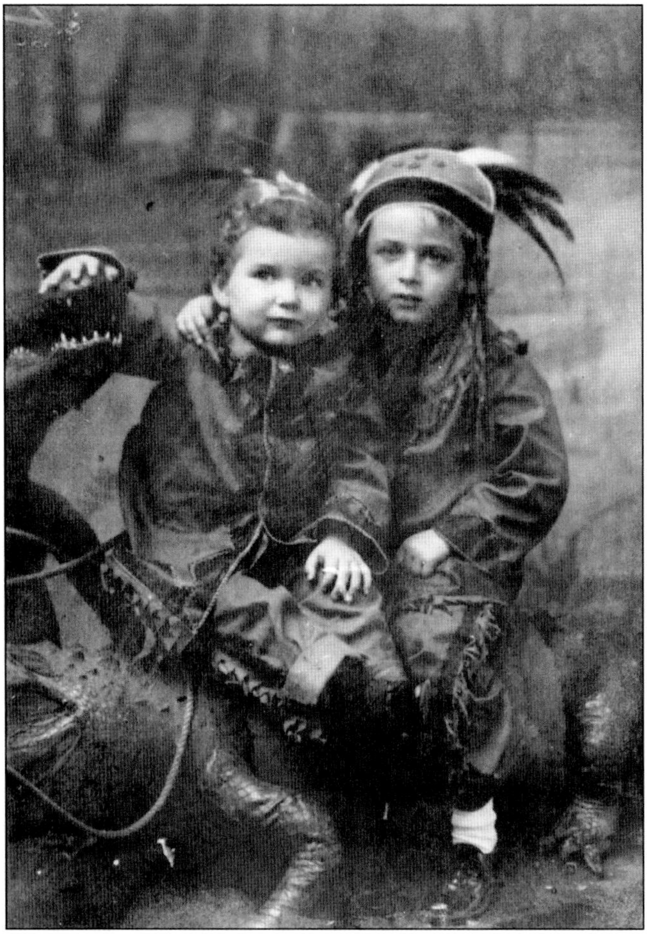

MAGID FAMILY ON SINGER SEWING MACHINE WAGON, 1908. Boruch Magid worked for the Singer Sewing Machine Company. He and his wife, Shaina "Jenny" Magid, are shown here with their children. Shaina is seated at left in the wagon, holding Louis (about four years old). Anna, about 13, is seated at center, and Bertha, about nine years old, is at right. Bertha later married Nat Shorstein. Doris was not yet born.

THERESA BUCKSBAUM AND MARTIN SECKBACH ON ALLIGATOR IN PLANT PARK, 1910. Many new Floridians took photographs posing on the state's symbol, the alligator, a native of the Florida Everglades. Luckily, the alligator in this photograph is not alive!

Louis and Toba Kasriel Wohl, 1907. Louis and Toba Wohl were Romanian immigrants who came to Tampa in 1897. They opened a general merchandise store, which became a family business. The family lived behind the store. The Wohl children included sons Joseph, Charles, and Isidor and daughters Clara, Sarah, and Elizabeth. Louis and Toba are seen here on their 15th wedding anniversary.

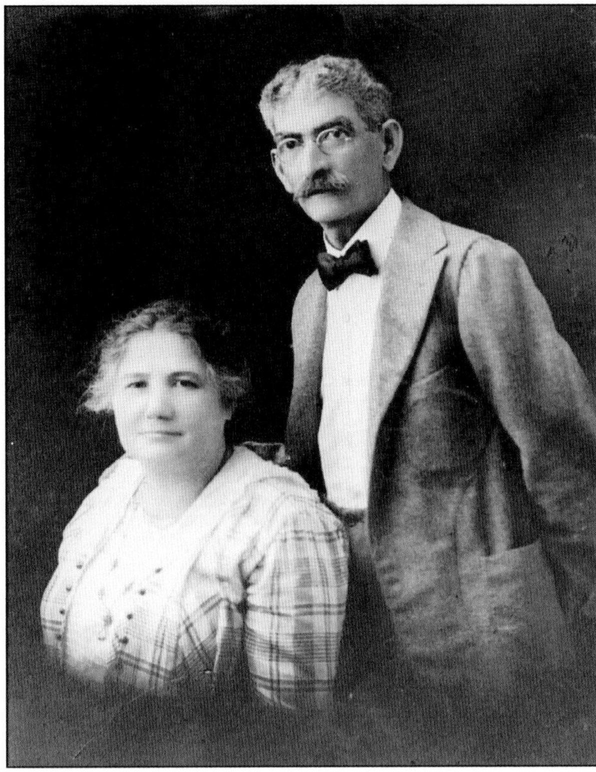

Bar Mitzvah Invitation for Joseph Wohl, 1907. When Joseph grew up, he married Rebecca "Beck" Goldberg. The couple had no children. Both were respected for their civic volunteer activities and their involvement with Rodeph Sholom. The American Association of University Women recognized Beck as the Outstanding Club Woman for 1955.

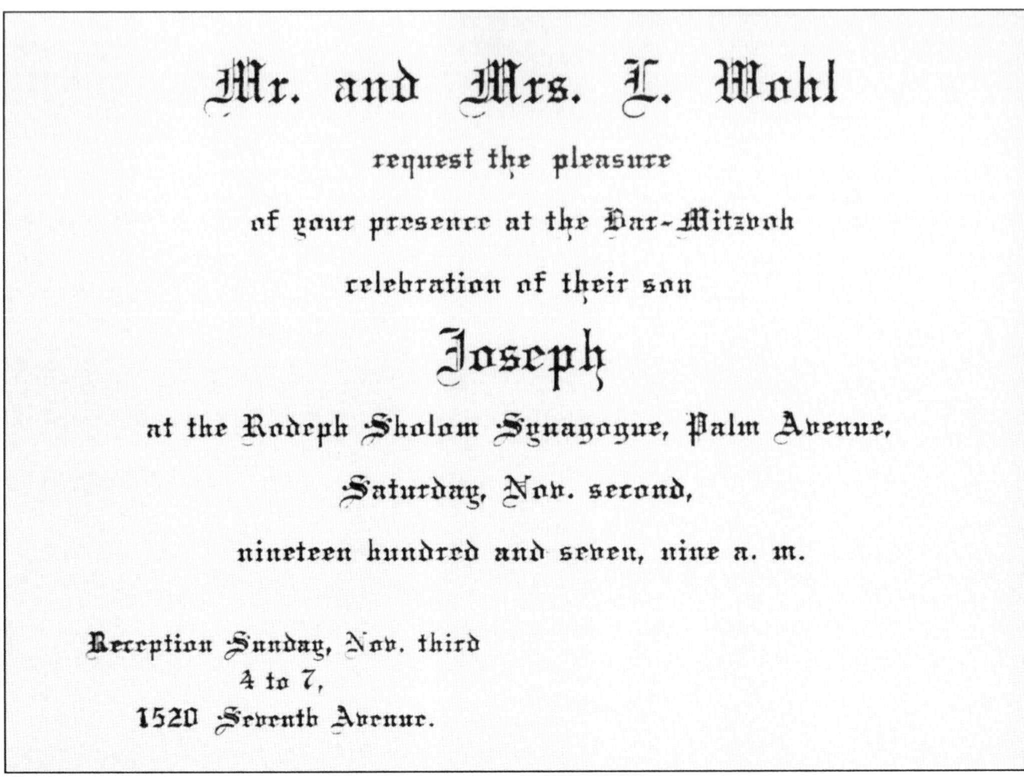

Mr. and Mrs. L. Wohl

request the pleasure

of your presence at the Bar-Mitzvah

celebration of their son

Joseph

at the Rodeph Sholom Synagogue, Palm Avenue,

Saturday, Nov. second,

nineteen hundred and seven, nine a. m.

Reception Sunday, Nov. third
4 to 7,
1520 Seventh Avenue.

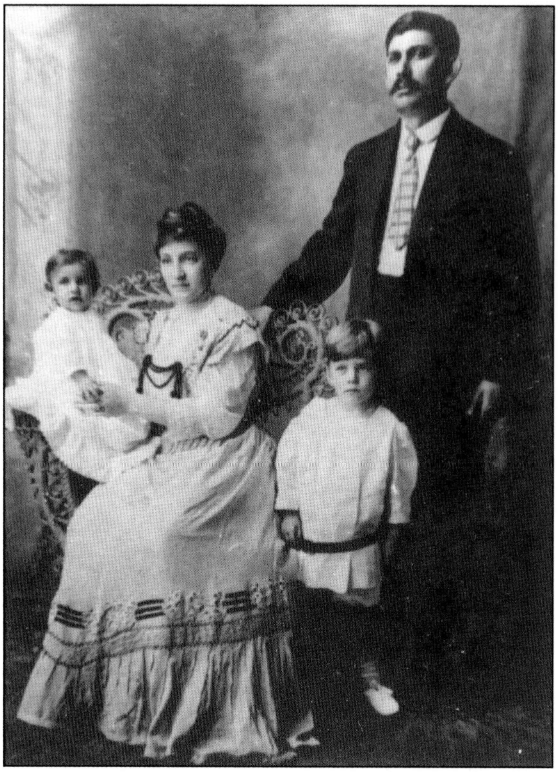

CRACOWANER FAMILY, 1909. Annie Streiffer and Daniel Cracowaner were both born in Iasi, Romania. When they immigrated to America, they each lived in New York for many years. The couple married in Jacksonville in 1904 and finally settled in Tampa. They are seen here with Minnie (left) and Irving.

BAR MITZVAH INVITATION OF IRVING CRACOWANER, 1918. Irving Cracowaner's bar mitzvah was held at Rodeph Sholom Synagogue in Tampa.

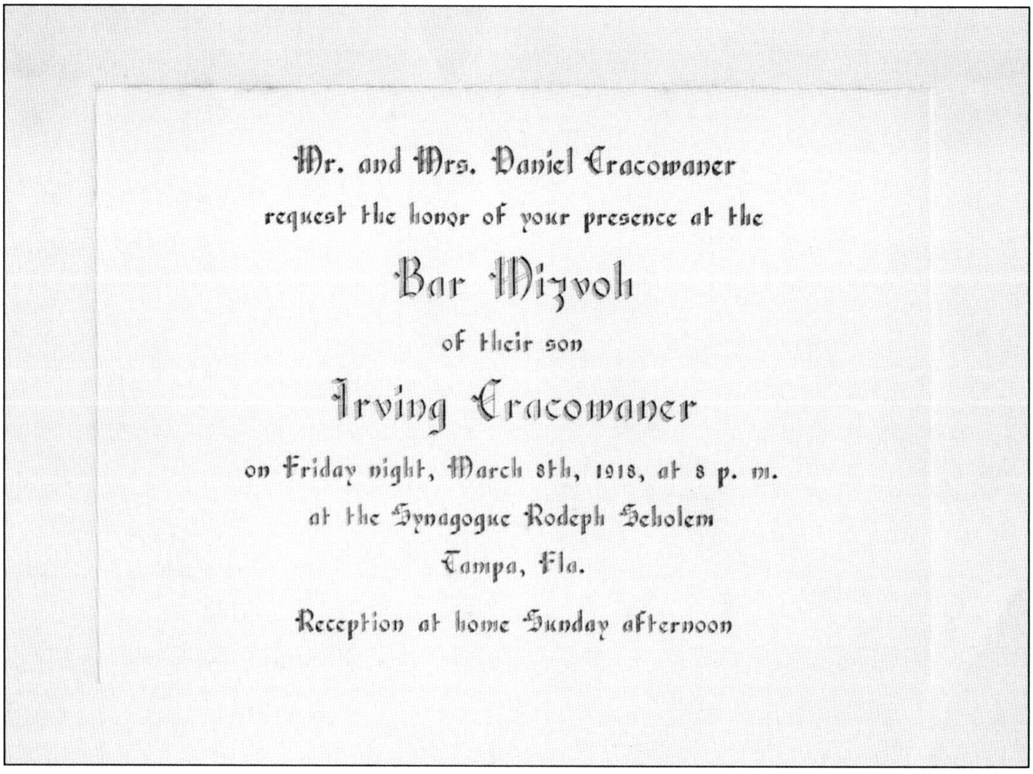

Mr. and Mrs. Daniel Cracowaner
request the honor of your presence at the
Bar Mizvoh
of their son
Irving Cracowaner
on Friday night, March 8th, 1918, at 8 p. m.
at the Synagogue Rodeph Scholem
Tampa, Fla.
Reception at home Sunday afternoon

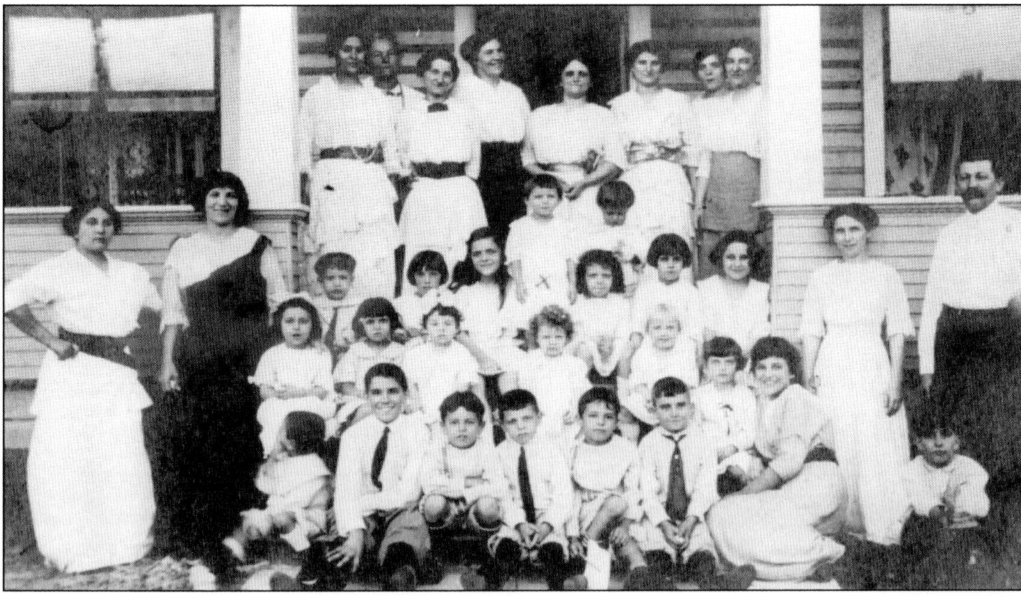

BETTY GOLDSTEIN'S THIRD BIRTHDAY PARTY, 1914. Like many Tampa pioneer Jews, Adolph Goldstein emigrated from Romania. He and his wife, Sabina Stein, were part of a "chain migration." Arriving in America around 1903, Adolph operated a gent's clothing store on Franklin Street until 1936. He also served on the city council in the 1920s. In this photograph, their daughter Betty is in the center of the second row, Adolph is standing at far right, and Sabina is next to Adolph. (See page 98.)

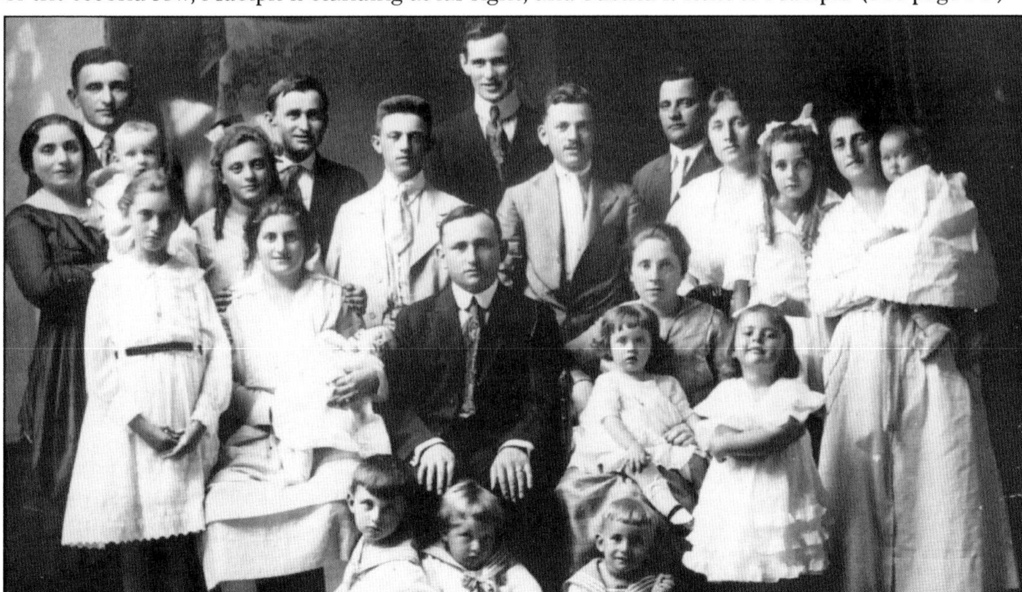

HAIMOVITZ AND SOLOMON FAMILY, C. 1919. Ben Haimovitz, like many pioneer Jewish Tampans, was a Romanian immigrant who trekked over land and sailed steerage to escape pogroms. Ben married Lillian Solomon in 1913. Molly Solomon and Abe Rippa arrived in 1908 so their children—Gus, Isador, Lillian, and Monis—could get a Jewish education. In this photograph, Lillian Solomon Haimovitz is at far right, holding a baby. Her husband, Ben Haimovitz, is second from left in back. (See page 121.)

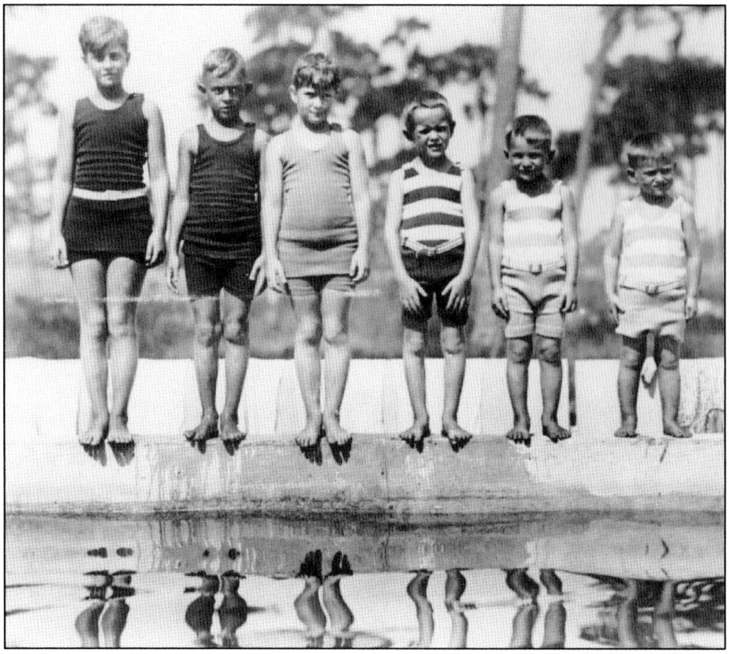

Nathan and Bess Rosenblatt's Children, 1925. Nathan and Bess Rosenblatt came to Tampa in 1912. Shown here are, from left to right, their children, Pauline, Nathan Jr. ("Sonny"), Isabel, Charlie, Eddie, and Frank. This photograph was taken at their home, 211 South Delaware Avenue in Tampa. (See pages 70 and 124.) (Courtesy of Dolly Williams.)

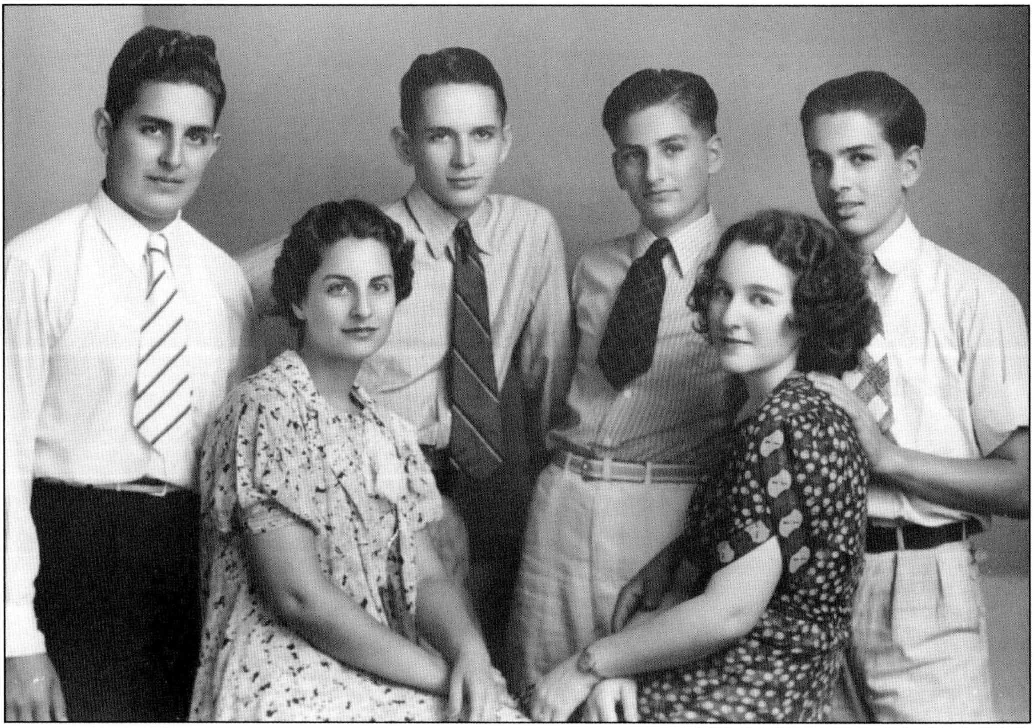

Rosenblatt Children, 1939. Shown here are, from left to right, (first row) Pauline and Isabel; (second row) Sonny, Charlie, Frank, and Eddie. Eddie died in college. Frank, Pauline, and Sonny remained in Tampa. Charlie was career military and then lived in Jacksonville. Isabel moved to Israel and is still there. (Courtesy of Dolly Williams.)

Two

GETTING ORGANIZED

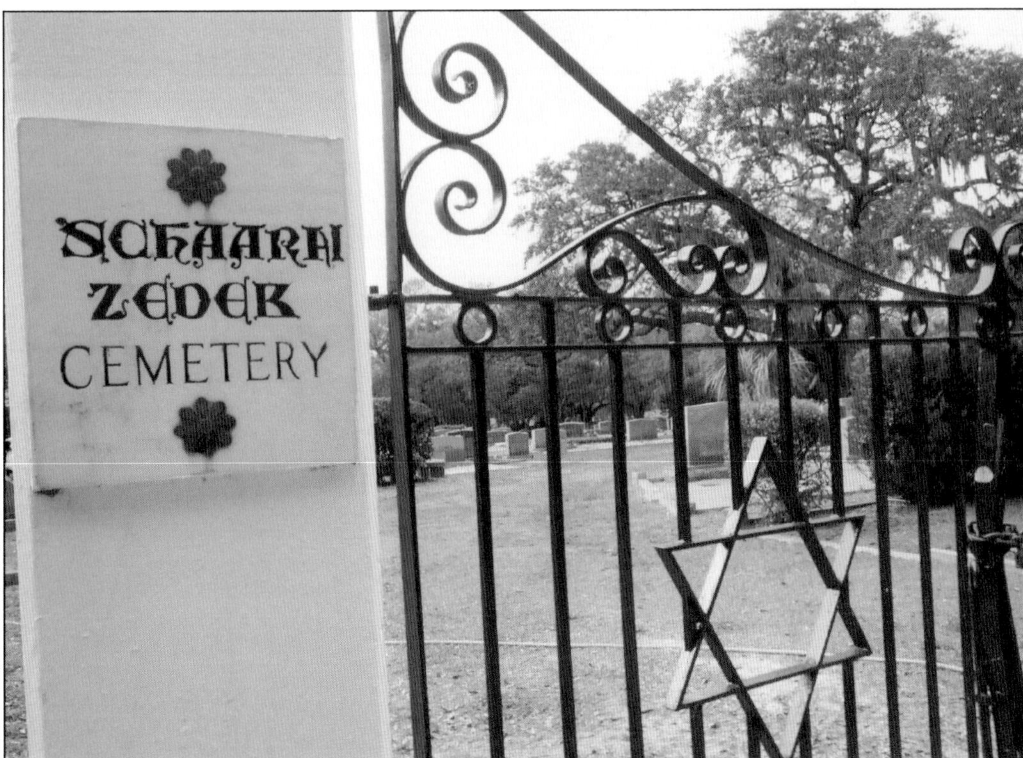

JEWISH CEMETERY GATE AND GRAVES. Historically, Jews create a cemetery when establishing a community. In Tampa, the congregation came first, but after two years of appealing to the Tampa City Council, Schaarai Zedek purchased a one-acre plot within the city's Woodlawn Cemetery in June 1896. The congregation pledged to organize a Hebrew Benevolent Society to fence and maintain the site. The oldest grave is that of S. Solomon, 1896.

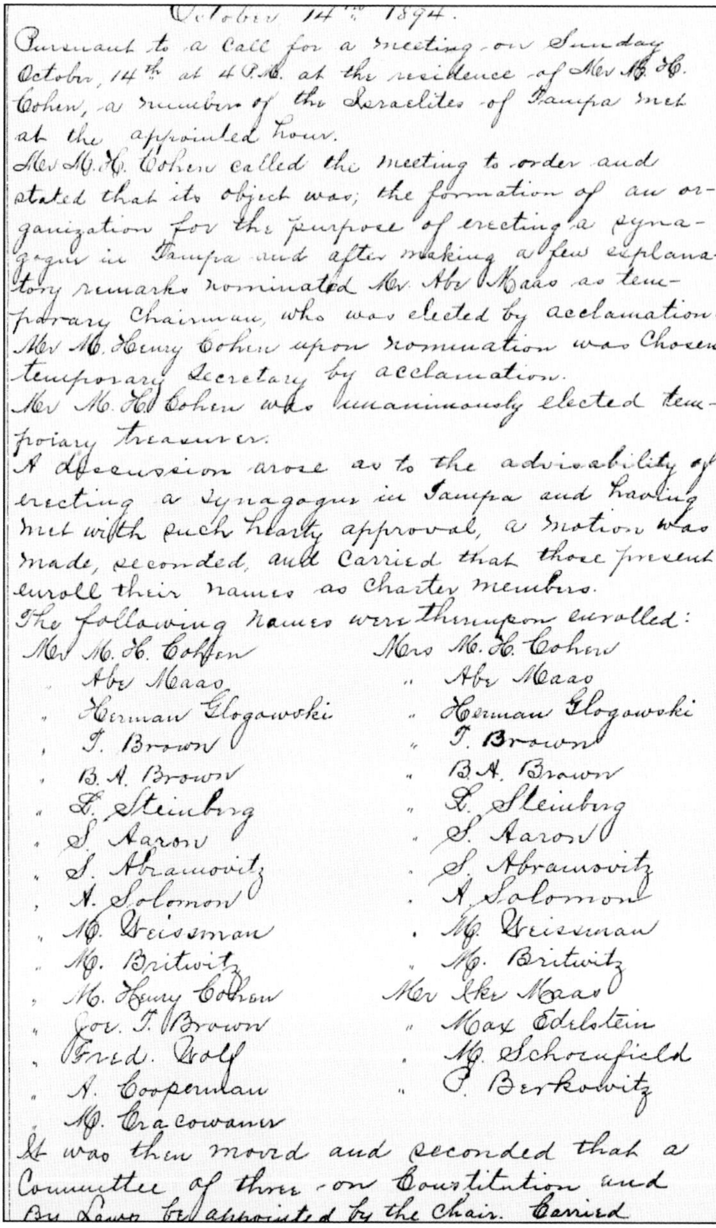

October 14th 1894.

Pursuant to a Call for a meeting on Sunday October, 14th at 4 P.M. at the residence of Mr M. H. Cohen, a number of the Israelites of Tampa met at the appointed hour.

Mr M. H. Cohen called the meeting to order and stated that its object was; the formation of an organization for the purpose of erecting a synagogue in Tampa and after making a few explanatory remarks nominated Mr. Abe Maas as temporary Chairman, who was elected by acclamation.

Mr M. Henry Cohen upon nomination was Chosen temporary Secretary by acclamation.

Mr M. H. Cohen was unanimously elected temporary treasurer.

A discussion arose as to the advisability of erecting a synagogue in Tampa and having met with such hearty approval, a motion was made, seconded, and Carried that those present enroll their names as Charter members.

The following names were thereupon enrolled:

Mr M. H. Cohen	Mrs M. H. Cohen
" Abe Maas	" Abe Maas
" Herman Glogowski	" Herman Glogowski
" I. Brown	" I. Brown
" B. A. Brown	" B. A. Brown
" L. Steinberg	" L. Steinberg
" S. Aaron	" S. Aaron
" S. Abramovitz	" S. Abramovitz
" A. Solomon	" A. Solomon
" M. Weissman	" M. Weissman
" M. Britwitz	" M. Britwitz
" M. Henry Cohen	Mr Ike Maas
" Jos. T. Brown	" Max Edelstein
" Fred. Wolf	" M. Schoenfield
" A. Cooperman	" P. Berkowitz
" M. Cracowaner	

It was then moved and seconded that a Committee of three on Constitution and By Laws be appointed by the Chair. Carried

PAGE FROM MINUTE BOOK FROM FORMATION OF CONGREGATION SCHAARAI ZEDEK, 1894. Congregation Schaarai Zedek (Gates of Righteousness) was founded as Orthodox, and most of the members lived downtown and along Seventh Avenue in Ybor City. Dr. D. Jacobson was the first rabbi, in 1896. In 1902, a group of "reformers" conflicted with the Orthodox congregants and gained control of the assets. In 1903, the congregation became Reform. The congregation's rabbis have been the following: H. Friedman (1901); Louis D. Mendoza (1902); Horace Wolf (1904); Henry Sande Stollnitz (1905–1906); Jacob Singer (1907); then, no rabbi served until George Benedict (1920–1923); I. Elliot Grafman (1924–1929) moved the congregation to a new building at the corner of Delaware Avenue and DeLeon Street; David L. Zielonka (1930–1970) moved the congregation to Swann and Lincoln Avenues in 1957; Frank Sundheim (1966–1986); and Richard Birnholz (1986–present). Today, the Reform congregation serves more than 1,000 families.

COURT CASE, 1902. More than 270 pages of testimony were taken in the case of *Congregation Schaarai Zedek v. Moses Henry Cohen* in the Sixth Judicial Circuit of the State of Florida. This page reflects the testimony of Dr. Louis Oppenheimer. The Orthodox faction brought the suit regarding "dirty tricks" used by the "Reformers" to take control of the congregation. Cohen represented the Reform faction, which won the case and remained Schaarai Zedek. The Orthodox left and formed Rodeph Sholom.

-157-

not a member, nor was I one of either side; I had no interest in either side; I was merely there in conformity with my principles of being a Jew and of my interest in seeing the Jewish people in harmony, and in conformity with the donation which I gave to this institution, amounting to $50 a year, for the purpose of harmonizing the Jewish people. My object in being present at that meeting was upon the solicitation of several of its members; I don't remember exactly who they were, Mr.Morris Falk being one, perhaps Mr.Glogowski can tell me who the others were, I have forgotten; at any rate, Mr.Maas, I believe, and Mr.Glogowski and Mr.Brash's father acting as Mr.Brash's substitute, and the minister of the congregation, and Mr.Falk, met me at my office for the purpose of harmonizing these factions and I, being looked upon as a neutral person and not taking sides with either one of those elements, and inasmuch as it was near to my heart to see the Jewish people harminious, thought I would have more influence in bringing those people together than anyone else. I didn't do this as a member, for I was not a member, wouldn't under any circumstances accept such a position in any creed of being a member of any creed; but did so because I am a Jew and I am proud to see Jews demonstrate those lofty characteristics which history has given to them, and would do all in my power to assist them in showing the world at large those characteristics; I think that is all.

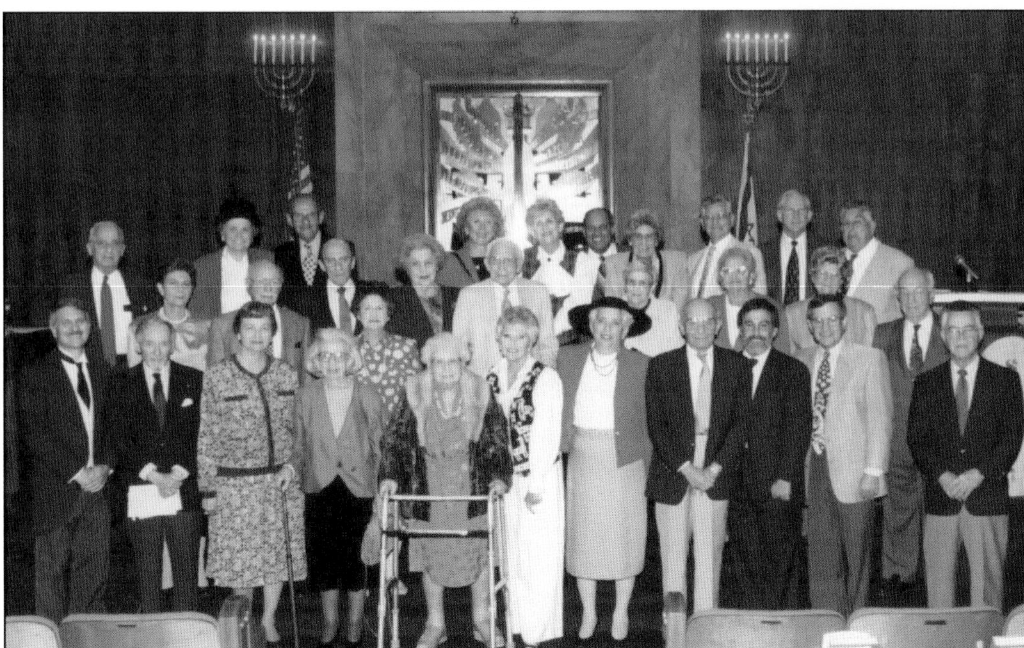

CONGREGATION SCHAARAI ZEDEK CENTENNIAL CELEBRATION, 1994. The women and men shown here have been members of the congregation for at least 50 years. (Courtesy of Schaarai Zedek.)

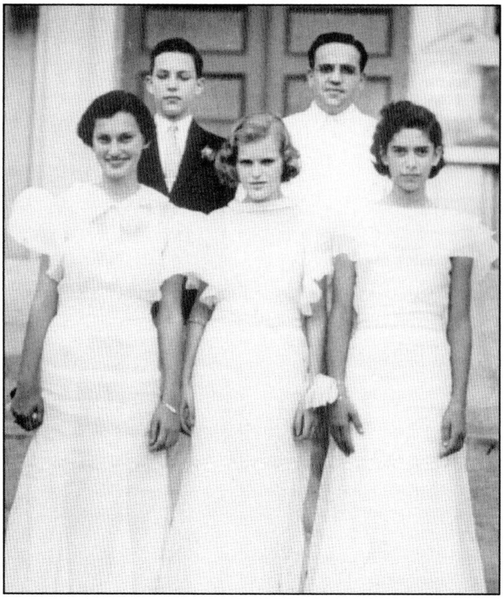

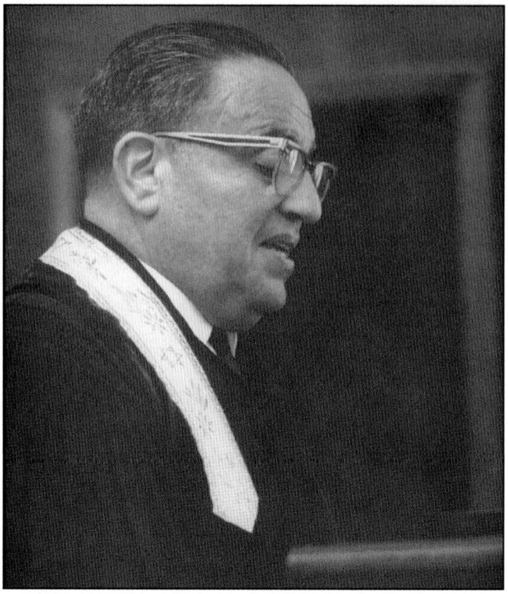

RABBI DAVID L. ZIELONKA. The above left photograph shows the Schaarai Zedek confirmation class of 1934. Shown are, from left to right, (first row) Shirley Scadrow, Ruth Shine, and Audrey Maas; (second row) Edward Zinkow and Rabbi David Zielonka. Known as a scholar and people person, Rabbi Zielonka served Congregation Schaarai Zedek from 1930 to 1970 and as emeritus until 1977. He and Clarence Darrow, known for defending John Scopes in the "Monkey Trial," joined other Tampa religious leaders in a Bible debate in 1931 (below). When the University of Tampa opened that year, Rabbi Zielonka served on the faculty and, in 1963, he became head of the Department of Religious Studies. When Rabbi Zielonka retired, one of his most prized gifts was a collection of letters from university staff and students whom he had counseled. The rabbi and his wife, Carol, were leaders in the religious and civic communities. (All, courtesy of Schaarai Zedek.)

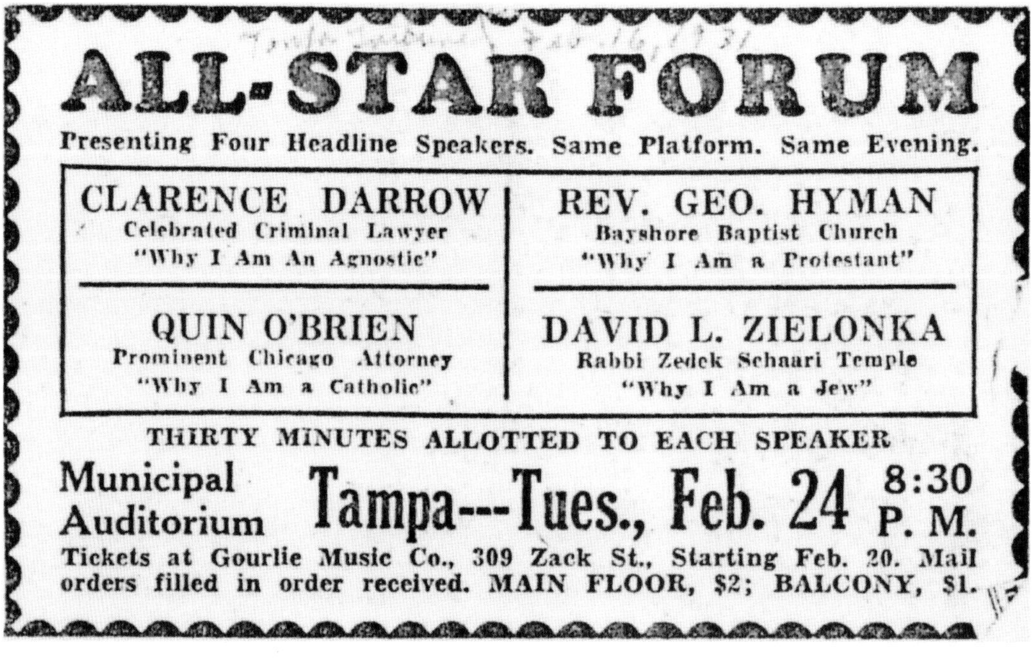

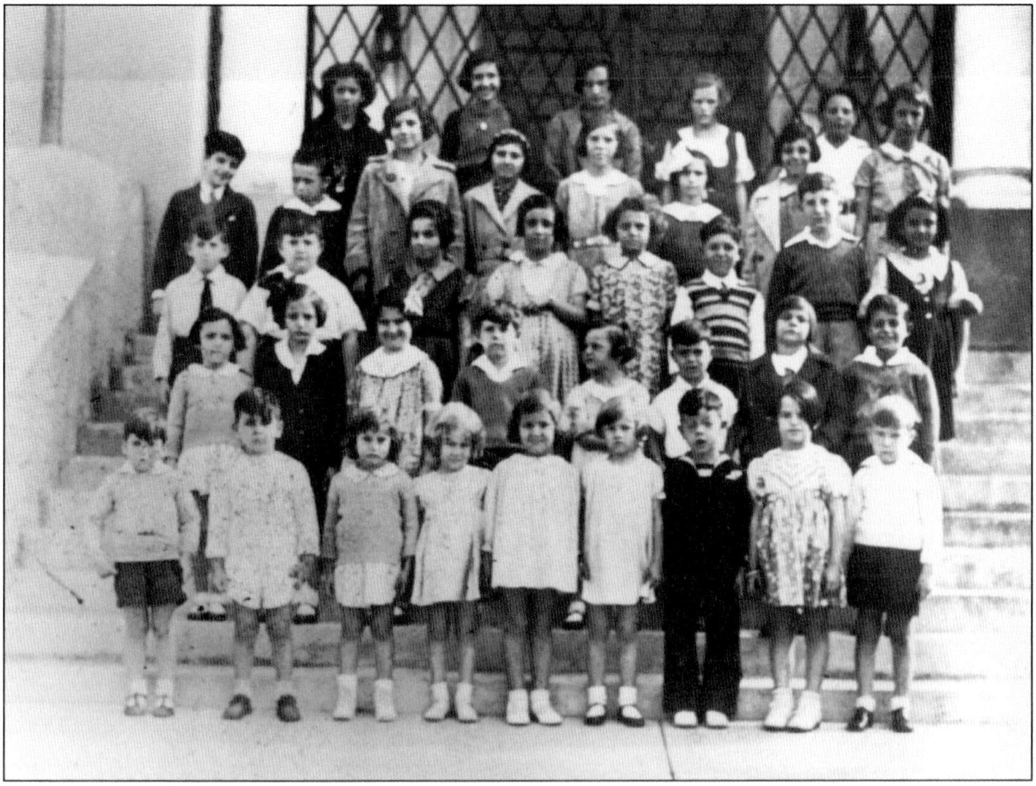

CONGREGATION SCHAARAI ZEDEK SUNDAY SCHOOL, 1935. These children attend religious school on Sundays to learn the history, traditions, and rituals of Judaism for the continuity of the Jewish people. (Courtesy of Schaarai Zedek.)

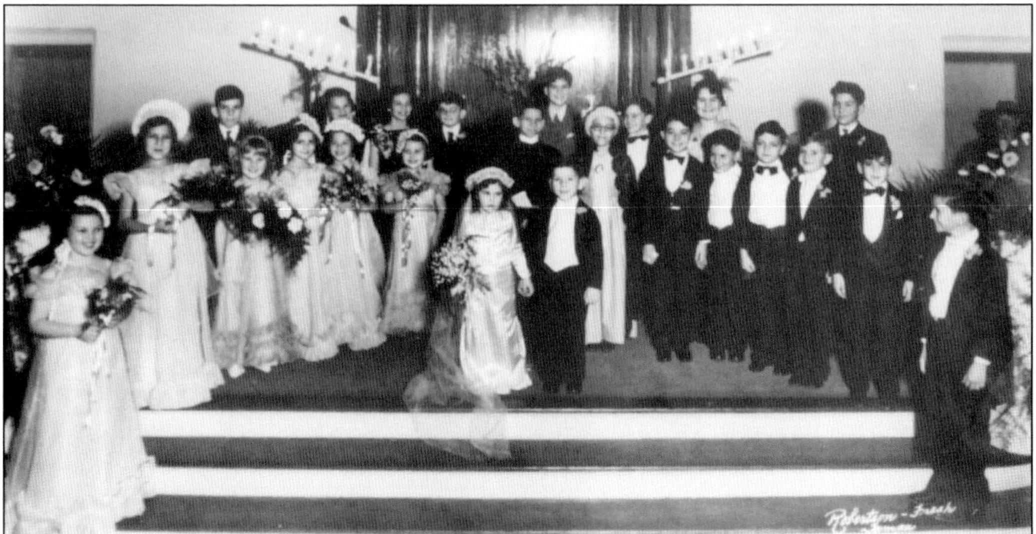

CONGREGATION SCHAARAI ZEDEK TOM THUMB WEDDING, 1936. This annual event, with children performing in a mock wedding, was held as a fundraiser for the congregation. Here, Walter Kessler is acting as the rabbi. Kessler grew up to be a president of the Tampa Jewish Federation, Congregation Schaarai Zedek, and Jewish Towers, and he has held many positions with the Shriners.

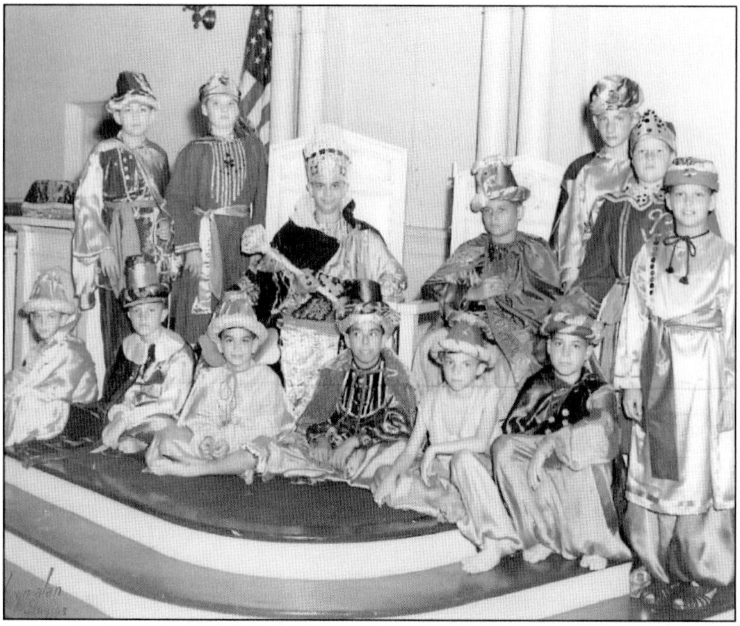

Schaarai Zedek Purim Play, 1948. Purim is a 2,600-year-old holiday celebrating the survival of the Jewish people. Queen Esther spoke out for her fellow Jews when threatened with annihilation by the Persian king's advisor, Haman. Among the children in this photograph are Richard Mensh, Myron Uman, Dan Rachelson, Judy Shirley Hirsh, Queen Judy Perlman Morris, Valerie Kaufman, David M. Zielonka, and Elliott Marcus. (Courtesy of Schaarai Zedek.)

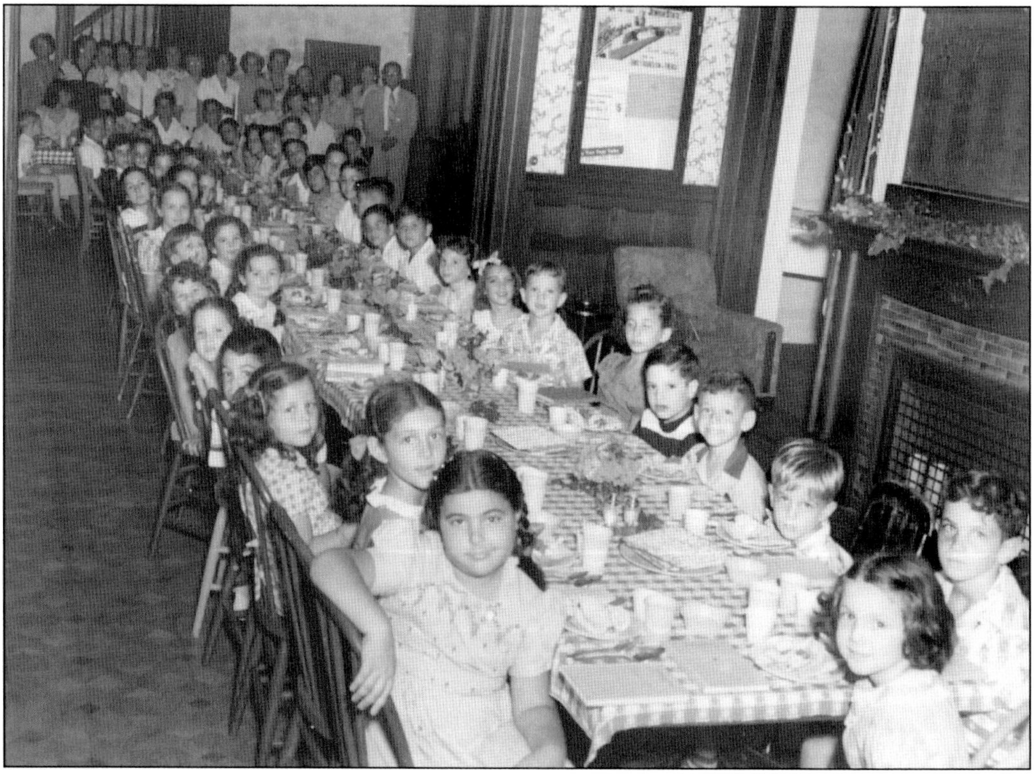

Schaarai Zedek Children's Seder, 1948. The festival of Passover is celebrated from the 15th through the 22nd of the Hebrew month of Nissan. It commemorates the emancipation of the Israelites from slavery in ancient Egypt more than 3,300 years ago. On the first night (some observe two nights), Jews gather to share a Seder, with wine, matzo, and other rituals, and read the story about freedom. (Courtesy of Schaarai Zedek.)

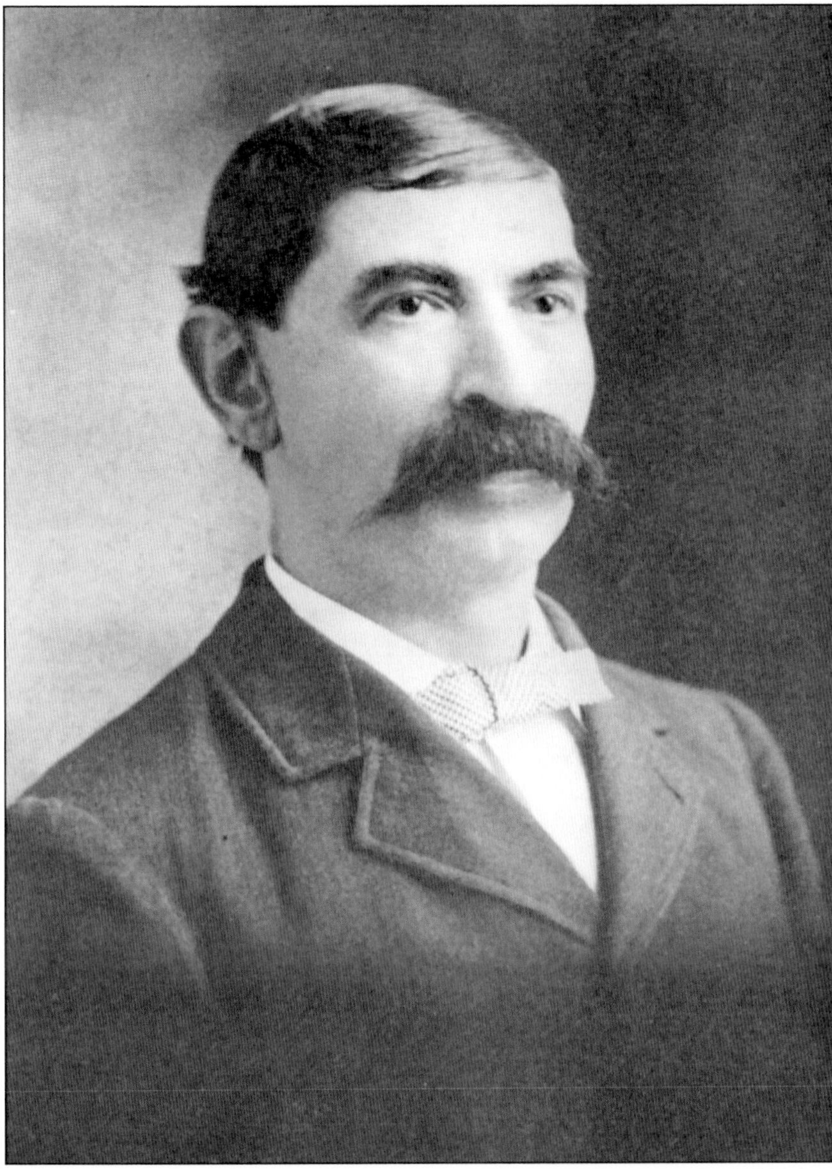

Julius Mairson, First President of Congregation Rodeph Sholom. In 1903, the Orthodox faction regrouped after the conflict. Starting with 26 families, Congregation Rodeph Sholom (Pursuers of Peace) purchased a modest structure on Palm Avenue in Ybor City, then tore it down for a larger structure in 1909. This building was in turn torn down in 1926 for a newer structure that was a symbol of Conservative Judaism. In 1955, the congregation erected the David Stein Educational Building and continued to grow. It then built a synagogue at its present site, on Bayshore Boulevard, in 1968. The congregation's rabbis have been the following: Julius Hess; Julius Shapo; Ralph B. Hershon (around 1917–1918 and again around 1928); Arthur Ginzler; Adolph Burger (in the 1920s and, following a term by Hershon, again from 1930 to 1942); Benjamin Eisenberg (1942–1945); Henry Wernick (1946–1953); Jerome Kestenbaum (1953–1959); Stanley Kazan (1959–1973); Sanford Hahn (1973–1979); Martin Sandberg (1979–1981); Kenneth R. Berger (1981–1989); Hillel Millgram (1989–1990); Arthur Lavinsky (1990–1995); and Marc S. Sack (1995–2013). Today, the congregation serves 430 families.

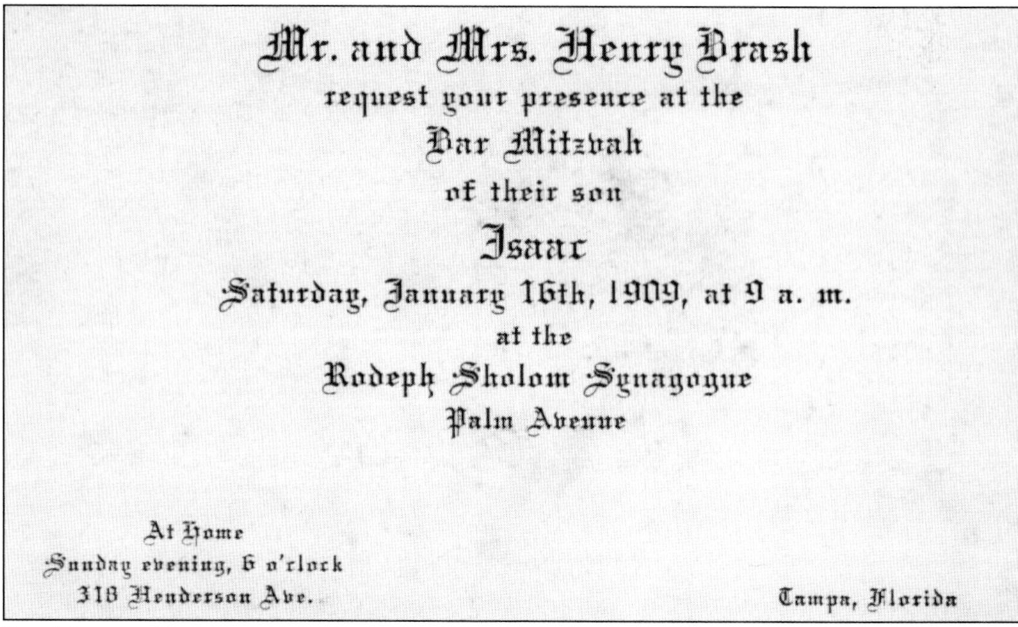

Mr. and Mrs. Henry Brash
request your presence at the
Bar Mitzvah
of their son
Isaac
Saturday, January 16th, 1909, at 9 a. m.
at the
Rodeph Sholom Synagogue
Palm Avenue

At Home
Sunday evening, 6 o'clock
318 Henderson Ave.

Tampa, Florida

BAR MITZVAH INVITATION FOR ISAAC BRASH, 1909. Isaac was the son of Sarah and Henry Brash. He was a haberdasher and a 63-year member of the Tampa Hillsborough Masonic Lodge No. 25 at the time of his death in 1983.

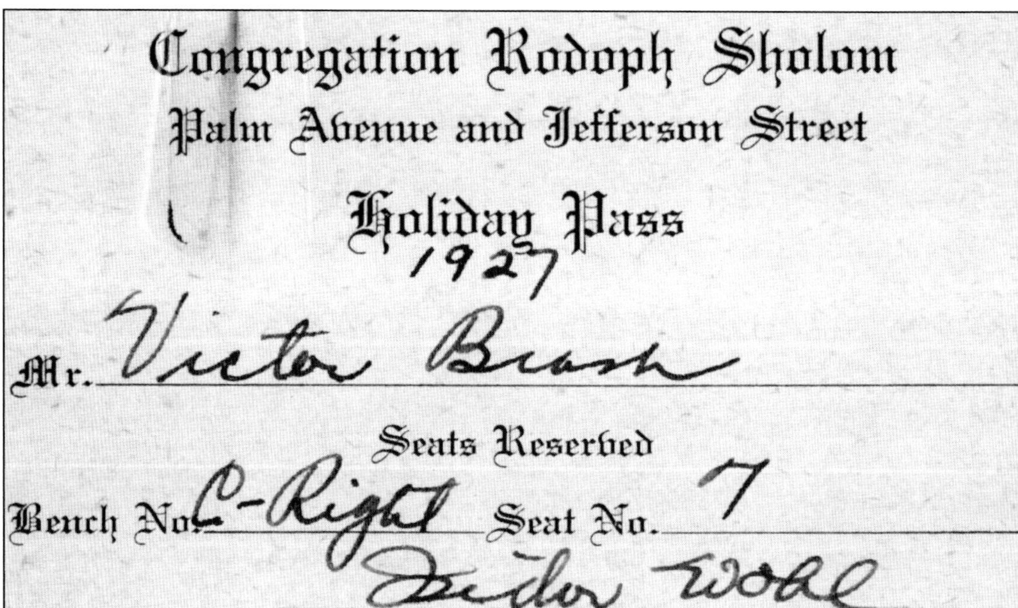

Congregation Rodoph Sholom
Palm Avenue and Jefferson Street

Holiday Pass
1927

Mr. Victor Brash

Seats Reserved

Bench No. C-Right Seat No. 7

RODEPH SHOLOM HIGH HOLIDAY TICKET, 1927. When Henry and Sarah Brash settled in Tampa in 1894, Henry opened a haberdashery store on Polk and Franklin Streets and quickly became involved in the community. He served the Masons for 33 years. Henry Brash (1857–1928) led the Orthodox group in the formation of Rodeph Sholom, which was named by his father-in-law, Solomon Zelnicker, who had served on the Confederate side in the Civil War. Henry wrote the original history of the congregation and, 42 years later, his son Victor updated it for the dedication of the new building in 1970.

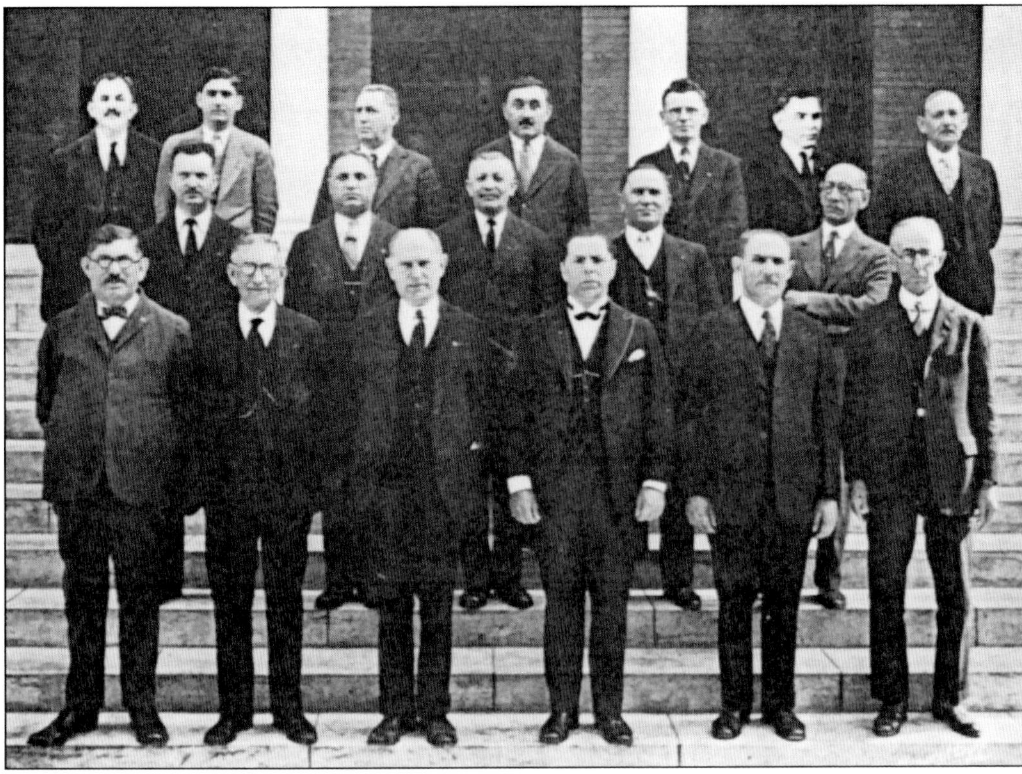

Rodeph Sholom Men's Group, 1920. Shown here are, from left to right, (first row) Dan Cracowaner, Louis Wohl, M.G. Rosenberg, Rabbi Hershon, David Stein, and Henry Brash; (second row) Murray Weisman, Max Argintar, Adolph Goldstein, Joe Abramowitz, and ? Gordon; (third row) Manuel Katz, Isadore Wohl, Jacob Buchman, Herman Perlman, Simon Essrig, Adolf Katz, and Morris Falk.

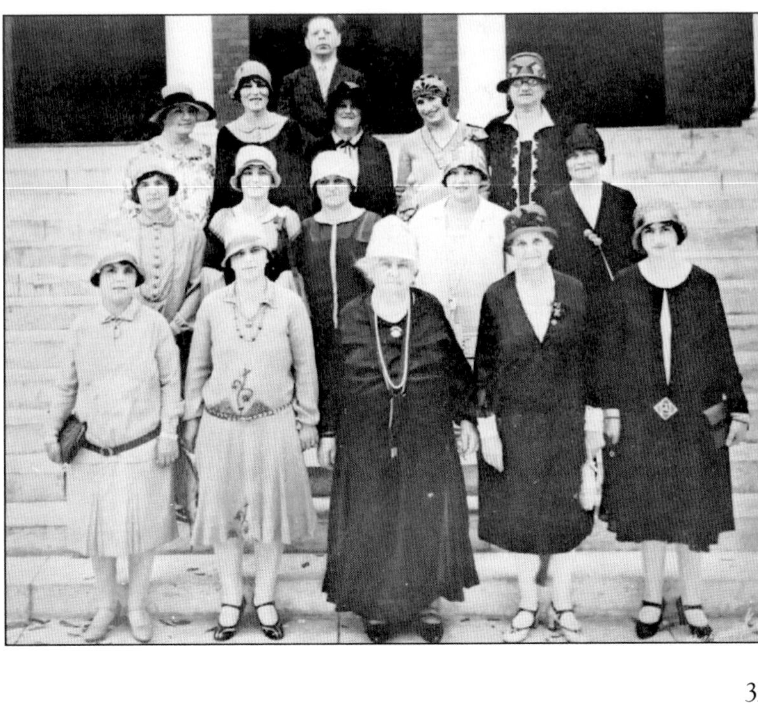

Rodeph Sholom Ladies Auxiliary, 1928. Shown here are, from left to right, (first row) two unidentified women, first president Mrs. Julius Mairson, Sarah Z. Brash, and Sarah Juster; (second row) five unidentified women; (third row) two unidentified women, Rose Kisler, Helen Wittner, and unidentified woman; and (fourth row) Rabbi Ralph Hershon.

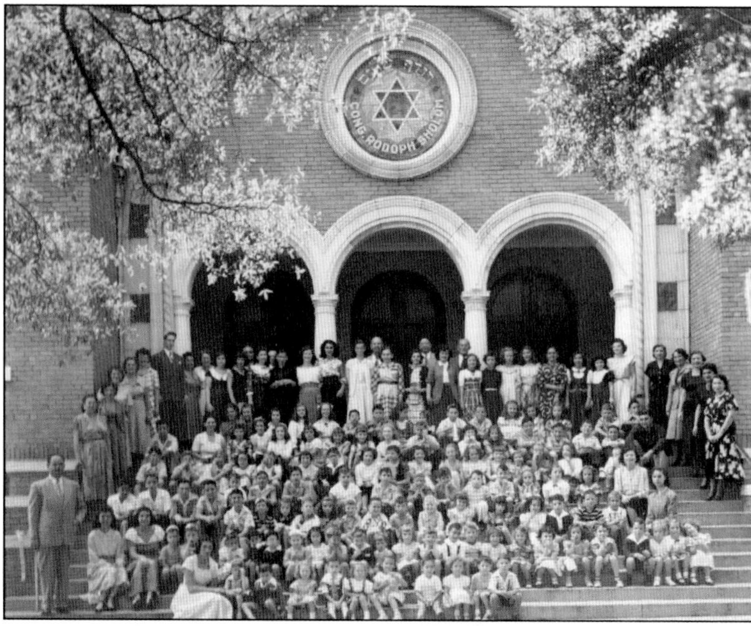

Rodeph Sholom Sunday School, 1937. Students of Rodeph Sholom's Sunday School gather on the synagogue's front steps.

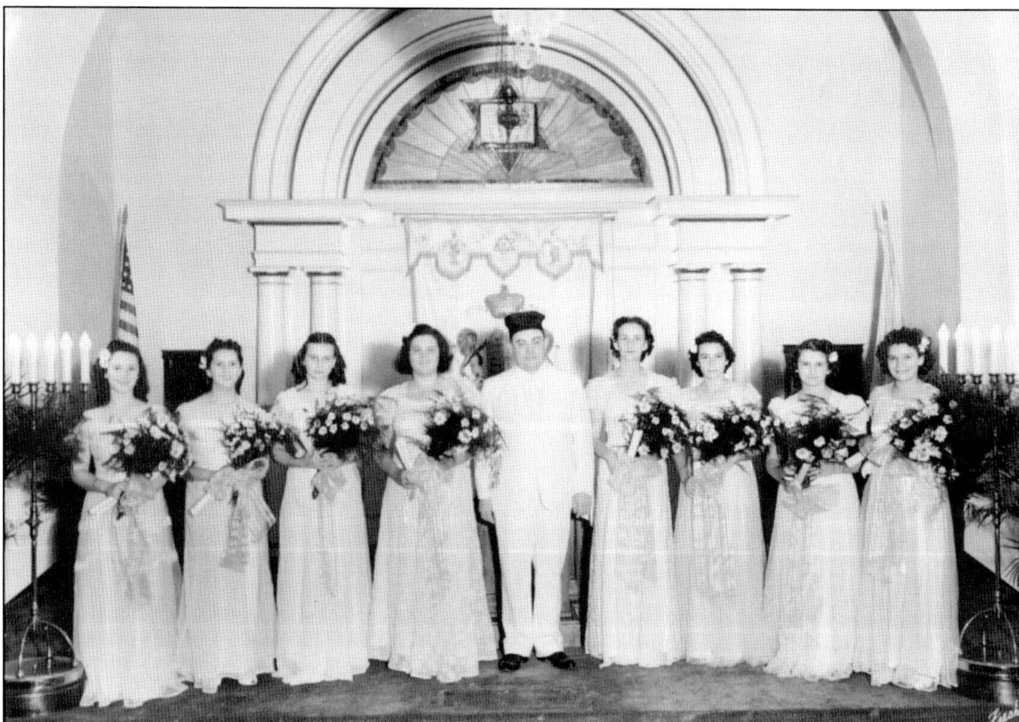

Rodeph Sholom Confirmation, 1940. This ceremony, conducted when the member is 16, follows years of religious study to affirm Jewish identity and is usually held on the festival of Shavuot, which celebrates the anniversary of receiving the Torah. Shown here are, from left to right, Adrienne (Blumberg) Tufeld, Judy (Nurwirth) Schwartz, Jackie Weber, Elinor (Rosenthal) Diamond, Rabbi Adolph Berger, Betty Fay Moses, Doris (Chaite) Rosenblatt, Joyce Lutz, and Mimi (Schill) Weiss.

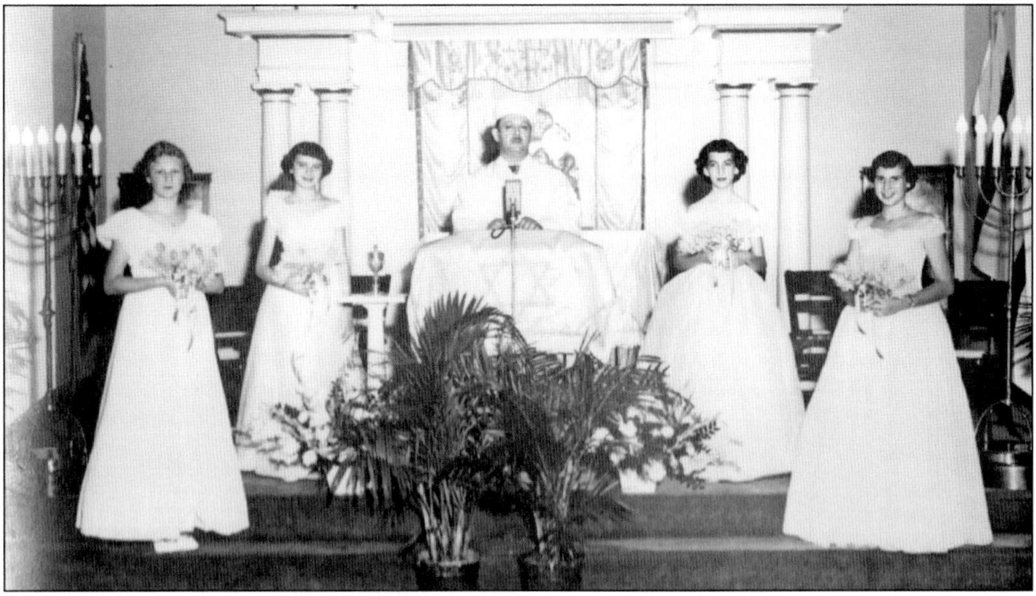

First Bat Mitzvah at Rodeph Sholom, 1952. This celebration, to mark a 13-year-old girl's acceptance of her responsibilities in the adult Jewish community, began in 1922 in Manhattan as a radical response to the Bar Mitzvah. In the 1950s, the popularity of the Bat Mitzvah ceremony spread across the country. Posing here are, from left to right, Ethel (Chaitow) Field, Elaine (Simovitz) Hilf, Rabbi Henry Wernick, Aimee (Salsbury) Mezrah, and Sandy (Schwartz) Turkel. (Courtesy of Sandy Turkel.)

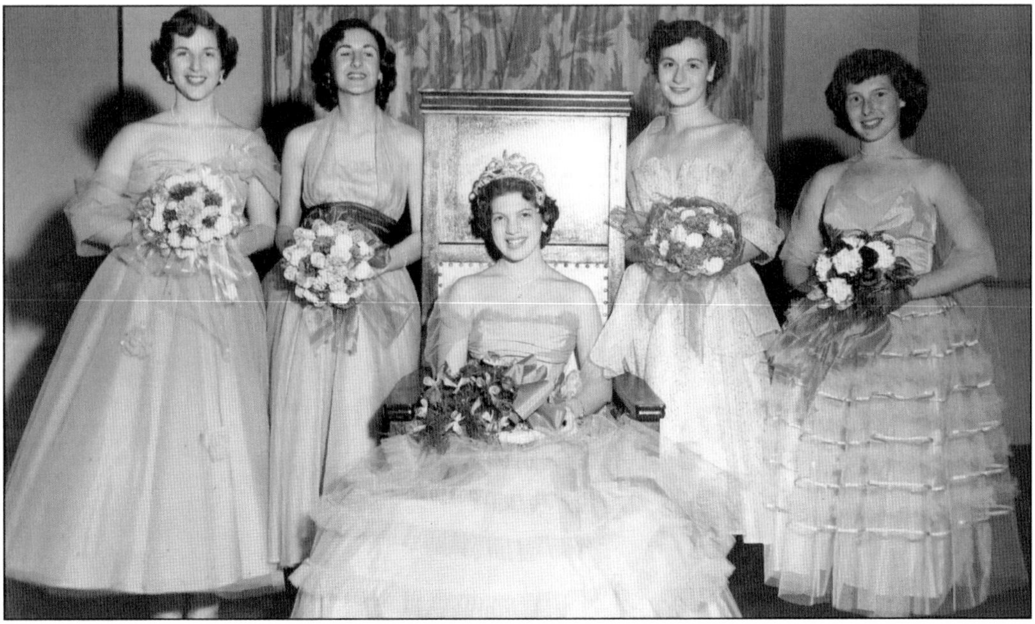

Rodeph Sholom Purim Ball, March 3, 1953. Purim balls began as a fundraiser for the congregation in 1934 and were held for about 30 years. Selected for the 1953 court were, from left to right, Ethel Friedman, Susan Ross, Queen Dale Salsbury, Barbara Levsky, and Goldie Rutkin. This event was held at the Tampa Terrace Hotel. Salsbury, 16, was a native of Tampa, as was her mother, Minnie Cracowaner Salsbury. (Courtesy of Rodeph Sholom.)

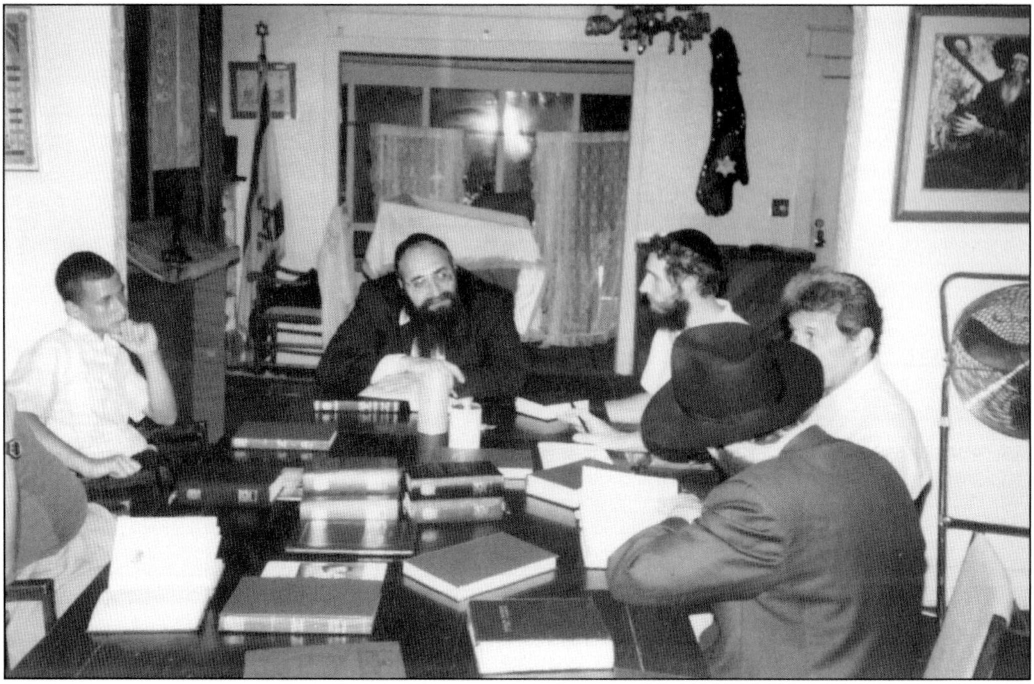

RABBI LAZER RIVKIN, 1993. Rabbi Rivkin came to Tampa from Brooklyn in 1976 to start the Young Israel and the Chabad groups. They started at 3721 Tacon Street and in 2010 moved to 13207 North Fifty-second Street, Temple Terrace. Here, Rivkin (at the head of the table) leads a study at the Young Israel Center with Yakov McKay (far left), Chaim Makarov (to the right of Rivkin), Steve Klein (far right), and a Yeshivah student (in hat). (Courtesy of Rabbi Rivkin.)

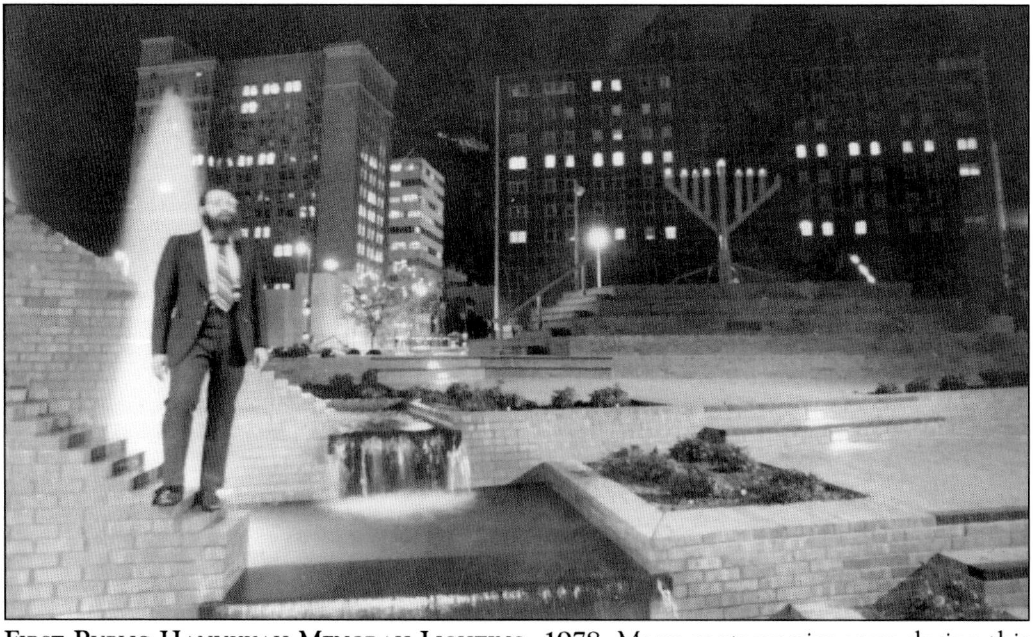

FIRST PUBLIC HANUKKAH MENORAH LIGHTING, 1978. Many controversies arose during this event, sponsored by Chabad at City Hall Plaza. The menorah is now lit every year in downtown Tampa. Here, Rabbi Lazer Rivkin leads the event. (Courtesy of Rabbi Rivkin.)

CHABAD SCHOOL STUDENTS, 1979. Rabbi Lazer Rivkin and Rebbetzin Dvorah Rivkin started Tampa's first Orthodox Jewish Day School, Torah Temimah Academy, in 1979. Rabbi Yossie Dubrowsky rejuvenated the school in 1983 as the Hebrew Academy, now located on Pennington Road in Tampa. (Courtesy of Rabbi Rivkin.)

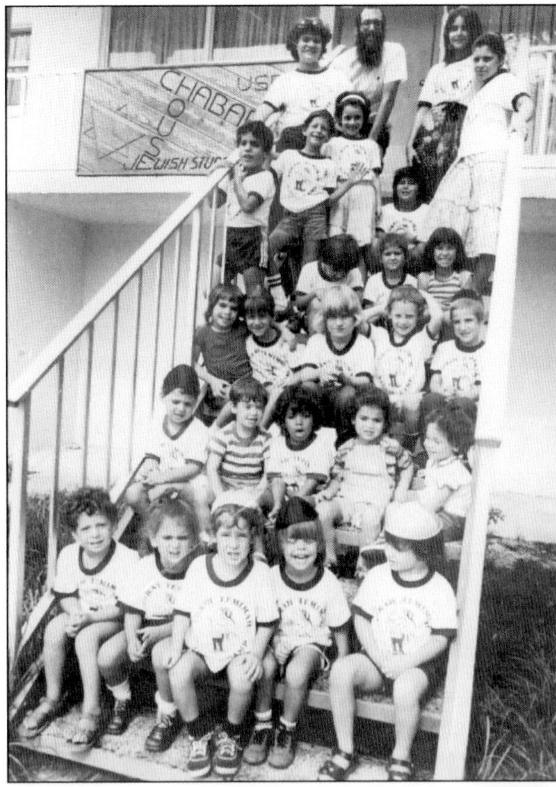

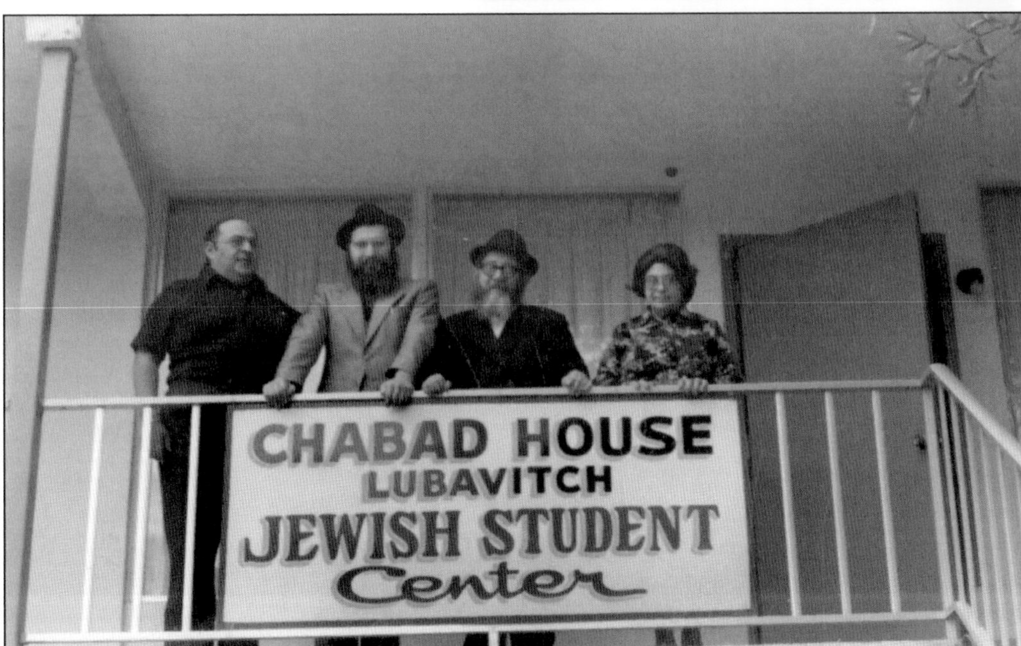

CHABAD LUBAVITCH JEWISH STUDENT CENTER, USF, 1976. Shown here are, from left to right, Al Mizrahi, Rabbi Lazer Rivkin, Rabbi Avraham Parshon, and Rebbetzin Sarah Parshon. (Courtesy of Rabbi Rivkin.)

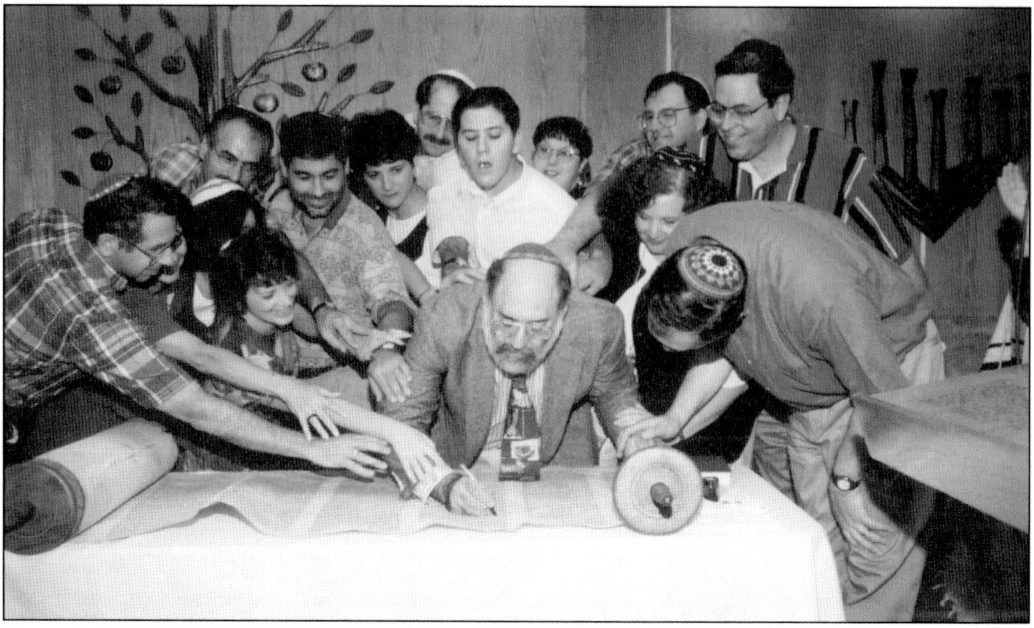

Congregation Kol Ami Torah Dedication, 1996. The congregation organized in 1978 to provide a Conservative focal point in North Tampa. Lay members conducted services until the first rabbi was hired in 1980. The original synagogue opened shortly before the High Holiday services in 1982. In 1998, it added a chapel, boardroom, and school wing. Dr. Mark Jaffe (wearing kippah) is on the lower right of the picture, his right hand on the Torah. To his right, with her left hand on the Torah, is Carol Jaffe. Dr. Steven Specter is on the far left, his right hand reaching out toward the Torah. Bruce Shanker, Dr. Kalman Pila, Judith Sachs, Marc Rosenwasser, and Leonard Marks are also pictured.

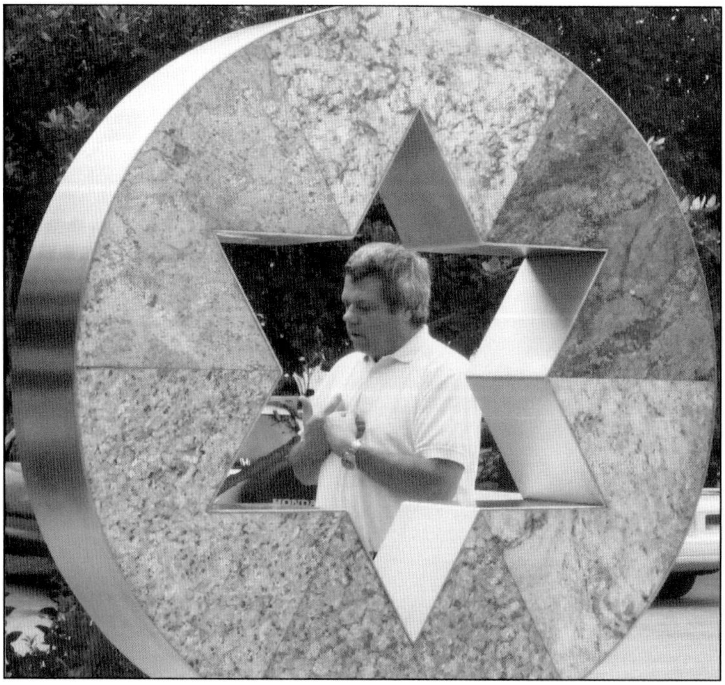

Kol Ami Star Garden Memorial, 2007. Bradley Arthur, a world-famous sculptor born in Tampa, is a member of Congregation Kol Ami. He designed and created the Jewish star sculpture at the front entrance, using stainless steel and six colors of granite on each side, representing the Twelve Tribes. His other works are in collections across the United States and Europe, and exhibition sites have included Lincoln Center in New York City and the Grand Palais in Paris.

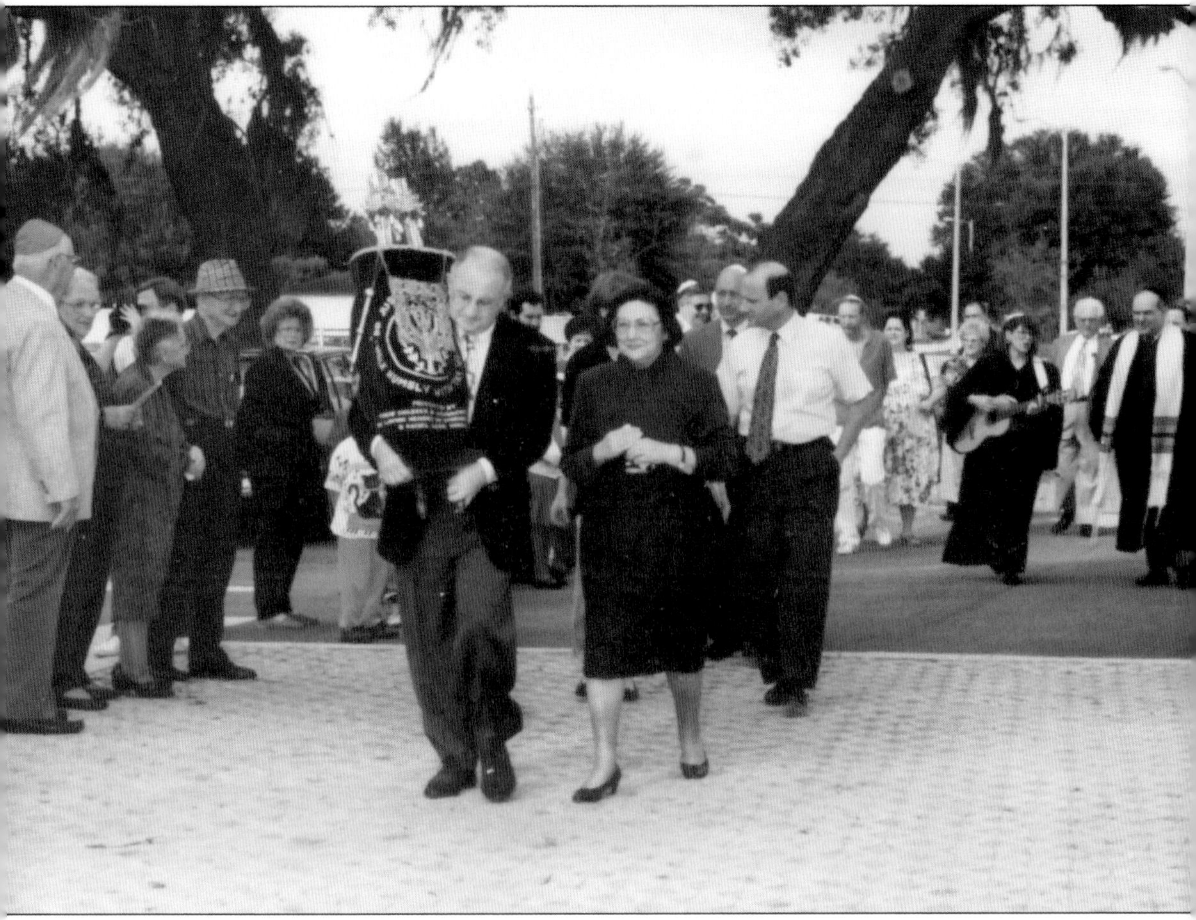

CONGREGATION BETH AM PARADING TORAH TO FIRST SANCTUARY, NOVEMBER 21, 1993. In 1986, eighty people met to form a Reform congregation in north Tampa. From left to right are Aaron and Kay Kraselski; Maize and Leo (with hat) Shaw (parents of Beth Am's first president, Dr. Maurice Shaw); an unidentified man behind Maize holding a camera; an unidentified woman to Leo's left; Dr. Maurice Shaw (Beth Am's first president) in the front, center, holding the Torah; Dr. Shirley Borkowf to his left; Steve Osheroff (behind Maurice Shaw); Paul Lewis (behind and to the right of Shirley Borkowf with the white kippah and sunglasses); Dr. Barry Kaufmann (with the jacket, tie, and white kippah); Ken Young (with white tie and white shirt); an unidentified man and woman; Vikki Silverman with a guitar (Beth Am's cantor from 1986 to 2012); Gold Brunhild (Vikki Silverman's mother, behind and to the right of Vikki); Dr. Ralph Golub (peeking out from behind Golda); Dr. Gordon Brunhild (Vikki Silverman's father, behind and to the left of Vikki with the jacket, tie, and white shirt); and Rabbi Earl Jordan (Beth Am's rabbi from 1990 to 1999, wearing a tallit).

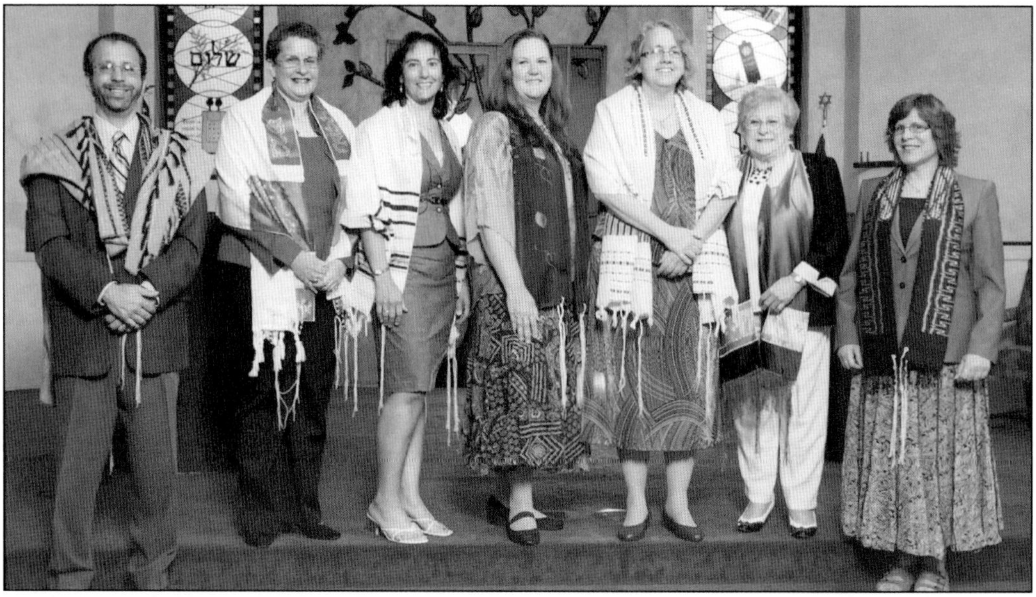

CONGREGATION BETH AM ADULT B'NOT MITZVAH, 2011. Posing here are, from left to right, Rabbi Jason Rosenberg, Sheryl Bowman, Wendy Hess, Caroline Roe, Irma Polster, Golda Brunhild, and Vikki Silverman. The congregation's fourth adult B'not Mitzvah class came to the Torah following two years of intensive study with Rabbi Rosenberg. Rabbi Janet Liss prepared the first class in 1989, and Rabbi Brian Zimmerman prepared the classes between 2001 and 2007. (Courtesy of Vikki Silverman.)

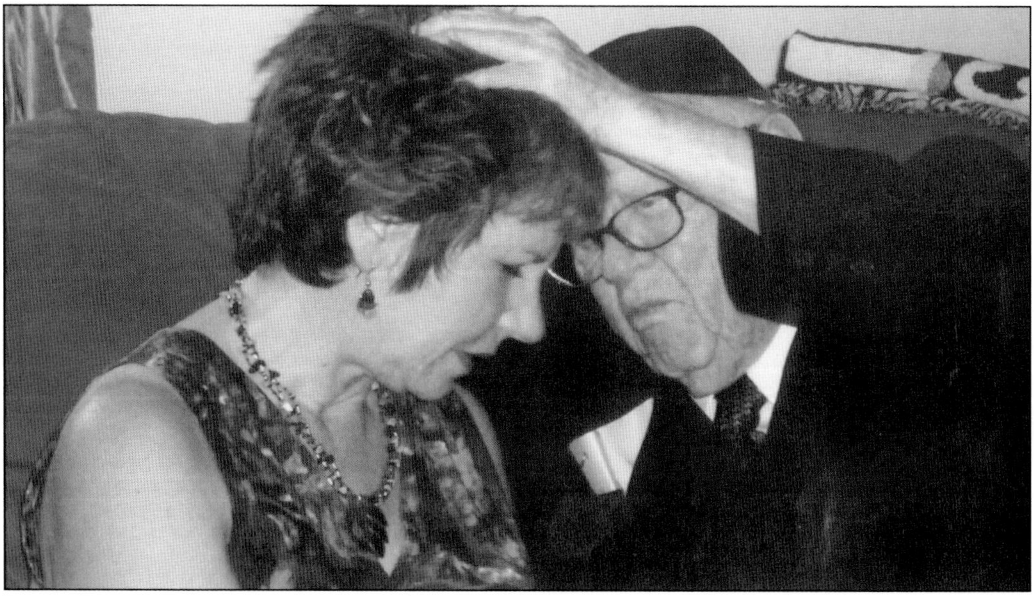

RABBI THEODORE BROD AND RABBI DEBRAH SHENEFELT OF CONGREGATION OR AHAVAH, JULY 31, 2006. Polish immigrant Rabbi Brod arrived in Tampa in 1958. He was the first to bring kosher slaughtering to Tampa, was a Talmudic scholar, and a practicing Kabbalist. Rabbi Debrah Shenefelt was his devoted student for 18 years and Rabbi Brod, despite his commitment to Orthodox practice, encouraged her to become a rabbi. Here, on his 92nd birthday, he blesses Shenefelt. (Courtesy of Debrah Shenefelt.)

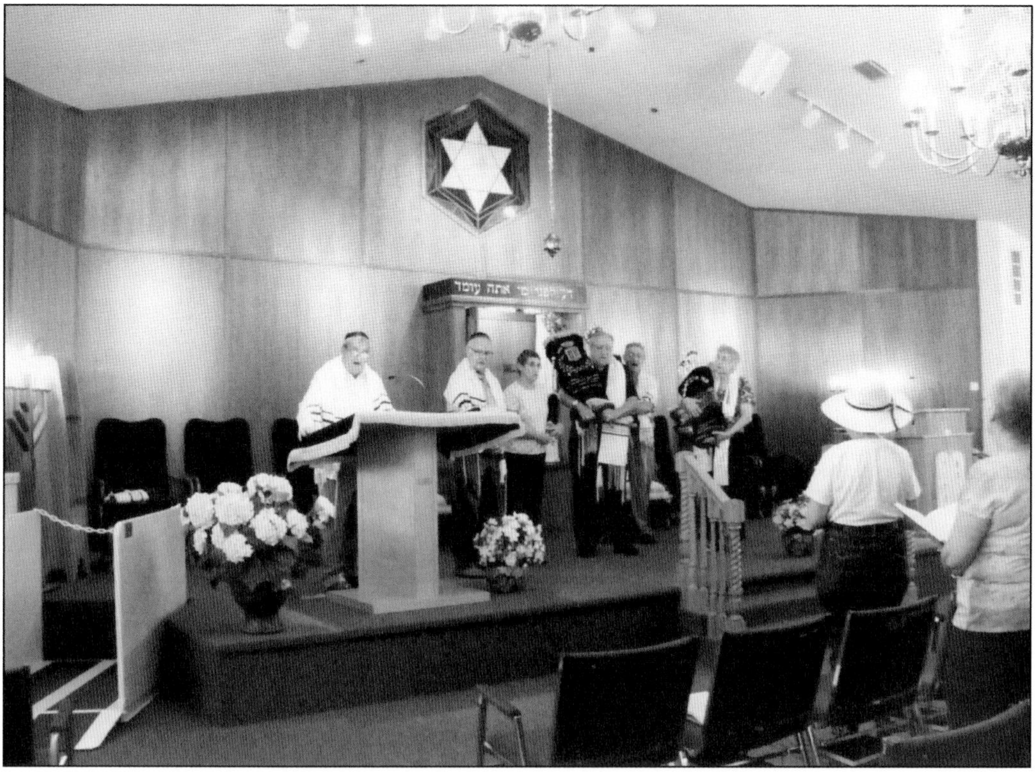

Beth Israel, the Jewish Congregation of Sun City Center, 2012. Shown here at a Simchat Torah celebration are, from left to right, Fred Levine, Bob Whiteman, Nina Malinak, Bernard Cohen, and Richard and Delyse Axinn. This congregation, founded in 1982, serves the Reform Jewish population in Sun City Center and includes a wide variety of Jewish traditions and experiences from a diversity of backgrounds.

National Council of Jewish Women Thrift Shop, c. 1950. Sarah Brash organized the Tampa section of the NCJW in 1924. One of its fundraisers was a thrift shop. Shown here are, from left to right, Bertha Magid Shorstein, Minnie Cracowaner Salsbury, two unidentified, Hannah Sandler, Sarah Wohl Juster, and Jean Witman.

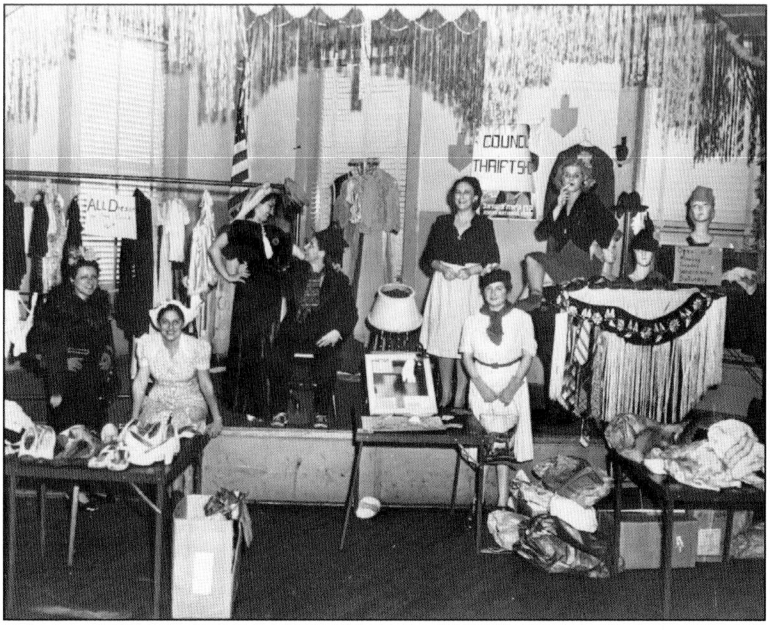

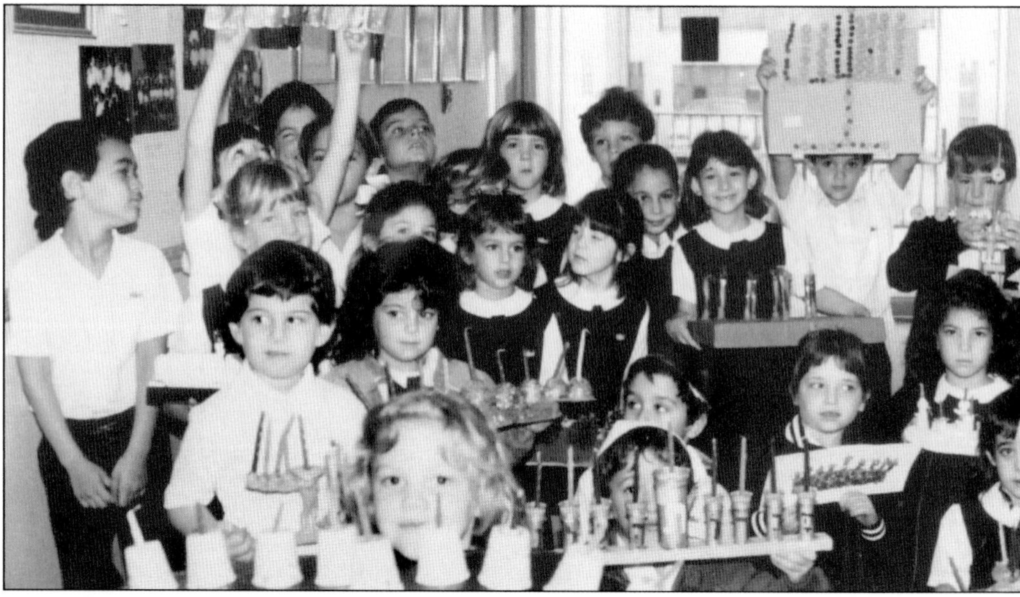

Hillel Community Day School Celebrating Chanukah, 1980s. In 1970, a group recognized the need for a Jewish day school in Tampa. Hillel began as a private school with 30 students in first through fourth grades at Congregation Rodeph Sholom. In 1984, the school moved to the JCC. By 1992, Hillel was open for kindergarten through eighth grade, and the 10-acre campus in North Tampa on West Fletcher Avenue was purchased, with additions constructed in 1999, 2003, and 2010.

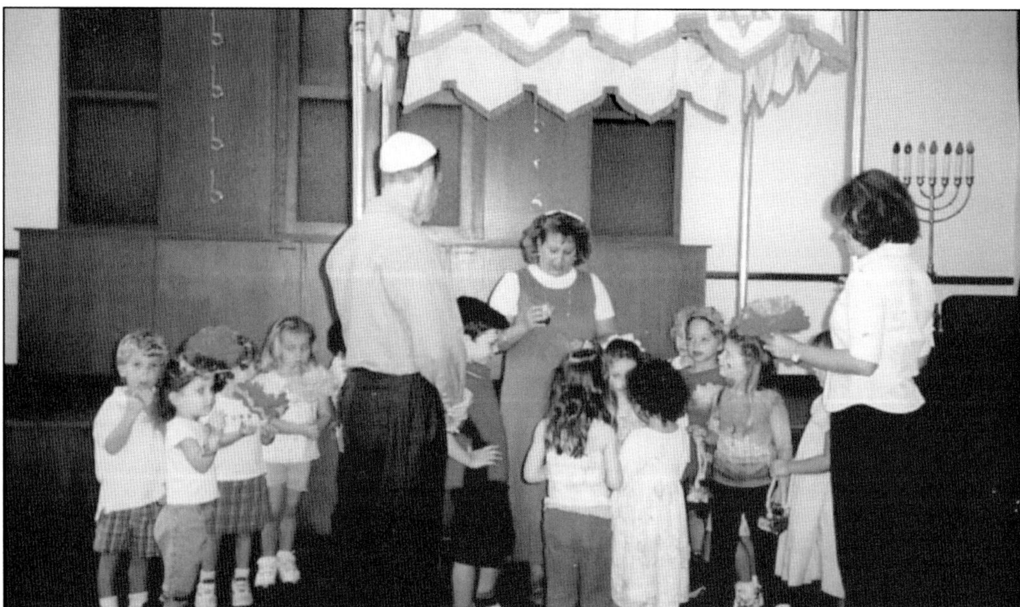

The Jewish Community Center and Federation Preschool South Branch. This school has been located at Rodeph Sholom since 1995 and has expanded from the original 67 children to more than 160 in the current school year. The goal is to create a meaningful educational experience for children with varied backgrounds. Judaism is explored through song, story, art, cooking, and movement. Jewish traditions are enriched through additional holiday and Shabbat activities.

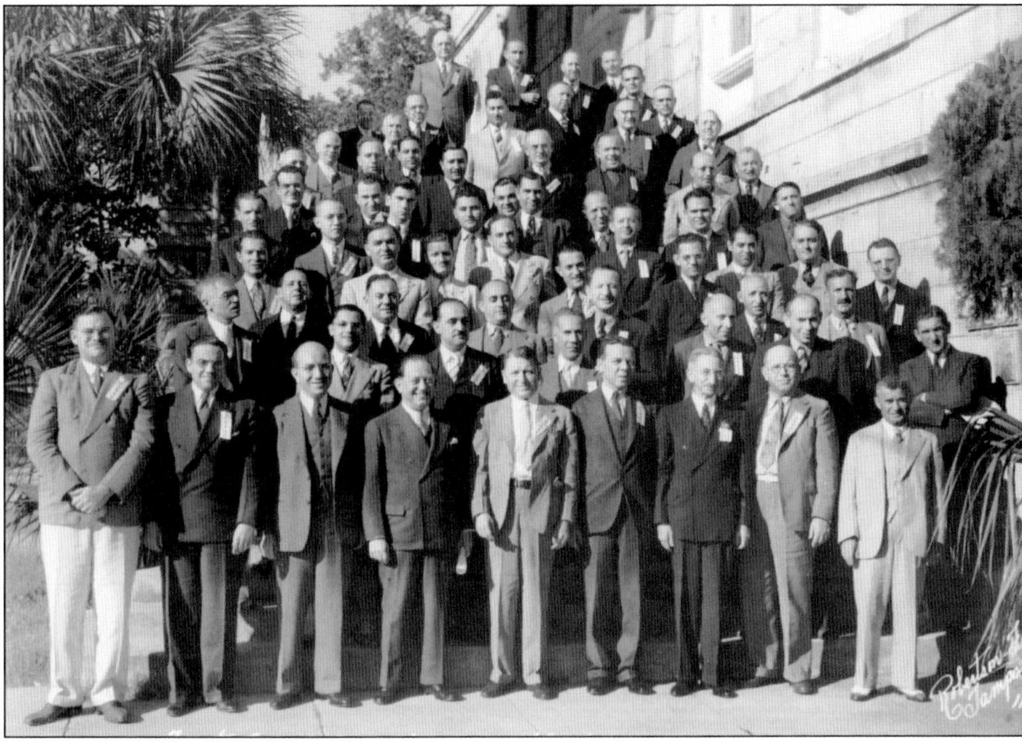

First Annual Conference of Florida B'nai B'rith Lodges, Tampa, 1937. Organized in 1843, this worldwide Jewish community service organization is a national and global leader in the fight against antisemitism and anti-Israel bias. The first lodge in Florida was in Pensacola in 1874.

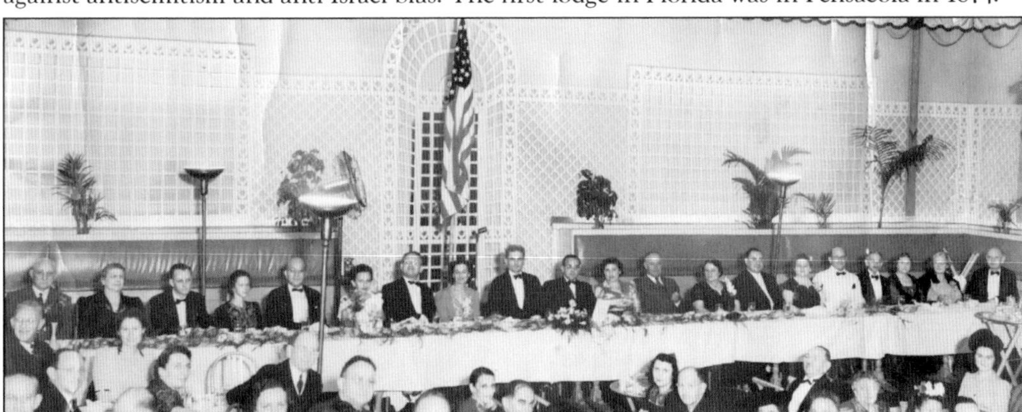

B'nai B'rith Meeting, Tampa, December 12, 1940. At this meeting, held at the Hillsborough Hotel, the address was given by Gov. Spessard Holland. From left to right are (foreground) David Stein, Hyman Wertheim (directly behind David Stein), unidentified, Gretchen Cohen, Rosa Hyman, Lil Stein, unidentified (behind Lil Stein), Maurice Stein, Hannah Sandler (Mrs. Harry N.), unidentified, Lillian and Joe Rosenthal, Gretchen Kotler, Abe Maas, unidentified, Bena Maas, unidentified, and Rebecca and Julius Silverman; (seated at table) Offim Falk, Emma Falk, two unidentified, Morrice S. Uman, Edith Uman, Sam Stein, unidentified, Governor Holland, Rabbi David Zielonka, Carol Zielonka, Mayor and Mrs. R.E.L. Chancey, Rabbi Adolph Burger, two unidentified persons, Judge M. Henry Cohen, Julia Wolf Cohen, Mrs. M.G. Rosenberg, and M.G. Rosenberg.

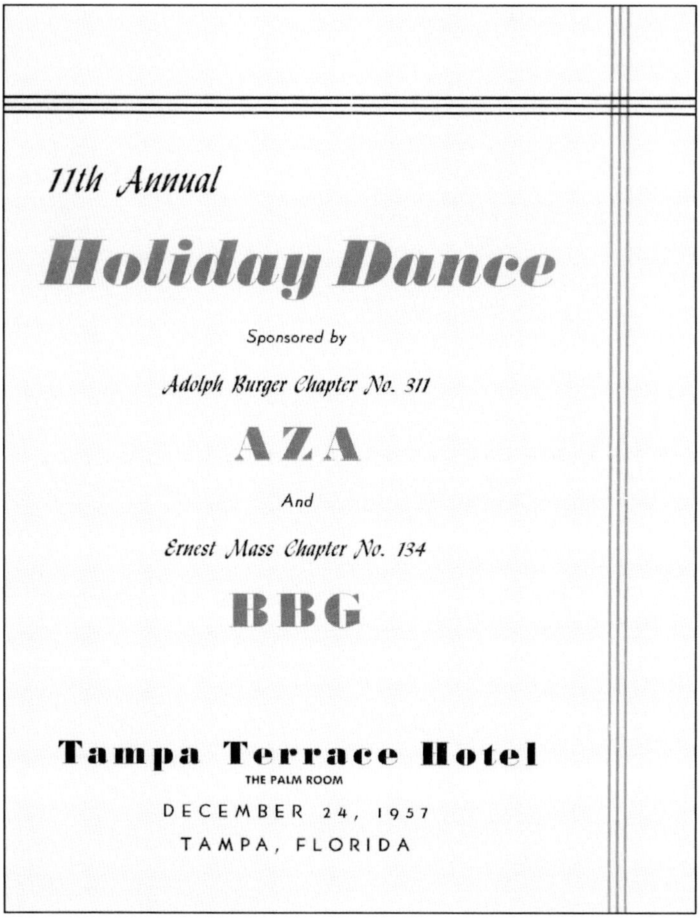

11th Annual

Holiday Dance

Sponsored by

Adolph Burger Chapter No. 311

AZA

And

Ernest Mass Chapter No. 134

BBG

Tampa Terrace Hotel

THE PALM ROOM

DECEMBER 24, 1957

TAMPA, FLORIDA

AZA Dance Program, 1957. The 11th annual Aleph Zadik Aleph Holiday Dance was held in the Palm Room of the Tampa Terrace Hotel.

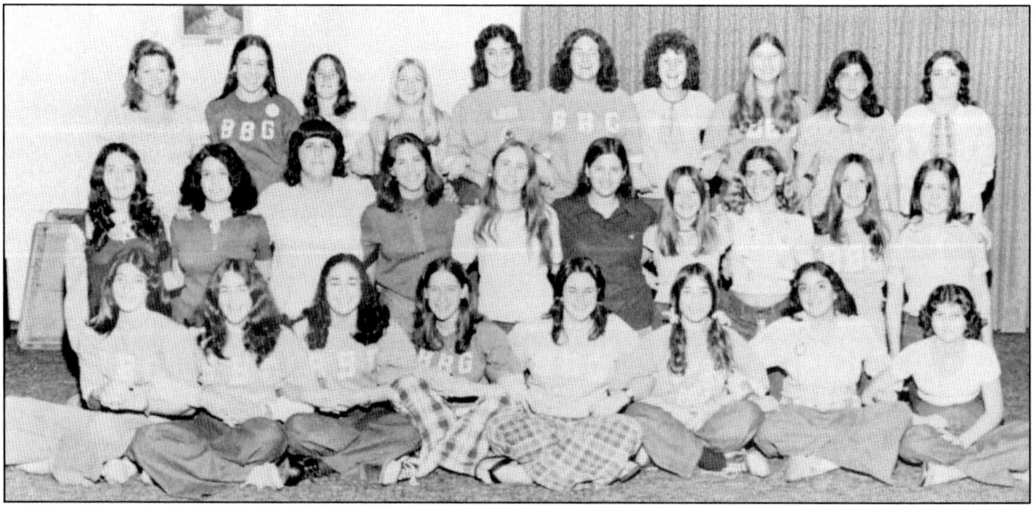

B'nai B'rith Girls, 1973. Since 1924 for Aleph Zadik Aleph (AZA) and 1944 for B'nai B'rith Girls (BBG), B'nai B'rith has sponsored youth organizations. AZA and BBG, composed of teen leaders, have more than 600 chapters worldwide. The organizations address critical issues while learning important skills such as public speaking, event planning, and project management.

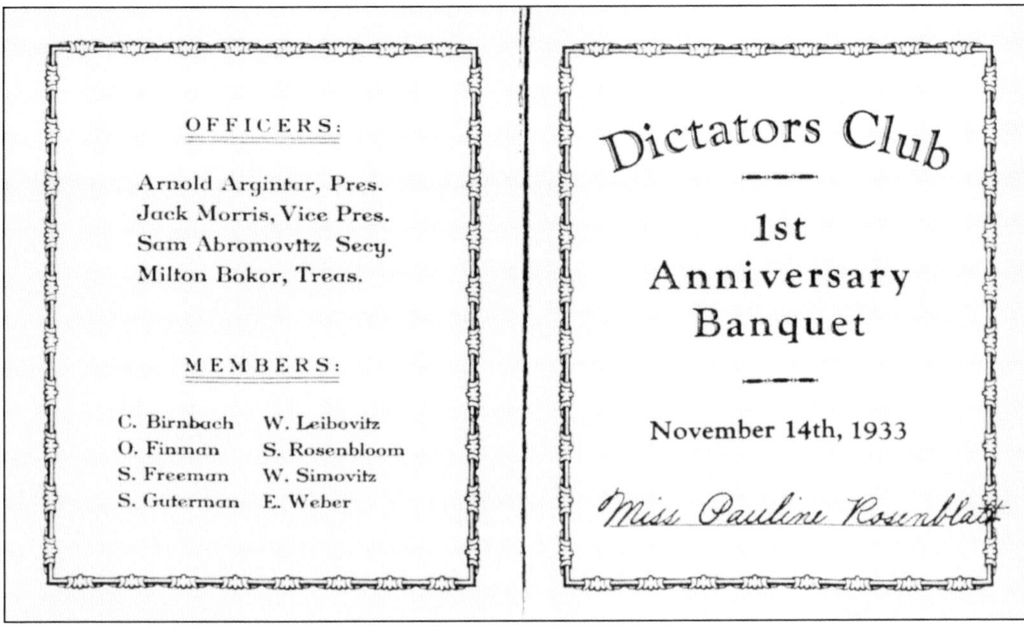

OFFICERS:

Arnold Argintar, Pres.
Jack Morris, Vice Pres.
Sam Abromovitz Secy.
Milton Bokor, Treas.

MEMBERS:

C. Birnbach	W. Leibovitz
O. Finman	S. Rosenbloom
S. Freeman	W. Simovitz
S. Guterman	E. Weber

Dictators Club

1st Anniversary Banquet

November 14th, 1933

Miss Pauline Rosenblatt

DICTATORS CLUB INVITATION, 1933. The Tampa Jewish community was very social, and clubs were formed based on the interests, affiliations, needs, and values of the participants. This was a men's social club.

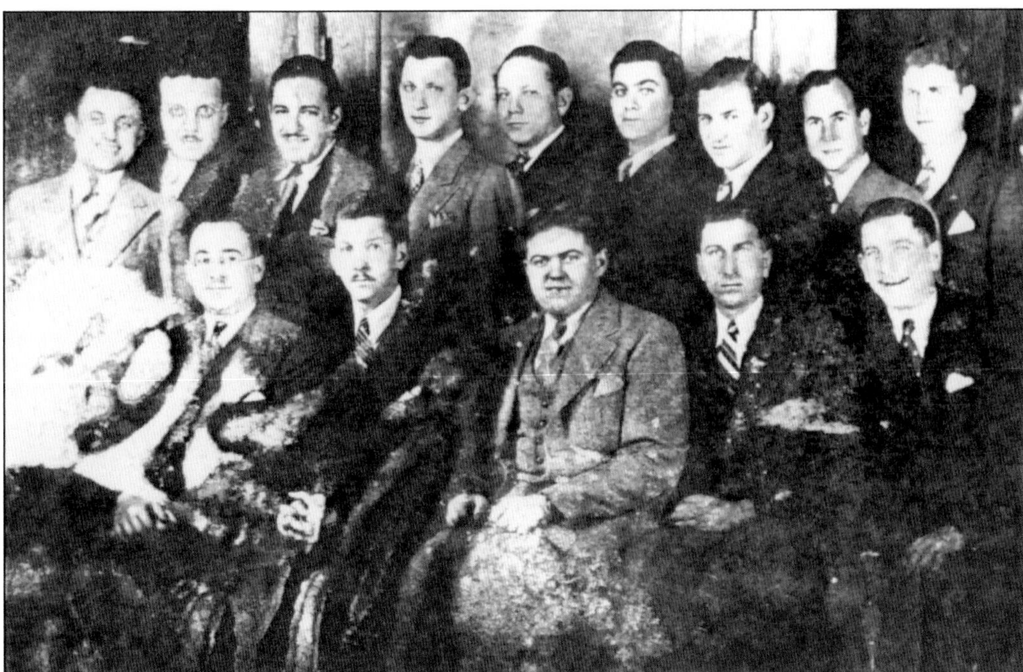

THE MERRY FELLOWS SOCIAL CLUB, 1939. Members shown here are, from left to right, (first row) Frederick Lebos, Leon Schwartz, Alex Bokor, Julius Silverman, and Irving Salsbury; (second row) William Simovitz, Adolph Weil, Sol Fleischman, Oscar Verkauf, William Wolfson, Simon Schwartz, Frederick Poller, Louis Augustine, and Nat Rabinowitz. The club bought radios as wedding gifts for its members.

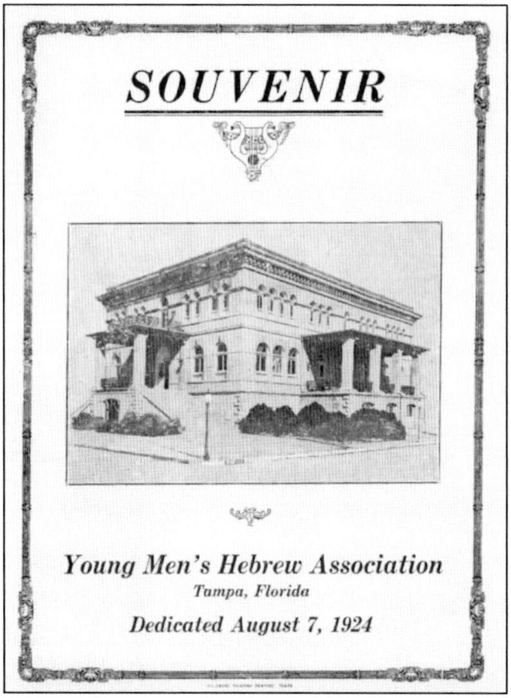
SOUVENIR

Young Men's Hebrew Association
Tampa, Florida
Dedicated August 7, 1924

YOUNG MEN'S HEBREW ASSOCIATION (YMHA) DEDICATION PROGRAM, 1924. Organized in 1906, this group secured a building at Ross and Nebraska Avenues for $26,000 to centralize Jewish activities. Abraham Finkelstein became the executive secretary, Rabbi Adolph Burger was the honorary president, and Samuel Feinberg was the president. Other board members were D. Stein, Sam Stein, Harry N. Sandler, Daniel Cracowaner, Sam Gordon, E.M. Bergman, E.H. Steinberg, and J. Buchman.

YMHA BASKETBALL TEAM, 1939. Posing here are, from left to right, (front) Paul Rippa; (first row) Sammie Argintar, Dick Kreutzman, Larry Waltzer, Mr. Finklestein ("Finky"), and Sam Kotler; (second row) Nathan Kreutzman, Dan Weinstein, Sally Kotler, and Archie Weiss.

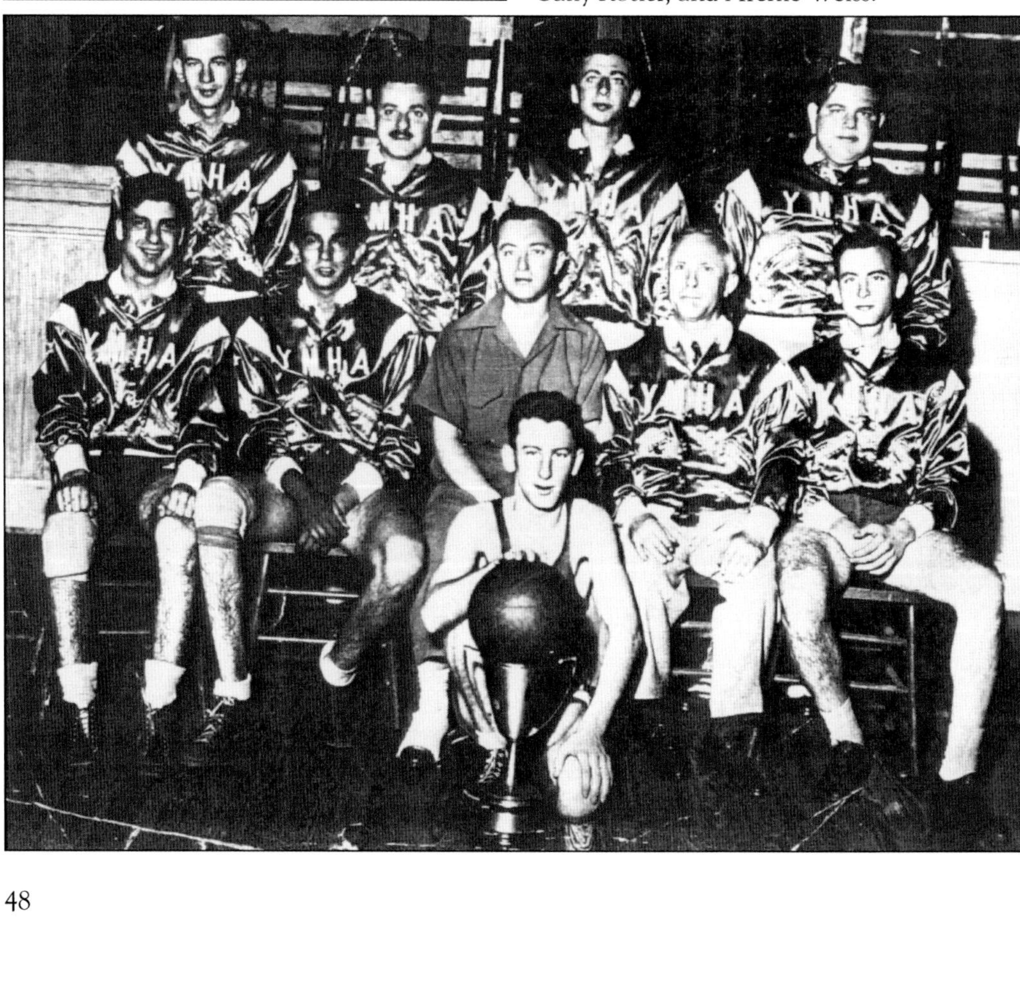

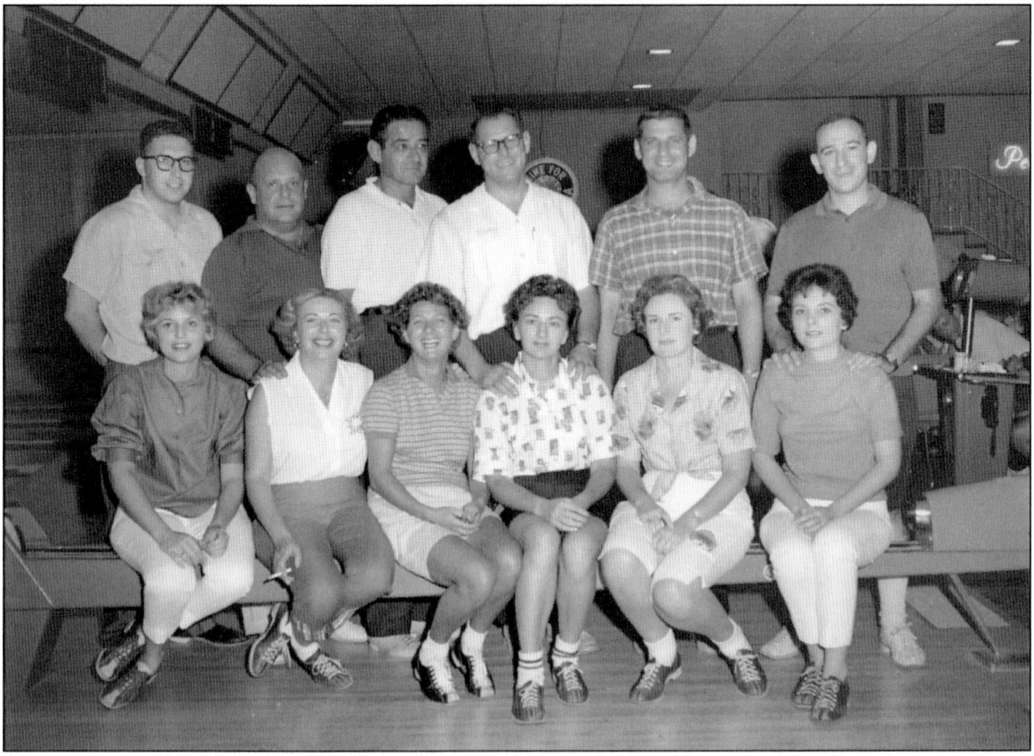

Tampa Jewish Community Center Bowling Team, 1960. The YMHA became the Jewish Community Center after World War II and moved to the former Peter O. Knight Mansion on Hyde Park Avenue. The organization offered a wide range of programming and activities to meet the needs of members of all ages, with a goal of Jewish continuity.

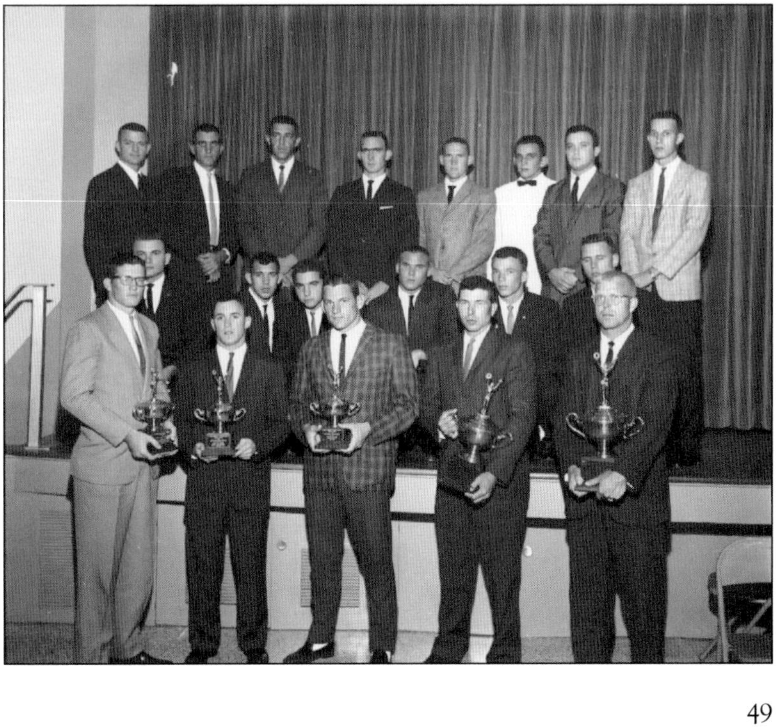

Tampa Jewish Community Center Sports Award Banquet, 1962. These young men were honored for their athletic achievements.

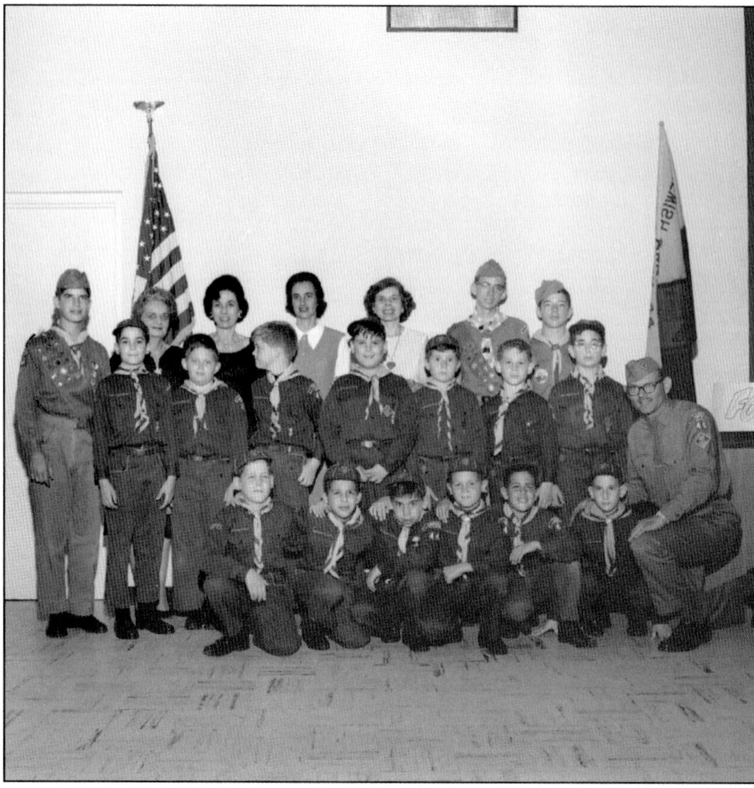

Tampa Jewish Community Center Cub Scouts, 1960s. The tradition of offering activities for all segments of the Jewish community carried over to the 1970s, when the JCC bought property on Horatio Street and erected its own building. The JCC remained there until 1993, when it moved to its North Tampa complex on Gunn Highway.

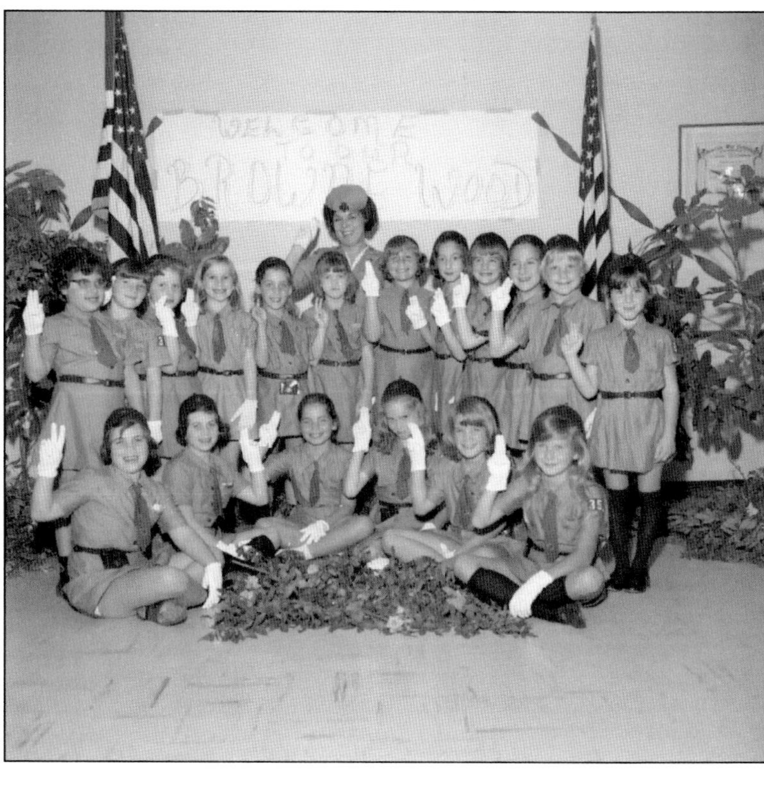

Tampa Jewish Community Center Brownies, 1968. With a population shift to South Tampa, currently, plans are moving forward for the Tampa Jewish Community Center and Federation to open a South Campus at the historic Fort Homer W. Hesterly Armory. It is projected to open in 2015.

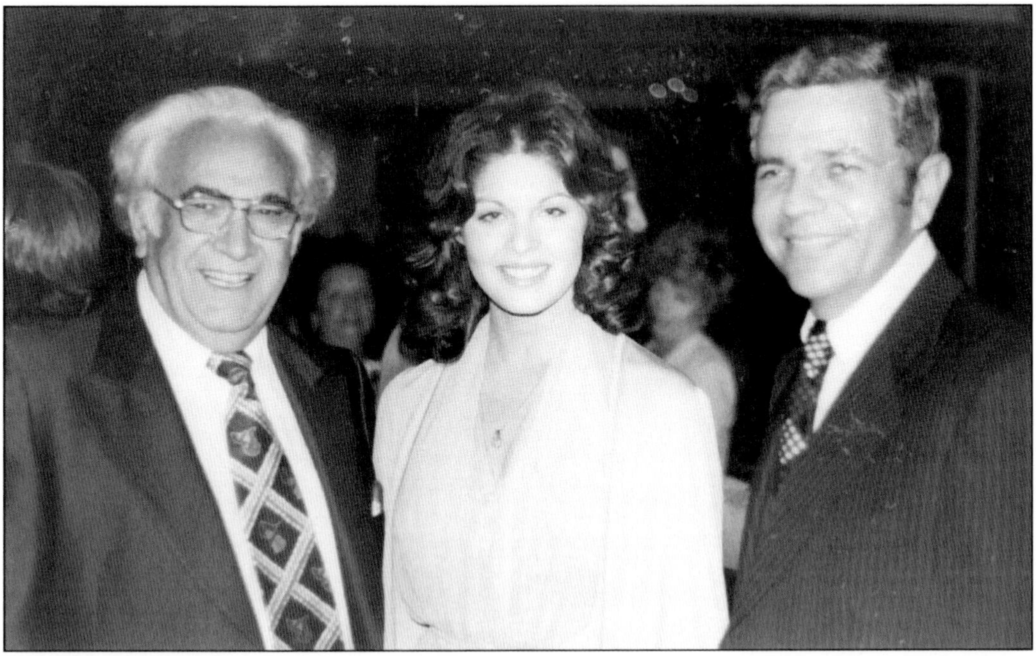

TAMPA JEWISH FEDERATION INITIAL GIFTS DINNER, 1976. Shown here are, from left to right, campaign chair Ben Greenbaum, Miss Universe (representing Israel) Rina Messinger, and president Joel Karpay. In 1941, a group of community leaders felt it was time to eliminate duplicate campaigns for Jewish causes and created the Jewish Welfare Federation. Ernest Maas was the first president. The Tampa JCC and Federation were brought together in 1996 after operating independently for more than 50 years. The mission is to support and enrich Jewish life and values in Tampa, in Israel, and worldwide, and to be a unifying force for Jewish activity. The annual campaign raises in excess of $2 million to fund local Jewish educational and social service organizations and to support Jews in need in Israel and around the world.

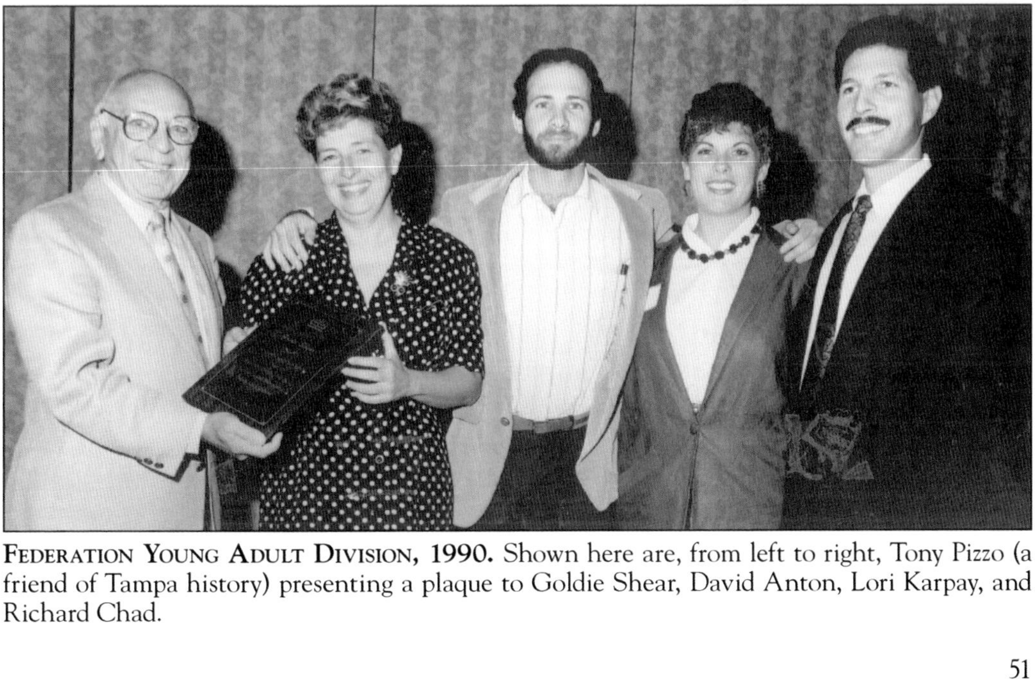

FEDERATION YOUNG ADULT DIVISION, 1990. Shown here are, from left to right, Tony Pizzo (a friend of Tampa history) presenting a plaque to Goldie Shear, David Anton, Lori Karpay, and Richard Chad.

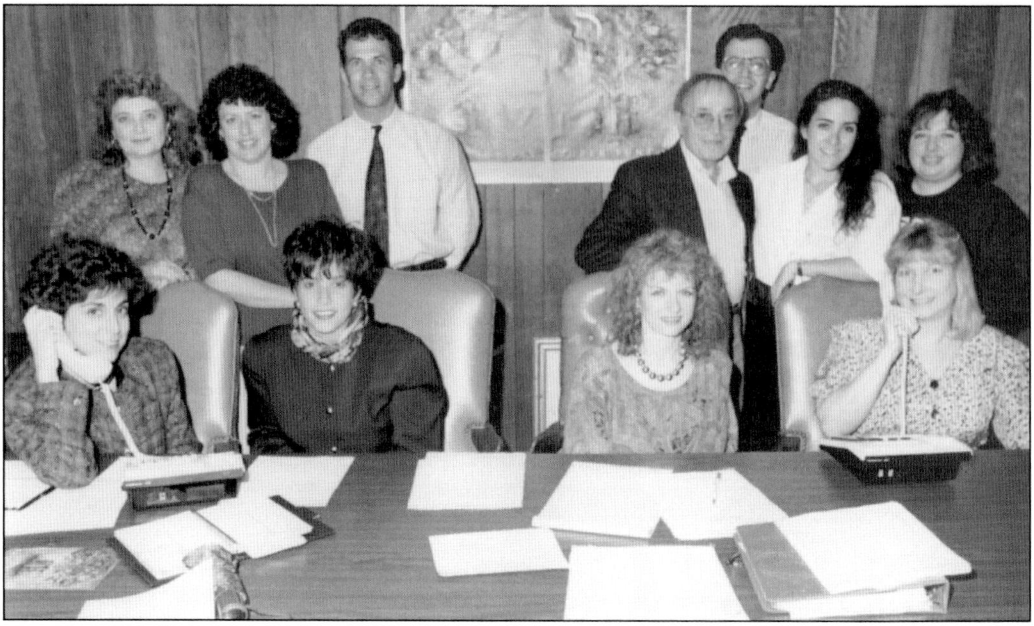

Federation Super Sunday Cabinet, 1993. Super Sunday is part of the annual fundraising appeal of the Tampa Jewish Federation. Shown here are, from left to right, (seated) Amy Schneirov, Barbara Rinde, Cindy Spahn, and Susan Kessler; (standing) Eva Aron, Ellyne Myers, Mark Wright, Sam Gross, Sanford Hoffman, Karen Brunhild, and Lynn Heller.

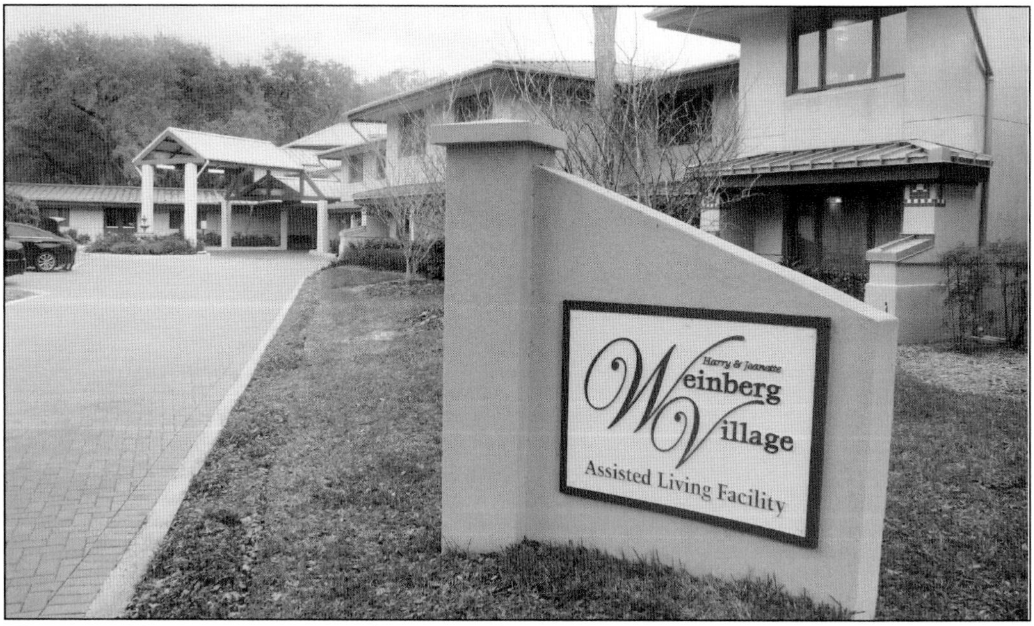

Weinberg Village, 2013. Weinberg Village was created in 1995 on the 21-acre campus of the Tampa Jewish Community Center (JCC) and Federation to celebrate the best in Jewish heritage, culture, traditions, and values, including kosher meals. The assisted living facility provides residential care for retirees and senior citizens with room for up to 95 residents. The organization partners with JCC Preschool North for intergenerational programming and activities. (Courtesy of Dr. Rob Norman.)

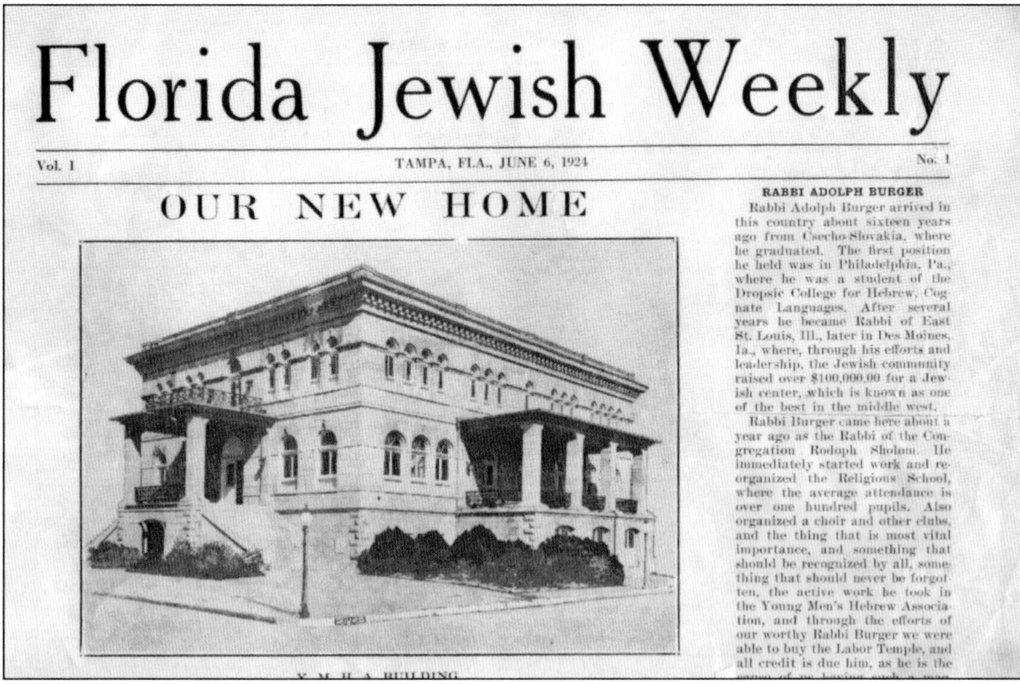

Florida Jewish Weekly

Vol. 1 TAMPA, FLA., JUNE 6, 1924 No. 1

OUR NEW HOME

Y. M. H. A. BUILDING

RABBI ADOLPH BURGER

Rabbi Adolph Burger arrived in this country about sixteen years ago from Czecho-Slovakia, where he graduated. The first position he held was in Philadelphia, Pa., where he was a student of the Dropsie College for Hebrew, Cognate Languages. After several years he became Rabbi of East St. Louis, Ill., later in Des Moines, Ia., where, through his efforts and leadership, the Jewish community raised over $100,000.00 for a Jewish center, which is known as one of the best in the middle west.

Rabbi Burger came here about a year ago as the Rabbi of the Congregation Rodoph Sholom. He immediately started work and reorganized the Religious School, where the average attendance is over one hundred pupils. Also organized a choir and other clubs, and the thing that is most vital importance, and something that should be recognized by all, something that should never be forgotten, the active work he took in the Young Men's Hebrew Association, and through the efforts of our worthy Rabbi Burger we were able to buy the Labor Temple, and all credit is due him, as he is the

FLORIDA JEWISH WEEKLY, VOLUME 1, NUMBER 1, 1924. This was the inaugural issue for this Tampa publication. Jewish newspapers have been published in Tampa since the 1920s to mobilize the community on issues and events and to increase awareness of news about the Jewish community, locally, nationally, and internationally.

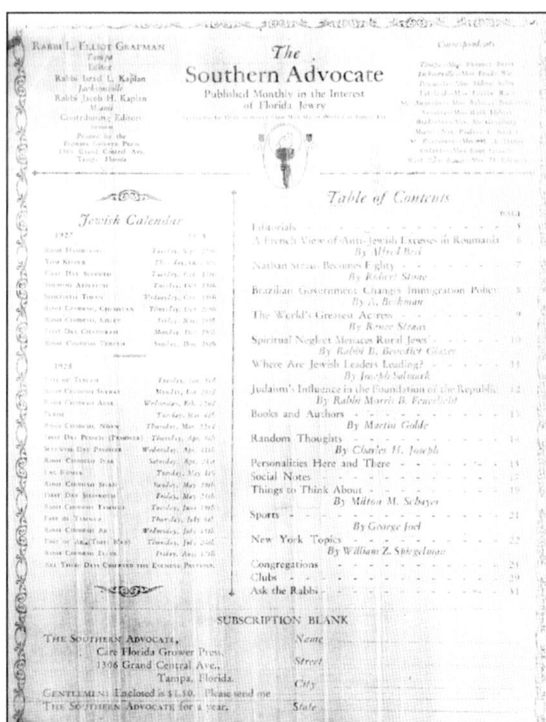

Rabbi L. Elliot Grafman
Tampa
Editor
Rabbi Israel L. Kaplan
Jacksonville
Rabbi Jacob H. Kaplan
Miami
Contributing Editors

The
Southern Advocate
Published Monthly in the Interest of Florida Jewry

Jewish Calendar

Table of Contents

	PAGE
Editorials	5
A French View of Anti-Jewish Excesses in Roumania — *By Alfred Berl*	6
Nathan Straus Becomes Eighty — *By Robert Stone*	7
Brazilian Government Changes Immigration Policy — *By A. Beckman*	8
The World's Greatest Actress — *By Renee Straus*	9
Spiritual Neglect Menaces Rural Jews — *By Rabbi B. Benedict Glazer*	10
Where Are Jewish Leaders Leading? — *By Joseph Salmark*	11
Judaism's Influence in the Foundation of the Republic — *By Rabbi Morris B. Feuerlicht*	12
Books and Authors — *By Martin Golde*	13
Random Thoughts — *By Charles H. Joseph*	14
Personalities Here and There	15
Social Notes	17
Things to Think About — *By Milton M. Schayer*	19
Sports — *By George Joel*	21
New York Topics — *By William Z. Spiegelman*	22
Congregations	25
Clubs	29
Ask the Rabbi	31

SUBSCRIPTION BLANK

The Southern Advocate,
Care Florida Grower Press,
1306 Grand Central Ave.,
Tampa, Florida.
Gentlemen: Enclosed is $1.50. Please send me The Southern Advocate for a year.

Name / *Street* / *City* / *State*

THE SOUTHERN ADVOCATE, PUBLISHED IN TAMPA, 1928. Rabbi Elliot Grafman was publisher and editor of this statewide Anglo-Jewish periodical. The paper published 11 monthly issues before the 1928 collapse of the real-estate boom, when advertising became a major challenge for Grafman. The *Jewish Floridian* also began publication in 1928, lasting until 1990. The entire run of the *Jewish Floridian* is part of the collections at the Jewish Museum of Florida.

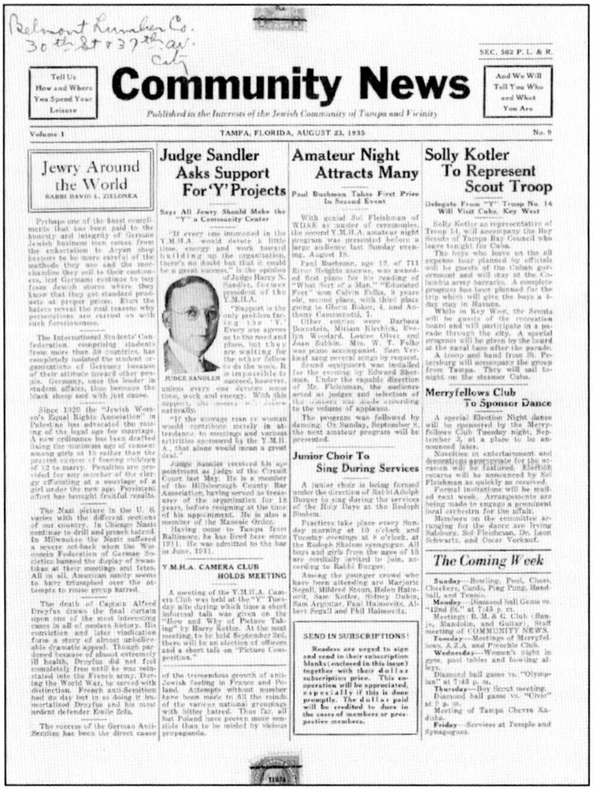

Tell Us How and Where You Spend Your Leisure

Community News

And We Will Tell You Who and What You Are

Published in the Interests of the Jewish Community of Tampa and Vicinity

Volume 1 — TAMPA, FLORIDA, AUGUST 23, 1935 — No. 9

Jewry Around the World

RABBI DAVID L. ZIELONKA

Judge Sandler Asks Support For 'Y' Projects

Says All Jewry Should Make the "Y" a Community Center

JUDGE SANDLER

Y.M.H.A. CAMERA CLUB HOLDS MEETING

Amateur Night Attracts Many

Paul Buchman Takes First Prize In Second Event

Junior Choir To Sing During Services

SEND IN SUBSCRIPTIONS!

Solly Kotler To Represent Scout Troop

Delegate From "Y" Troop No. 14 Will Visit Cuba, Key West

Merryfellows Club To Sponsor Dance

The Coming Week

COMMUNITY NEWS, 1935. Founded in 1935, this was a weekly local newspaper about and for the Tampa Jewish community. Ben Haimovitz's daughter Florence Haimovitz Rosenberg was the editor. Florence also was a social worker for the Florida Department of Children and Families for more than 20 years.

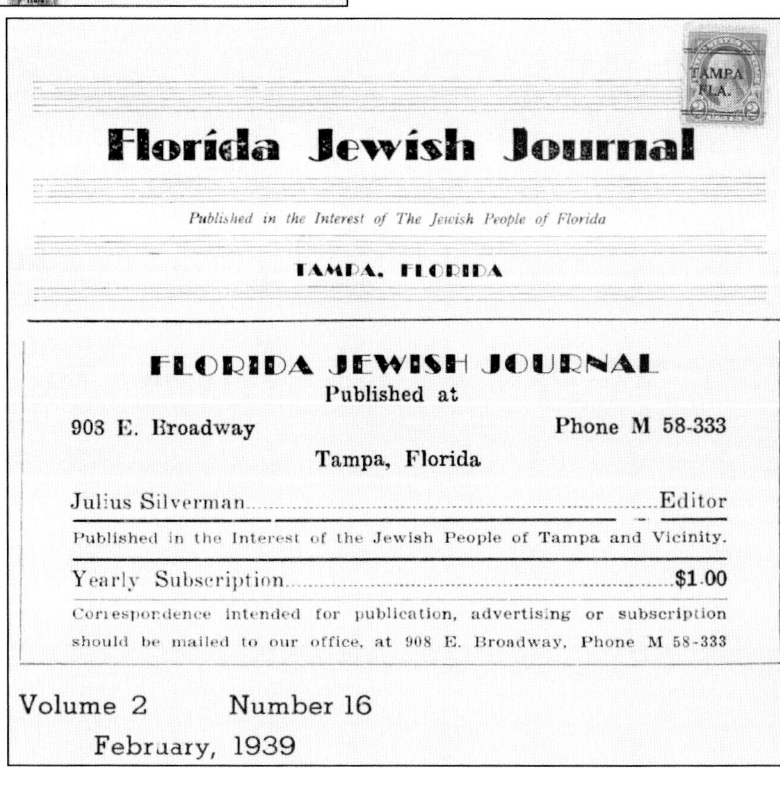

Florida Jewish Journal

Published in the Interest of The Jewish People of Florida

TAMPA, FLORIDA

FLORIDA JEWISH JOURNAL
Published at

903 E. Broadway — Phone M 58-333

Tampa, Florida

Julius Silverman .... Editor

Published in the Interest of the Jewish People of Tampa and Vicinity.

Yearly Subscription $1.00

Correspondence intended for publication, advertising or subscription should be mailed to our office, at 908 E. Broadway, Phone M 58-333

Volume 2 Number 16
February, 1939

FLORIDA JEWISH JOURNAL, 1939. The *Florida Jewish Journal* was based at 908 East Broadway. For $1, a reader could get a year's subscription.

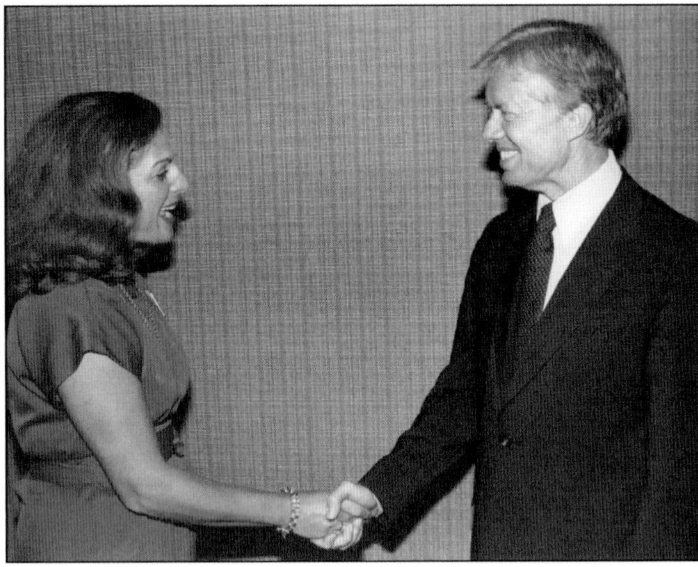

THE *JEWISH FLORIDIAN* OF TAMPA. In 1979, the year the paper began publication, the founding editor, Judith Rosenkranz (shown here), was invited to a meeting of Florida newspaper editors, where Pres. Jimmy Carter greeted them. Fred Shochet published the *Jewish Floridian of Tampa* for nine years. Rosenkranz has served as president of both the Jewish Federation of Tampa (1984–1986) and Women of Reform Judaism (1993–1997). (Courtesy of Judith Rosenkranz.)

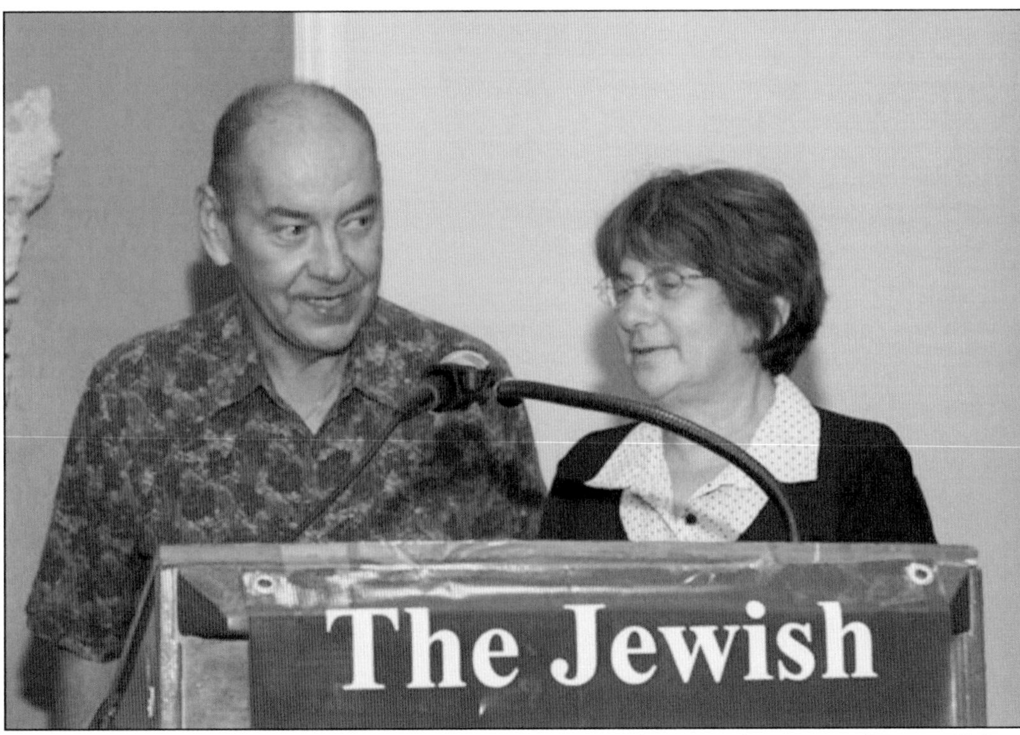

KAREN AND JIM DAWKINS, 2009. "When we were journalists at other papers (*Tampa Tribune* and *Evening Independent* in St. Petersburg), we worked hard, but didn't have time for life. We did not have the time to be involved in the Jewish community. But this [founding the *Jewish Press of Tampa*] allowed us to combine professional journalism with Judaism." These words sum up the Dawkinses' commitment as they started the *Jewish Press of Tampa* in 1988 in their home. (Courtesy of *Jewish Press*.)

INAUGURAL EDITION

Jewish Press of TAMPA

serving the Hillsborough County Jewish Community

VOLUME 1 NUMBER 1 Tampa, Florida, JULY 22, 1988 • 8 AV 5748 8 Pages • 30 Cents

Federation delays allocations, extends 1988 Campaign until end of August

• Related VIEWPOINT column, PAGE 2

Faced with budget requests higher than funds raised so far, The Tampa Jewish Federation Board has voted to extend the 1988 Campaign through the end of August and delay approving allocations to local and national agencies.

Calling it a "crisis" situation, Campaign officials said an additional $150,000 is needed before Aug. 31 to meet just the minimum needs of the Tampa Jewish community.

To date, the 1988 Tampa Jewish Federation/United Jewish Appeal Campaign has raised $1,103,000, a 9 percent increase over the same cards last year.

However, there is still nearly $100,000 in pledges received in 1987 that have not been realized for the 1988 campaign, according to Walter Kessler, 1988 campaign chairman and new Federation president.

"It is imperative that we receive these and other commitments before the end of August so that we can budget on a maximum result," he said.

For each dollar raised in the campaign, 50 cents goes to UJA. The other 50 percent is split among other agencies with local beneficiary agencies such as the Jewish Community Center, Tampa Jewish Family Service, Hillel School and Community High School receiving a major portion of the funds.

This year, these local and national agencies have requested allocations totaling $563,000. If the Federation were to budget on a campaign figure equal to last year, there would be more more than $75,000 in necessary budget requests that

CAMPAIGN continued on PAGE 2

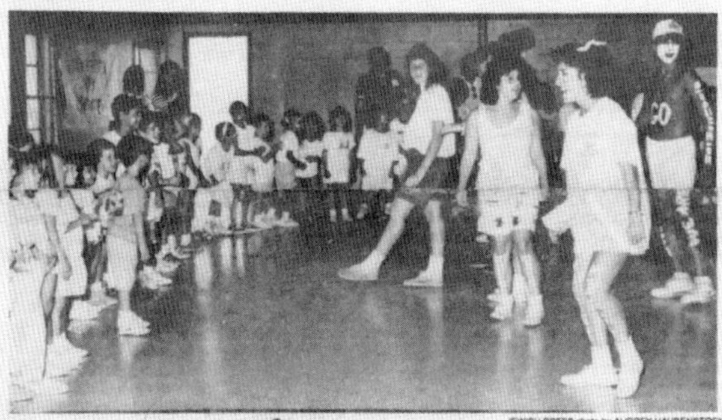

JEWISH PRESS photo by AUDREY HAUBENSTOCK

Blue versus white makes for three days of fun

The Maccabee Games (Color War) featuring three days of fun and competition, blue versus white, got under way Tuesday at the JCC Main Branch Summercamp. Here counselors, their bodies covered with blue and white paint, rouse the group with cheers. Counselors are Susan Bruemmer, Michelle DeCroes, Charles Silver and Brad Ivers.

PROFILE: Walter Kessler, new Federation president

Upcoming years seen as bright with potential for Federation, community

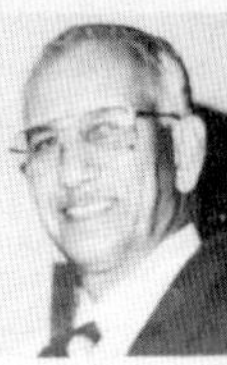

WALTER H. KESSLER

Walter H. Kessler, newly elected president of the Tampa Jewish Federation, sees the next two years as a challenge not only for himself, but also for the Tampa Jewish community.

"I see a lot of potential for growth," Kessler said.

In the public sector, Tampa is heralded as the nation's next great city. As the area grows, Kessler believes the Jewish population also will increase, and the existing Jewish community needs to be ready.

There's a definite need to increase the philanthropic base, he said, through Campaign, TOP and Menorah Manor, plus to increase the level of activities and programs available for Tampa's Jewish population.

Kessler sees the Federation as the central address for the county's Jewish community because the Federation is the umbrella organization representing all the agencies and organizations and also is the organization which channels community contributions to provide financial support through the agencies such as the JCC, Tampa Jewish Family Service and Hillel School.

The new Federation president, who served as General Campaign chairman for the past two

KESSLER continued on PAGE 2

Tampa doubles number of charitable grants to non-profit groups through TOP

Charitable grants by the Tampa Orlando Pinellas (TOP) Jewish Foundation topped the $1 million mark during the fiscal year ending June 30. Meanwhile, the amount of grants distributed to Tampa non-profit groups more than doubled over the previous year.

TOP, the endowment arm of the three Federations, made a total of 320 grants totaling $1,019,499 during the past year. That is an 8 percent increase over the previous year when $940,133 was distributed to 302 non-profit groups.

Just over half of the money, $530,530, was allocated directly to the three Federations served by TOP. Federation beneficiary agencies received 15 percent of the total allocations, $157,469. Another 21 percent, $210,54, went to other Jewish organizations such as ORT, Hadassah and Chabad, with the remaining 12 percent, $120,995, going to non-Jewish organizations.

In Tampa, 70 grants totaling $194,342 went to 24 non-profit groups, compared to last year when $81,849 was distributed. The TOP grants in Tampa represented 19 percent of the Foundation's total allocations for 1987-88.

In Orlando, 139 grants totaling $372,948 was given to 58 groups. However, that figure represents a $71,000 decrease in allocations.

Pinellas County had the highest amount allocated during the year with 111 grants made to 32 organizations. That was 44 percent of all money allocated by TOP. In 1986-87, TOP allocations totaled $414,333.

TOP Executive Director Mark Glickman said he was

TOP continued on PAGE 4

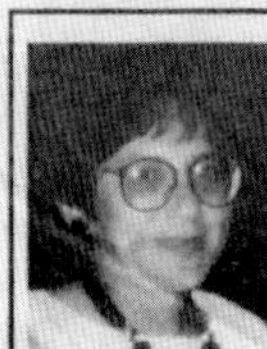

KAREN WOLFSON DAWKINS

Karen Wolfson Dawkins to head Tampa edition of Jewish Press

The Jewish Press you are now reading is the first edition of the *Jewish Press of Tampa*, a privately-owned Jewish community newspaper published in the Tampa Bay area.

The paper's debut marks a cooperative agreement between the paper's publishers, Wolfson-Dawkins Publications, and the Tampa Jewish Federation to bring a locally produced Jewish community newspaper to Hillsborough County.

The birth of this paper is occurring as the Jewish Press celebrates its second anniversary of publication in Pinellas County with the separate *Jewish Press of Pinellas County*.

"The debut of the *Jewish Press of Pinellas County* two years ago and that of the *Jewish Press of Tampa* today, we believe, is part of a changing trend in Jewish newspapers, in areas where Jews are definitely the minority," said Jewish Press owner & publisher Jim Dawkins.

"Desktop publishing has made local publication possible," Dawkins said, "while the changing character of the general and Jewish populations has made Jewish papers even more necessary."

"Assimilation and minority-status has made the Jewish paper important as a vehicle to promote Jewish identity," Dawkins said.

"Federations have long entered into cooperative agreements with Jewish papers, ensuring the existence of the paper by guaranteeing subscription costs and providing the most economical method for Federations to reach their constituents.

JEWISH PRESS continued on PAGE 3

JEWISH PRESS OF TAMPA, FIRST EDITION, 1988. Celebrating 25 years of service in providing biweekly news and issues of importance, in cooperation with the Tampa JCC & Federation, Karen and Jim Dawkins have kept the Tampa Jewish community informed, cohesive, and responsive. The co-owners moved to their Largo office in 2002. Karen's dad, Harold Wolfson, has been the volunteer production manager. (Courtesy of *Jewish Press.*)

Three

In Business and Professions

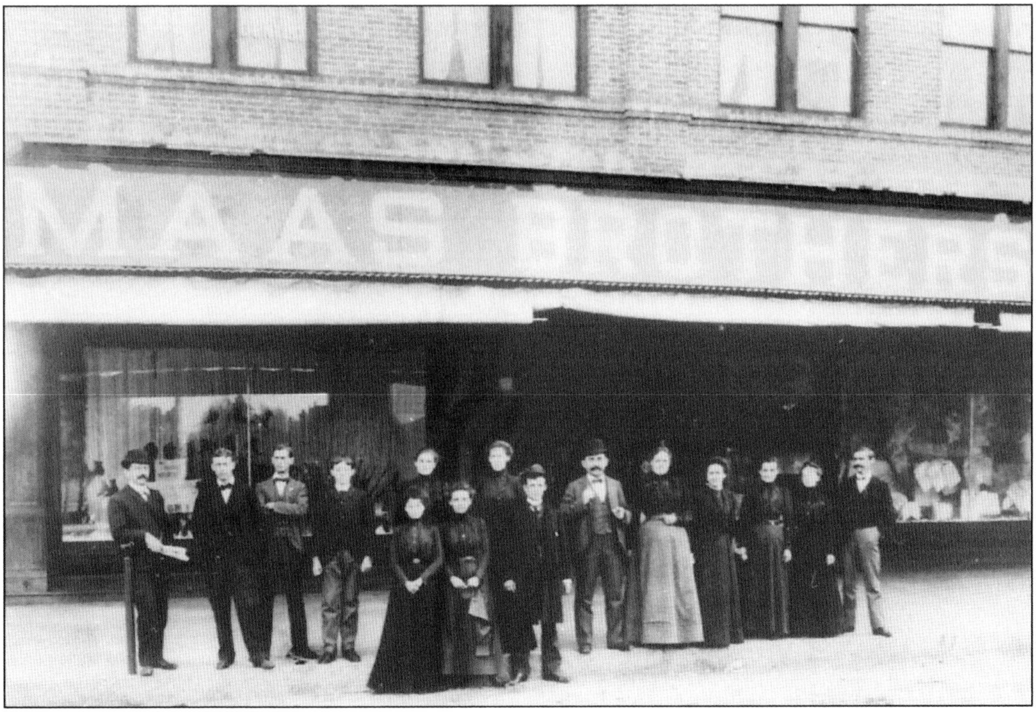

Maas Brothers, c. 1898. German immigrant Abe Maas opened his first store, Dry Goods Palace, in 1886. His brother, Isaac, joined him the following year to form Maas Brothers. Here, a group of the Maas family and employees stand in front of the second location, in the Krause Building at Franklin and Zack Streets, which operated for 23 years. Maas Brothers grew to be Tampa's leading department store, with a chain of 39 stores in 100 years.

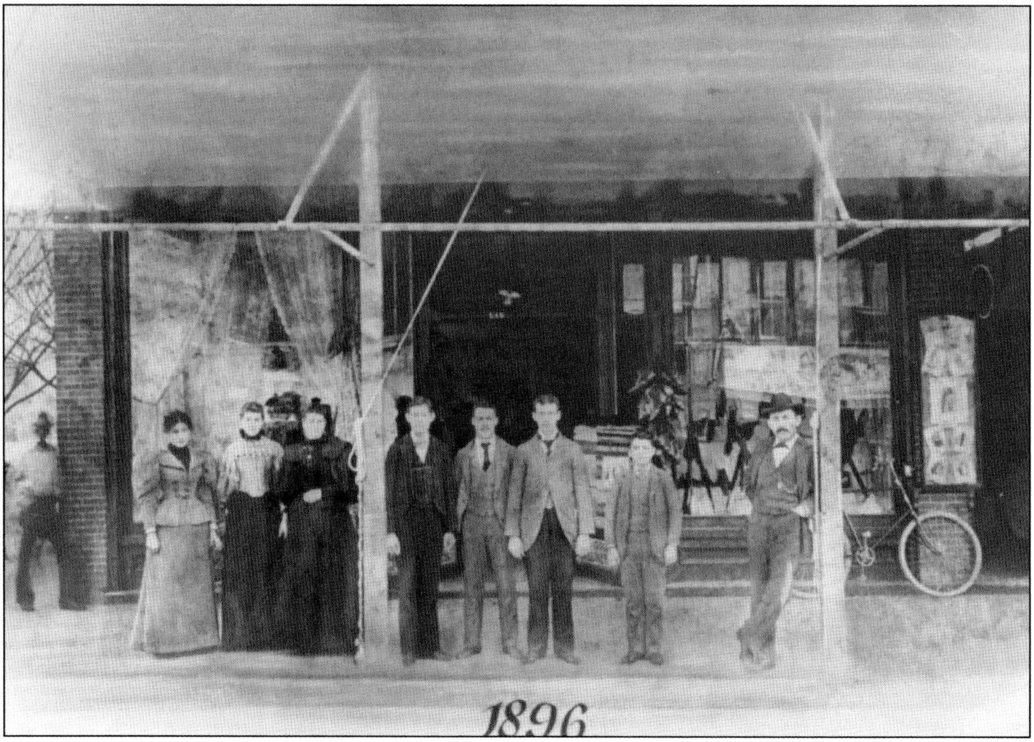

Maas Family in Front of Dry Goods Palace, 1896. Abe Maas opened his first store with his wife, Bena, in a 23-foot-by-90-foot room in the two-story J.C. Field Building, shown here, at Franklin and Twiggs Streets. Abe Maas is on the far right, leaning against a column. His cousin Ernest Maas is to his left.

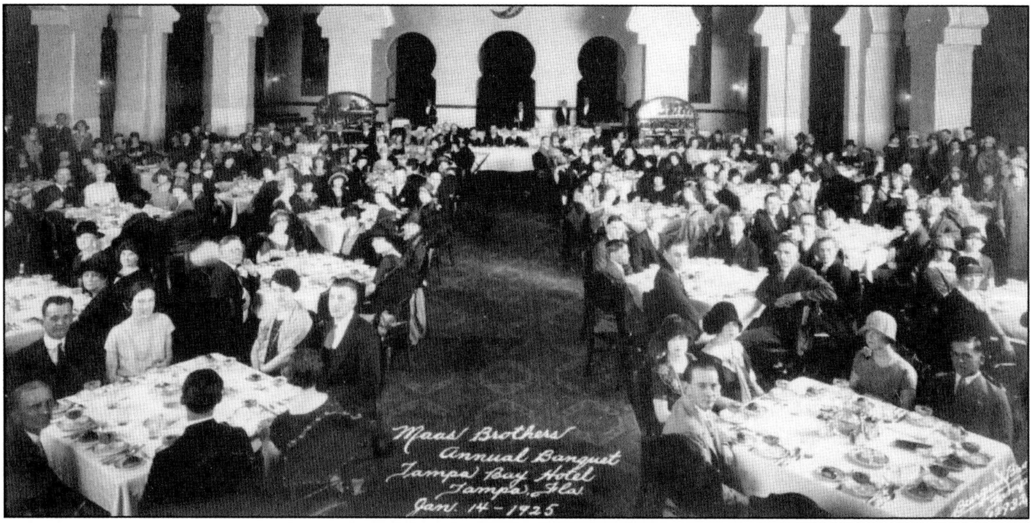

Maas Brothers Annual Employee Banquet, 1925. The business acumen and untiring energy of the Maas brothers was instrumental in the growth of the business. By 1921, the store occupied 25,000 square feet, the sales force had grown from 3 employees to more than 100, and capital expanded from $625 to $250,000. The company went from being one of the smallest to the largest exclusive ladies furnishing goods houses in the state.

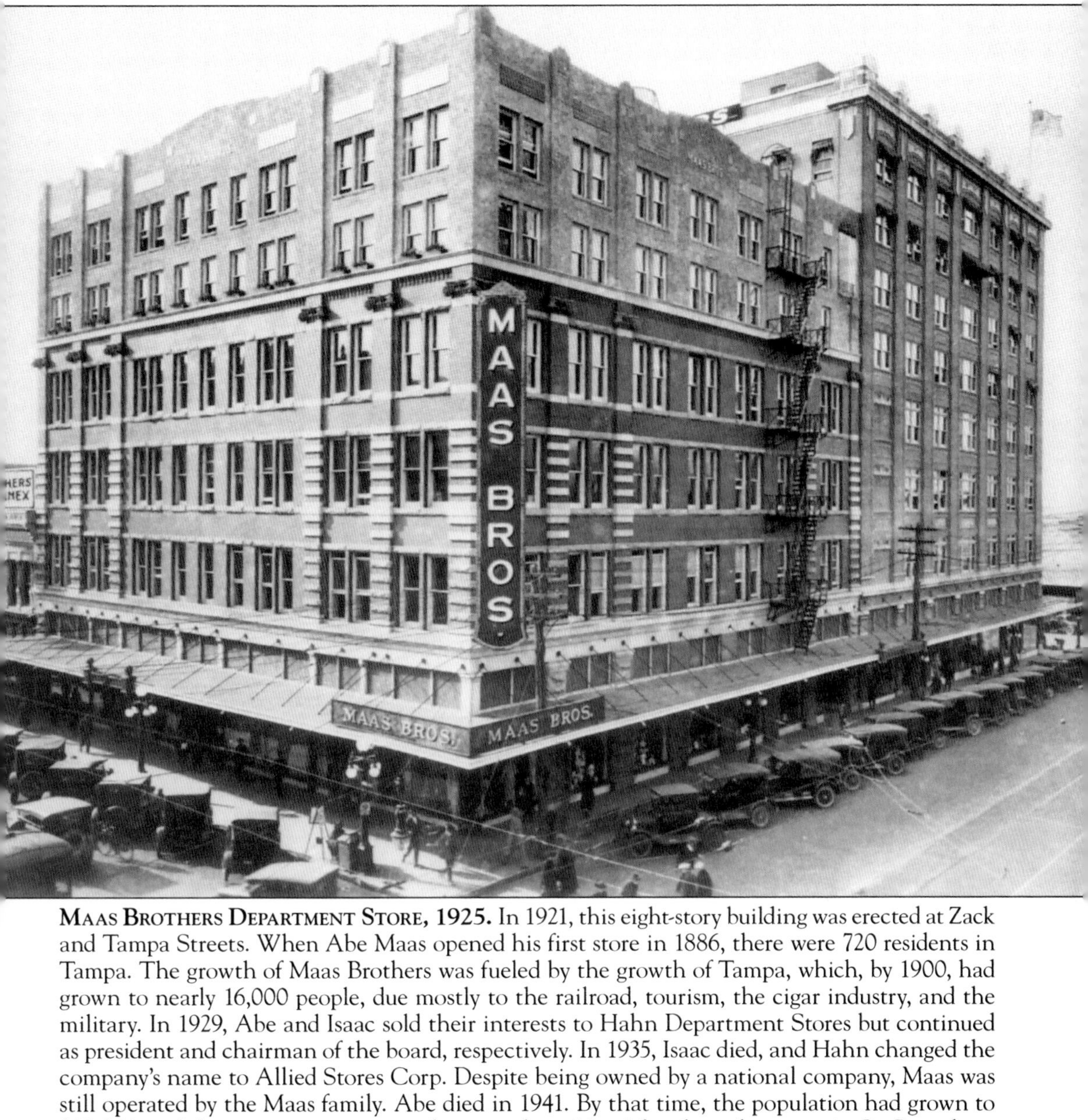

MAAS BROTHERS DEPARTMENT STORE, 1925. In 1921, this eight-story building was erected at Zack and Tampa Streets. When Abe Maas opened his first store in 1886, there were 720 residents in Tampa. The growth of Maas Brothers was fueled by the growth of Tampa, which, by 1900, had grown to nearly 16,000 people, due mostly to the railroad, tourism, the cigar industry, and the military. In 1929, Abe and Isaac sold their interests to Hahn Department Stores but continued as president and chairman of the board, respectively. In 1935, Isaac died, and Hahn changed the company's name to Allied Stores Corp. Despite being owned by a national company, Maas was still operated by the Maas family. Abe died in 1941. By that time, the population had grown to 500,000 and the west coast was greatly expanding. Maas' first branches were in St. Petersburg (1948), Lakeland (1954), Sarasota (1956), Clearwater (1961), and then Fort Myers. In 1987, the Maas Brothers chain absorbed the Jordan Marsh stores and, in 1991, Maas was closed. When Maas was merged with Burdine's (now Macy's) in 1991, all 39 stores were renamed, the doors to the central office were closed, and the Maas building sat abandoned until it was demolished in 2006.

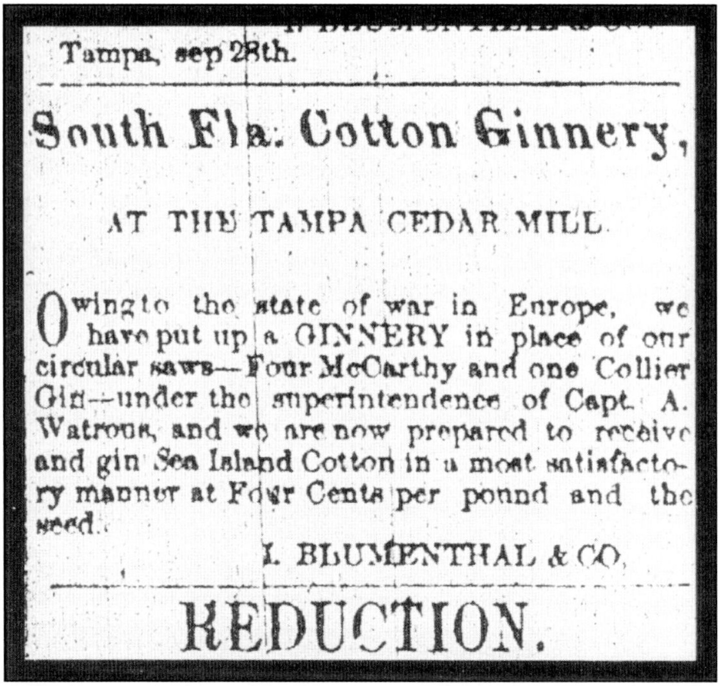

Tampa, sep 28th.

South Fla. Cotton Ginnery,

AT THE TAMPA CEDAR MILL.

Owing to the state of war in Europe, we have put up a GINNERY in place of our circular saws—Four McCarthy and one Collier Gin—under the superintendence of Capt. A. Watrous, and we are now prepared to receive and gin Sea Island Cotton in a most satisfactory manner at Four Cents per pound and the seed.

I. BLUMENTHAL & CO.

REDUCTION.

Isidore Blumenthal's Ginnery Advertisement, 1870. Abe Maas was not the first Jewish merchant in Tampa, as others had come and gone two decades prior to his arrival. An immigrant from Bavaria, Isidore Blumenthal came to Tampa in 1869 and opened a cedar mill and store, including a fur business. Blumenthal led Tampa's business community for at least three years before a national depression destroyed the city's economy and again delayed the arrival of a railroad. (See page 97.) (Courtesy of UF.)

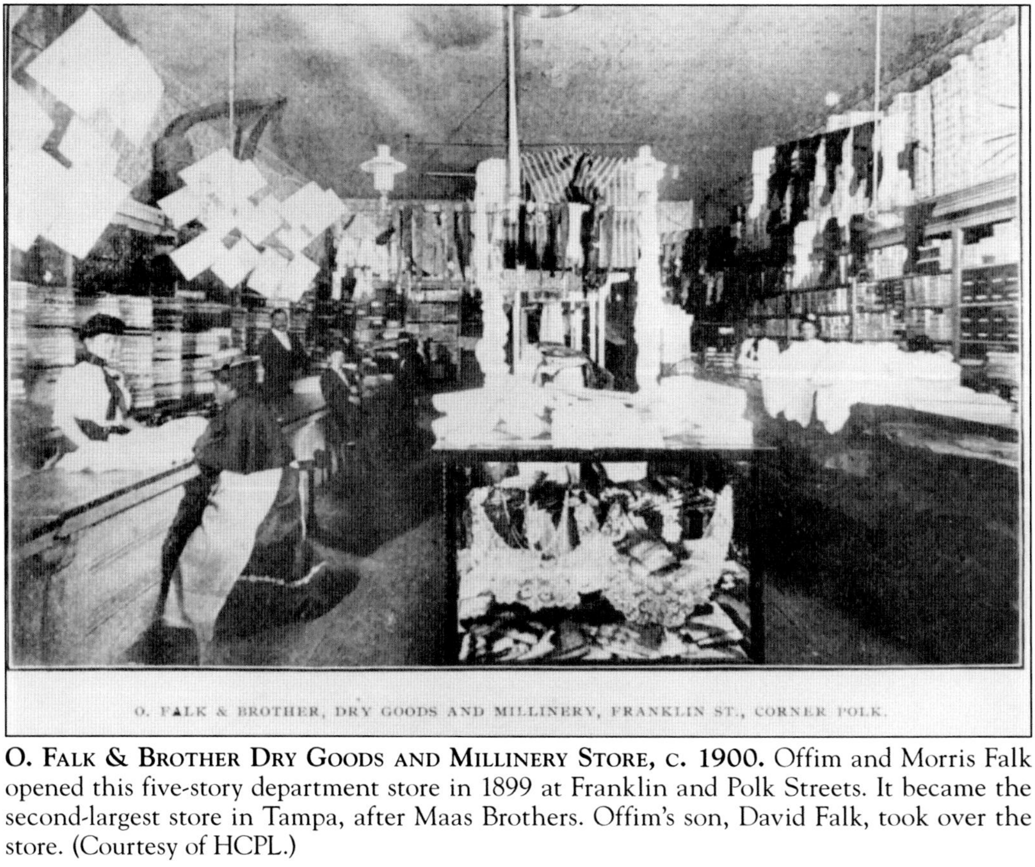

O. FALK & BROTHER, DRY GOODS AND MILLINERY, FRANKLIN ST., CORNER POLK.

O. Falk & Brother Dry Goods and Millinery Store, c. 1900. Offim and Morris Falk opened this five-story department store in 1899 at Franklin and Polk Streets. It became the second-largest store in Tampa, after Maas Brothers. Offim's son, David Falk, took over the store. (Courtesy of HCPL.)

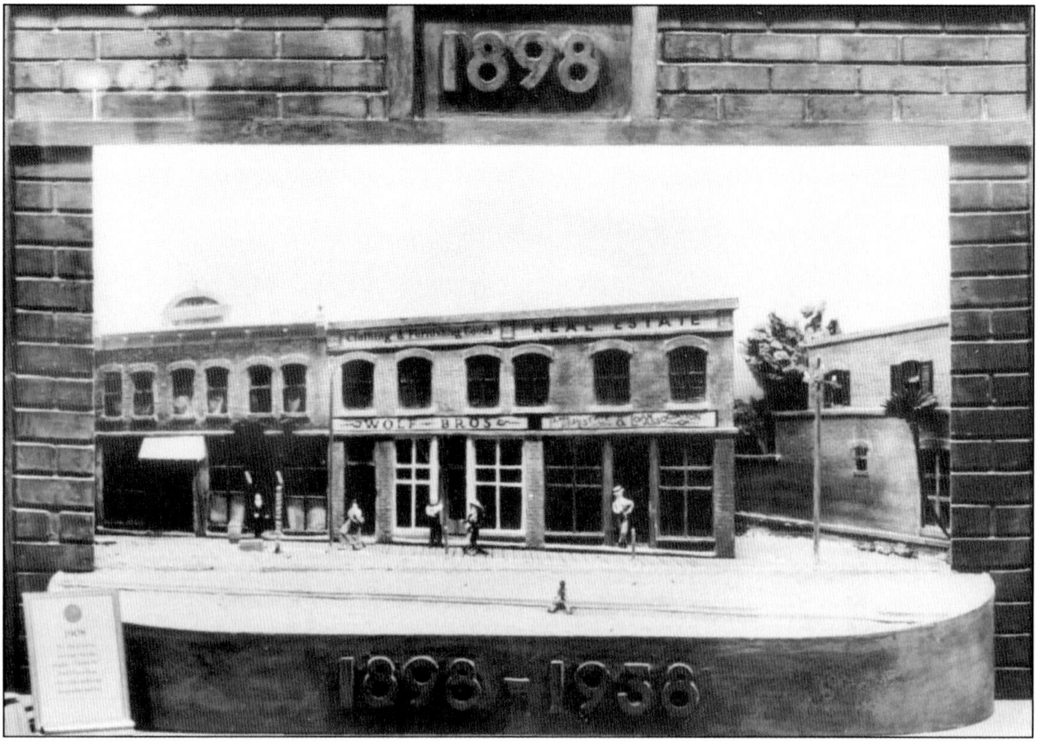

Wolf Brothers, 1908. When brothers Fred and Morris Wolf arrived in Tampa, they were employed with their brothers-in-law, Abe and Isaac Maas, until 1898, when Morris set up his own business with $200.

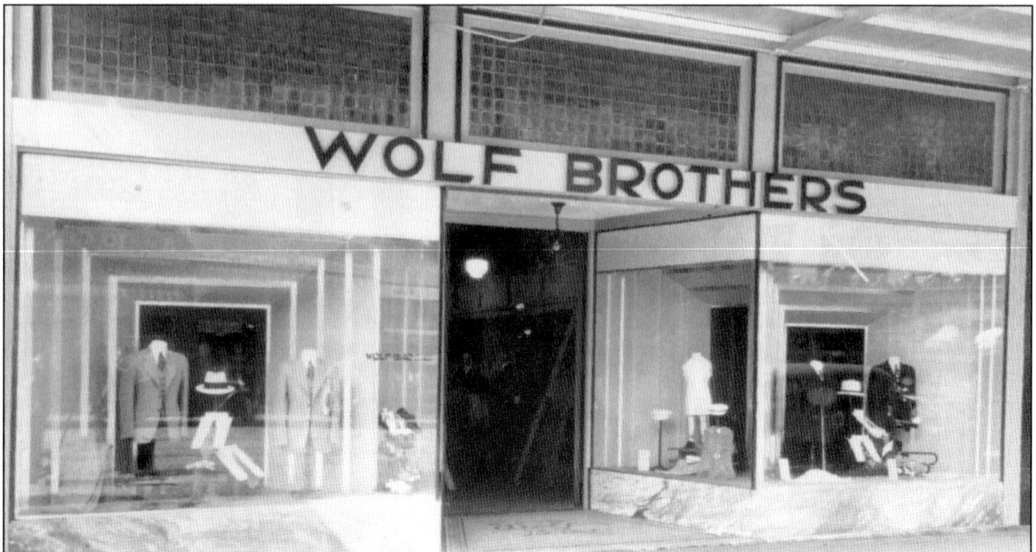

Wolf Brothers, 1932. In 1899, Fred joined Morris and Wolf Brothers, which operated for 94 years, selling men's fine clothing. Fred married Thekla Strauss in 1898, and they had two children, Joseph and Harold. Morris married Caroline Baer around 1912, and the couple had three children, Bernice, Mildred, and Dolly.

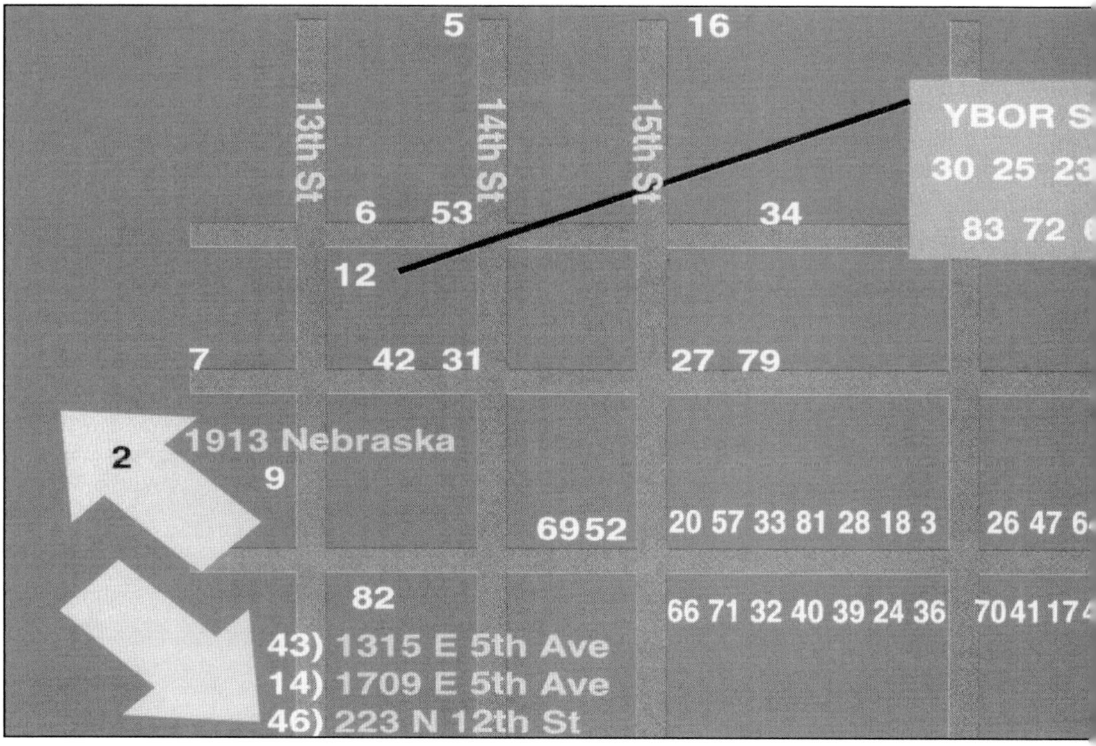

Ybor City Map of Jewish Businesses, 1920s–1970s. Ybor City, founded in 1886, has been transformed from the days when Romanian, Russian, and German Jewish immigrants arrived and energized the business community with their merchandising skills. What remains are some storefronts and signs that represent the impact of this group of people on the history of Ybor City. The map above shows many Jewish businesses that were in Ybor City during the 50-year period from 1920 to

1. Rodeph Sholom Synagogue
2. Knesses Yisroale Synagogue
3. (Meyer) Kisler Pharmacy
4. YMHA
5. American Pipe & Plumbing (Irv & Roy Salsbury)
6. House of a Million Auto Parts (Phil Grubstein & George Ichill)
7. Milchman Kosher Deli [2]
8. William Bass Scrap Metals
9. Grocery (front) Printing (rear) (Julius Silverman)
10. Finman Kosher Market
11. Elozory Furniture Store
12. Blue Ribbon Supermarket (Bobo Families) [1]
13. Tick/Reznick Bags & Drums
14. (2nd Ybor Post Office) Hallmark Emblems (Klein, Weissmans, etc.)
15. West Coast Army Store (became Fremacs Mens Wear) (Fred & Mack Perlman and Sam, Alex, & Milton Bokor)
16. (Max) Star Grocery
17. Max Argintar Pawn & Clothing [1]/Martin's Uniforms [4]
18. Adam Katz Family Clothing (Harry Wilderman)
19. Liberty Mens Store (Abe Herscovitz)
20. Curtis Gimpel, Office Machines
21. Dr. I. Einbinder, Dentist (upstairs)
22. Blue Ribbon Supermarket [2]
23. Isadore Davis Department Store
24. Rophies Mens Wear [3]
25. Style Hat Shop (Alma Fleischman)
26. Rainbow Mens Wear (Abe & Sam Verkauf)
27. Adorable Hat Store (Tillye Simovitz/Waltzer/Freedman)
28. Isadore Segall Ladies Wear
29. Russells Ladies Wear (Russell & Jean Bernheim)
30. David Kasriel Dept. Store/The Jewel Box (Buddy Levine; then Dave Kartt)
31. Louis Wohl Household Supplies [1]/ The Palace (Louis & Mark Shine) [1]
32. Max (& Sam) Argintar Mens Wear [2]
33. Rophies Linens [1 & 2]
34. Joseph Kasriels Ladies Dept. Store
35. Louis Wohl & Sons Restaurant Supply [2]
36. Silver's 5-10¢ and $1.00 Stores
37. Bond Shoe Store (Jack Woolfe)
38. Weber Ladies Uniform Dress Mfg.
39. United Shoe Store (Leon Woolfe)
40. Rippa Ladies Wear (Bob Rippa's Grandfather)
41. Haber's Ladies Wear (Bob Rippa's Grandfather)
42. Ida's Ladies Ready to Wear (Max & Ida Goodrich) The Palace [2]
43. Economy Ladies Wear (Oscar Poller)
44. David Stein Furniture Co.
45. Abe Wolfson Mens Wear

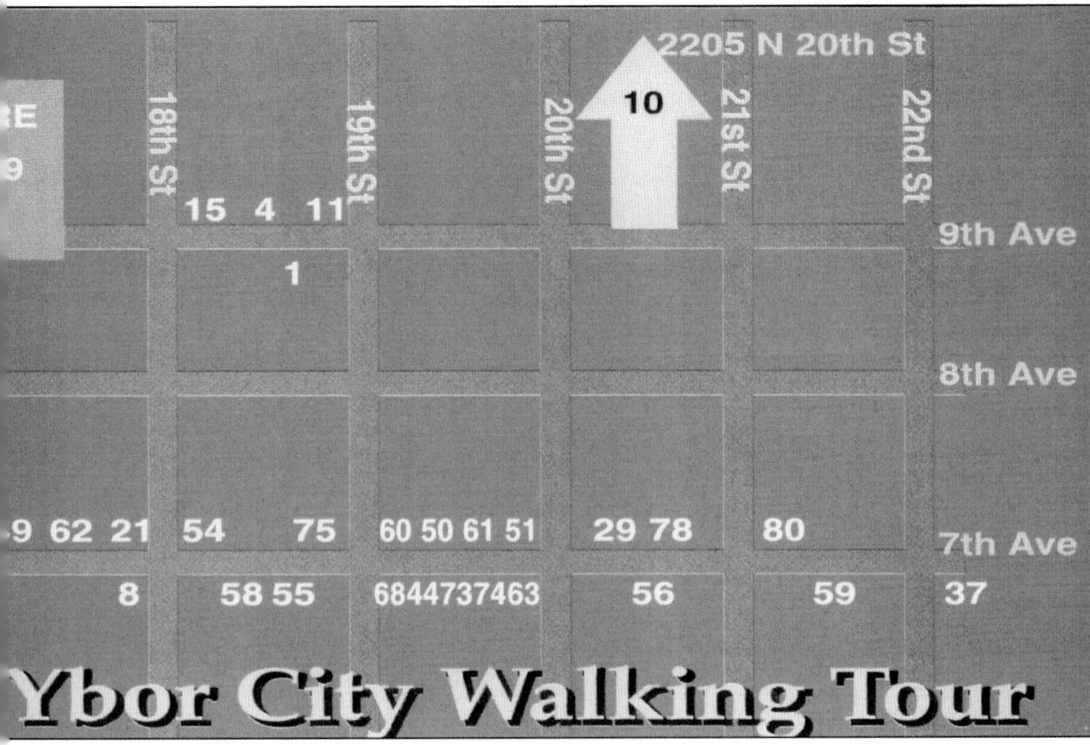

1970. The map and list reflect the memories of Irving Weissman and his friends. The mid-1920s was the height of the number of Jewish merchants in Ybor, primarily on Seventh Avenue, or La Setima. Some businesses had existed prior to this time frame, and others were not in operation for the entire duration of this period. In this list of businesses, the numbers before the name match the location on the map, and the numbers in brackets after the name indicate sequential locations.

46. Pollers Ladies Wear (Nathan Poller)
47. Wolfson's Trimming Store (Adam Wolfson & Son, William)
48. Modern Home Furnishings (Louis Buchman & Son "Booky")
49. Manuel Aronovitz Store
50. Herman Aronovitz Clothing Store/ (Buddy) Arnold's Shoes & Art Supply
51. Dayan Linens (Victor Dayan) [2]
52. Dayan Linens (Nissam Day) [1]
53. Little Katz Fabrics (Fannie Katz & nephew Irving) Edwards Childrens Store (Morris Weisman & Son, Edward)
54. Steinbergs
55. Ike Weiss Department Store/Sunshine Department Store [2] (Manuel Leibovitz & Sons)
56. Milton Schwartz Tire Co.
57. Sunshine Department Store [1]
58. Philip Weissman Clothing [2]
59. Philip Weissman Clothing [1]
60. Louie's Department Store (Soloman Simovitz & Sons)
61. Buchman's Department Store & Royal Palm Window Shades (Jacob Buchman Family) [1]
62. Martin's Uniforms (Spicola) [6B]
63. Red Globe Store (Joseph Weissman) Martin Uniforms (Howard & Irving Weissman) [2 & 6A]
64. Royal Palm Window Shades [2]/Martin's Uniforms [5]
65. Leader Dry Goods & Notions (Toba Margolis & Daughter Cecelia) Milchman Watch & Jewelry Repair
66. Red Globe Store [1]/ A & Z Restaurant Supply (Anton & Zack) [2]
67. Julius & Fannie Buckman Store
68. Sam Hartzman (2nd Hand Suits)
69. Weissman Clothing Store [3]; then to Martins Uniforms [1]
70. Charles Haimovitz Mens Store (Barney Haimes' Father)
71. The Leader Clothing Store (Hyman Golden)
72. Corona Brush Co. (Gregory & David Waksman)
73. Louis Markovitz Clothing
74. Ozias Meerovitz Mens Store
75. Tampa Typewriter Service (Martin Haas)
76. Southern Iron & Bag (Louis Gordon)
77. Zack Restaurant Supply [3A]
78. Peretzman Scrap Iron & Metal
79. Hillsborough Plumbing Supply (William & Bootsie Oster)
80. Anton Restaurant Supply [3B]
81. (Leo) Chardkoff Bag Co.
82. A & Z Restaurant Supply [1]
83. West Coast Salvage & Iron [1] (Sidney Bernstein)
84. West Coast Salvage & Iron [2] (Sol Walker & Co. Scrap Iron)

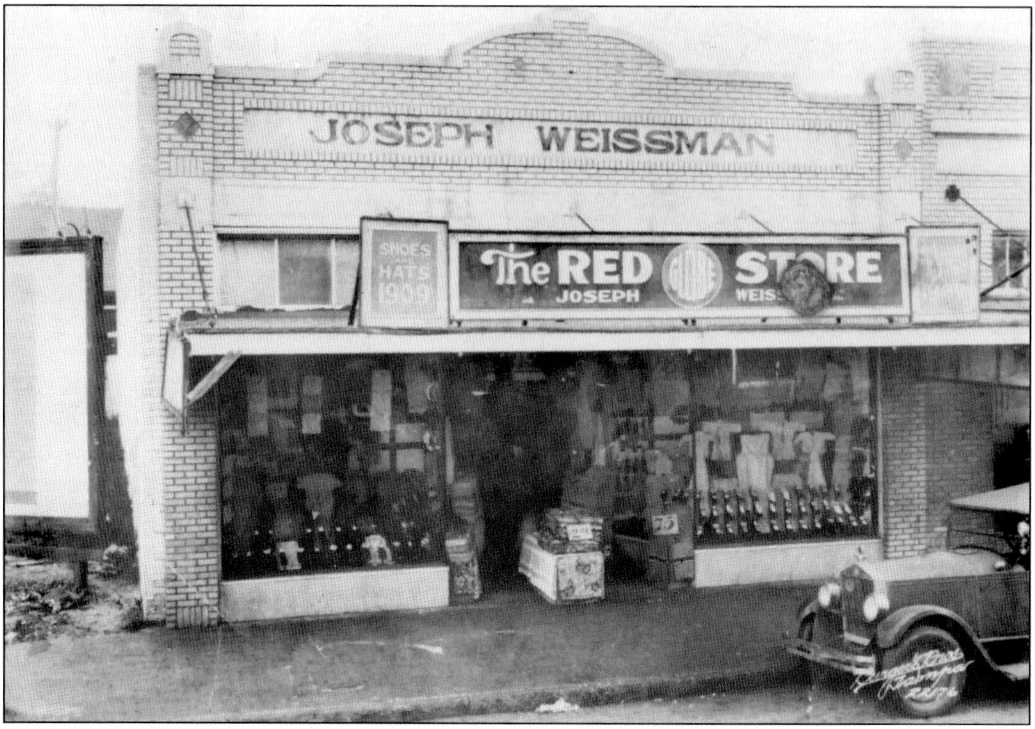

RED GLOBE CLOTHING STORE, 1920. Joseph Weissman came to Ybor City from Romania in 1913. After serving in World War I, he and his wife, Sylvia Margolis, opened the Red Globe Clothing Store in 1920. The store's name underwent changes, first to Weissman's Clothing Store, eventually becoming Martin's Uniforms. Joseph's son, Irving, was so involved in creating Menorah Manor to serve the senior population, that the adult day center is named for him.

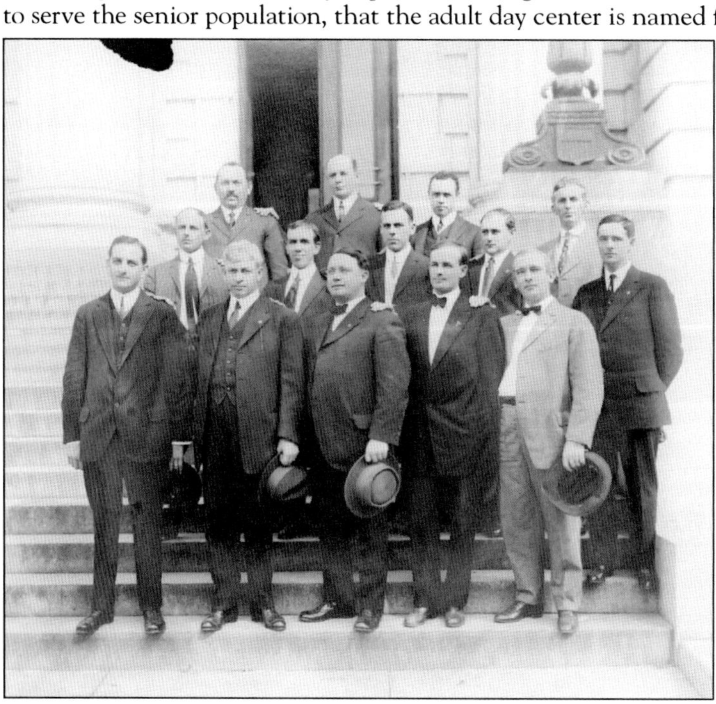

BUSINESSMEN IN FRONT OF COURTHOUSE ON FLORIDA AVENUE, C. 1920. Jewish businessmen were very involved in promoting and supporting both economic and civic life in Tampa. Jerome Waterman (first row, far left) became president of Maas Brothers. Also seen here are Abe Maas (third row, far left) and Fred Wolf (third row, second from left). (Courtesy of TBHC.)

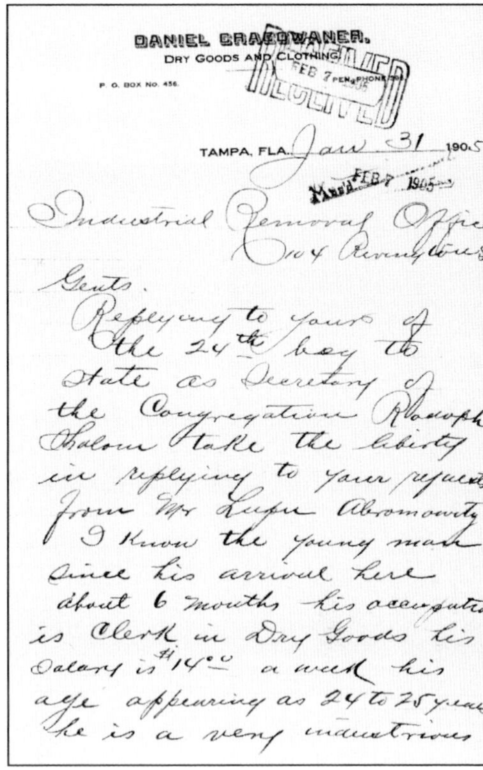

DANIEL CRACOWANER,
DRY GOODS AND CLOTHING.
P. O. BOX NO. 456.

TAMPA, FLA. Jan 31 1905

Industrial Removal Office
104 Rivington St

Gents.

Replying to yours of the 24th beg to state as Secretary of the Congregation Rodoph Sholom I take the liberty in replying to your request from Mr Lupu Abromowitz

I Know the young man since his arrival here about 6 months his occupation is Clerk in Dry Goods his Salary is $14.00 a week his age appearing as 24 to 25 years he is a very industrious

LETTER TO INDUSTRIAL REMOVAL OFFICE (IRO) ABOUT AID FOR IMMIGRANT, 1905. In the early 1900s, Romanian Jews fled to New York, and the Romanian Committee was organized to help relocate the immigrants to other cities and help them find employment. This committee soon became the IRO, under the Jewish Agricultural Society. This letter was written by Daniel Cracowaner, as secretary of Rodeph Sholom, asking for assistance for a recent immigrant.

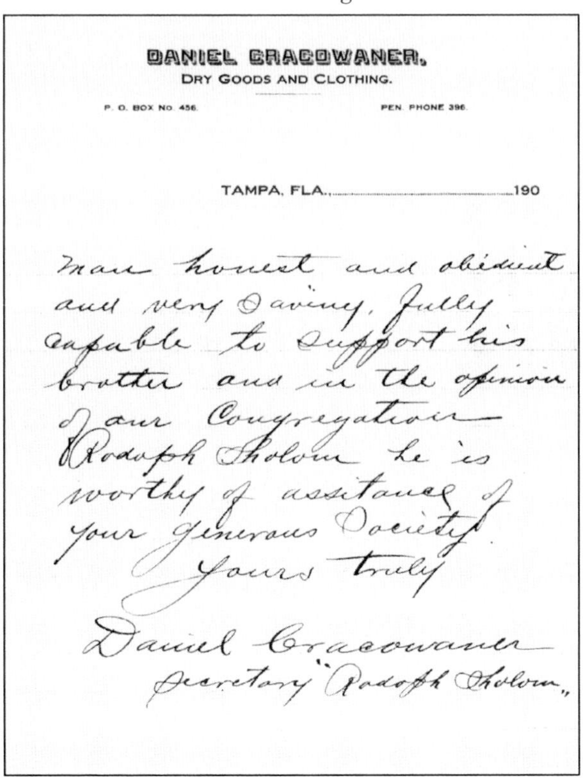

DANIEL CRACOWANER,
DRY GOODS AND CLOTHING.
P. O. BOX NO. 456. PEN. PHONE 396.

TAMPA, FLA.,.................190

man honest and obedient and very Saving, fully capable to support his brother and in the opinion of our Congregation Rodoph Sholom he is worthy of assitance of your Generous Society.

Yours truly

Daniel Cracowaner
Secretary "Rodoph Sholom"

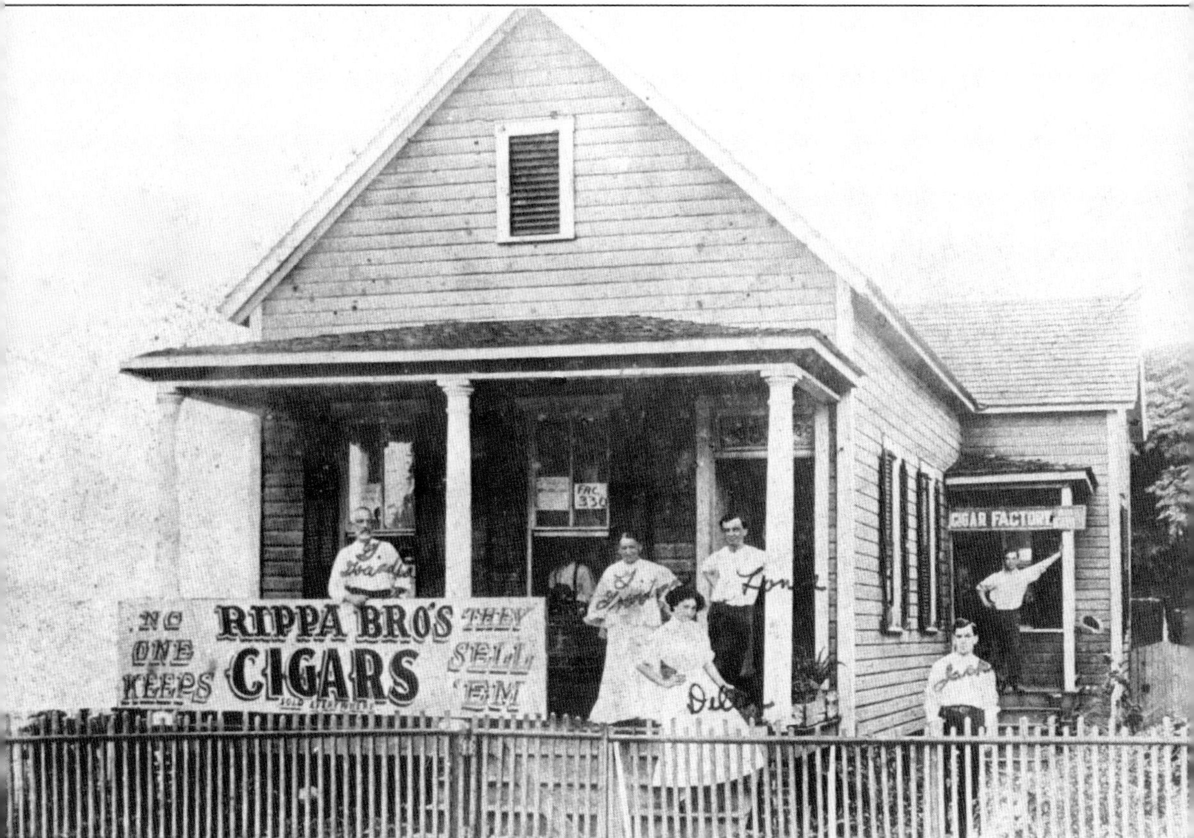

Rippa Family Cigars, 1904. Most Jews in Ybor City were merchants but some were involved in cigar production. In 1888, due to the persecution of Jews in Romania, the Rippa families became part of a chain migration to Key West. From there, the cigar factory was moved to Ybor City, where the Rippas produced their own brand. Shown here are, from left to right, David (b. 1843), Toba (b. 1845), Della, Louis, and Jack. The man on the far right, rear, is unidentified.

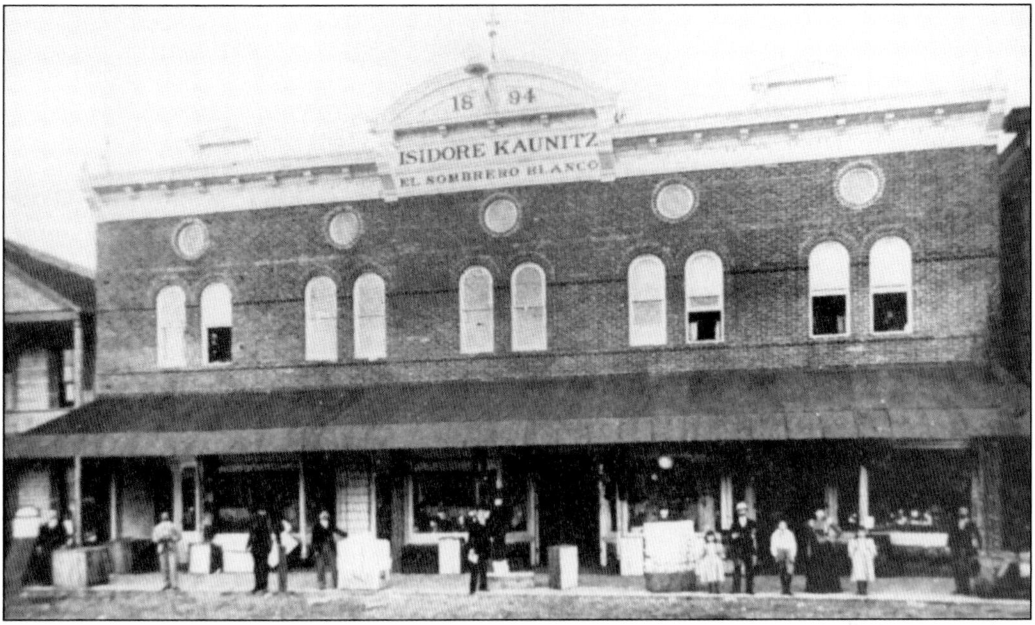

El Sombrero Blanco Clothing Store, 1894. Isidor Kaunitz was attracted to Ybor City when it became a center of growth with Henry Plant's South Florida Railroad (1884). Named for Kaunitz's signature white hat, this was the first store for Ybor City's earliest Jewish merchant and the destination for Romanian immigrants for their first jobs. Records indicate that Isidor and his wife, Rebecca, had three children, Elizabeth, Julius, and Ernestine.

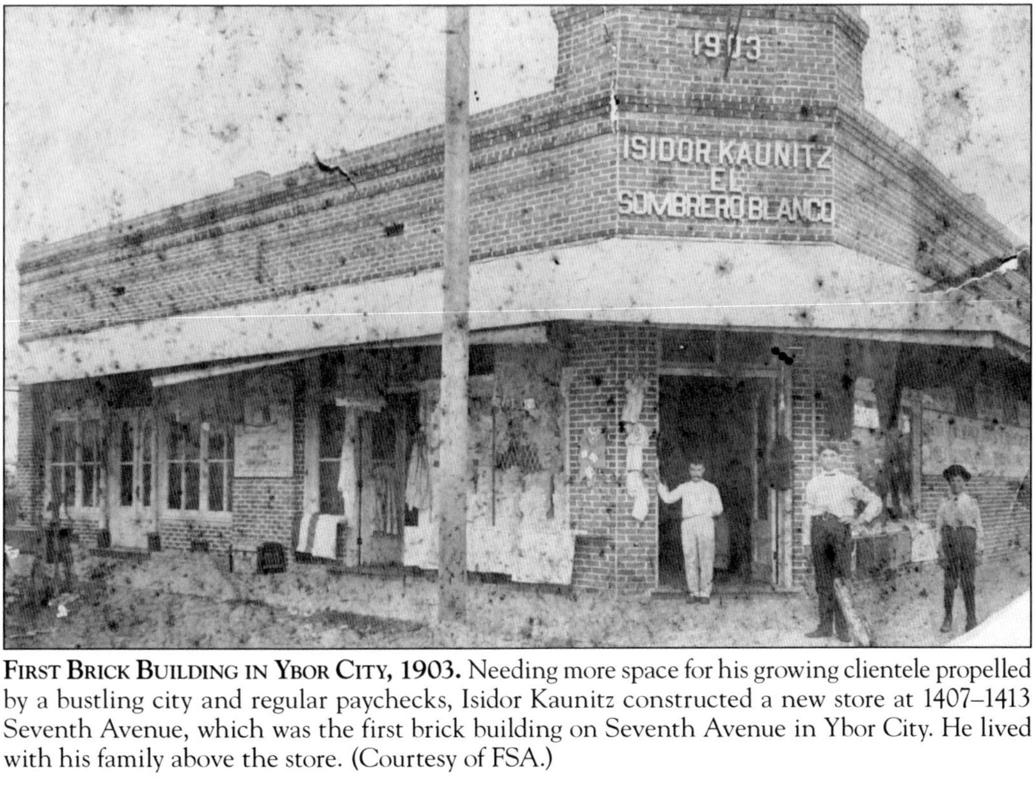

First Brick Building in Ybor City, 1903. Needing more space for his growing clientele propelled by a bustling city and regular paychecks, Isidor Kaunitz constructed a new store at 1407–1413 Seventh Avenue, which was the first brick building on Seventh Avenue in Ybor City. He lived with his family above the store. (Courtesy of FSA.)

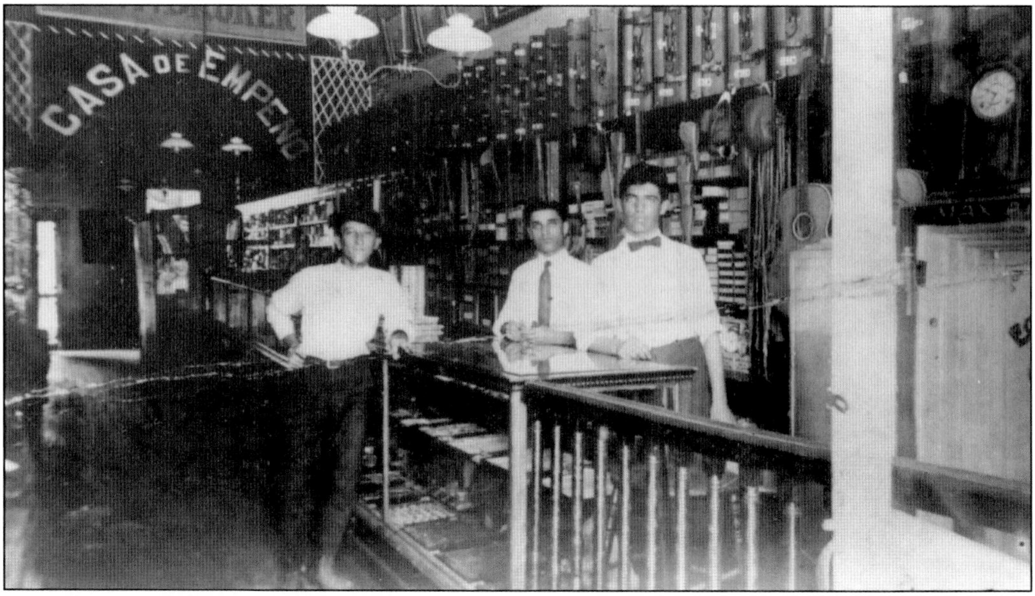

Max Argintar Store, 1908. Originally, the store had a pawnshop portion, including cases filled with jewelry and walls with musical instruments. Max (center) is seen here with his cousin Sender (right). Later that year, after a fire on his block, Max moved the establishment and dropped the pawnshop. His store featured clothing and became known for quality menswear. The man at left is unidentified.

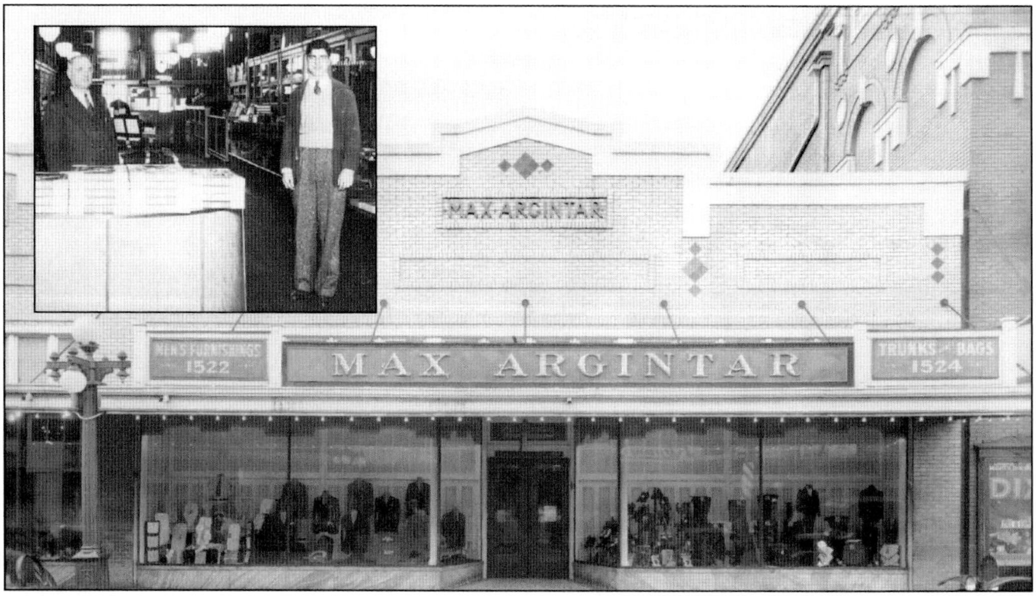

Second Argintar Store Exterior, 1937. Max Argintar's son, Sammie, (Max is standing at left, Sammie is standing at right in the inset photograph) began working full time at Argintar's in 1937. In 1964, he and his wife, Dorothy, took over the business until it closed in 2004 after 96 years of continuous, family-run operation. Old-timers have memories of the clothes they bought from Argintar's, which was an important part of the community. The mostly Latin and black customer base remained loyal during urban renewal. Even after closing, the building with the Argintar sign remains in Ybor City.

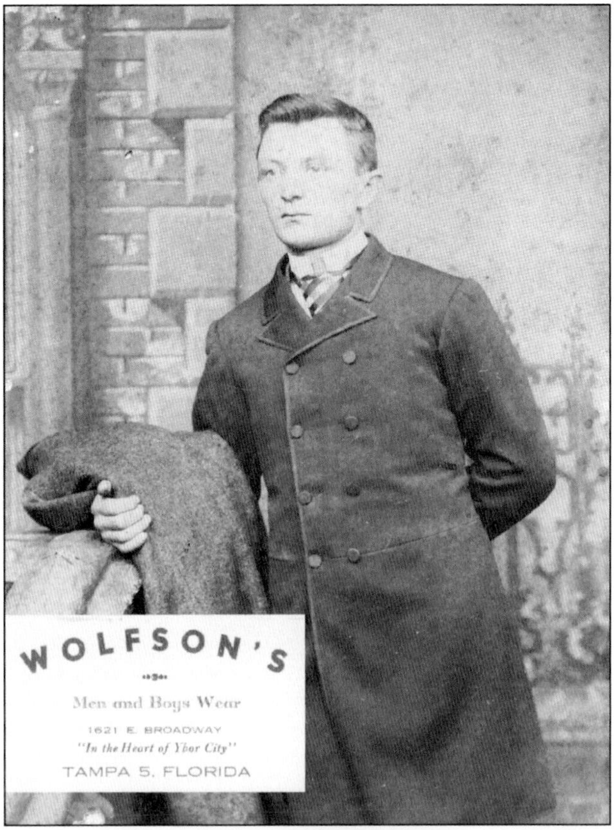

ADAM WOLFSON. Adam joined his brother, Louis Wolfson, in Key West around 1888. By 1920, he moved to Tampa with his sons, Abraham and William. Adam built a brick structure, in which he started Wolfson's Trimming Store and Wolfson's Men & Boys Wear on Seventh Avenue in Ybor City. "Wolfson 1922" is engraved into the top of the building, which remains. The Trimming Store was famous throughout the South for decades.

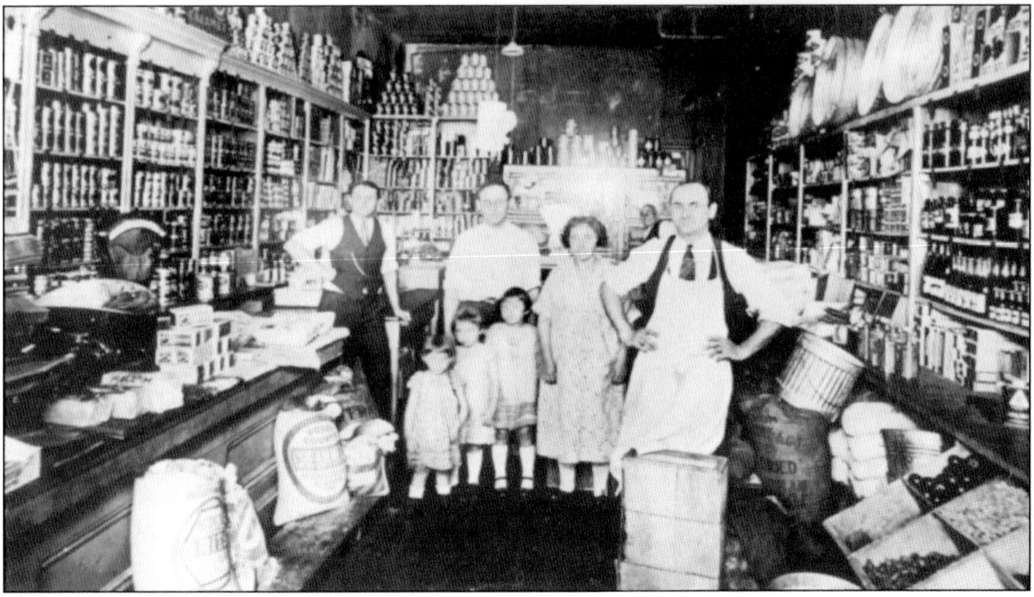

STAR GROCERY, 1927. Max Star was born in Poland as Mendel Staroletni in 1891, was drafted into the Russian Army in 1915, then came to Tampa via Japan. Here, Max (wearing an apron) and Sarah Star pose in their grocery store with three daughters, from left to right, Mary, Lillian, and Dorothy (Skop). Their son Albert was at school. Others in this photograph are unidentified.

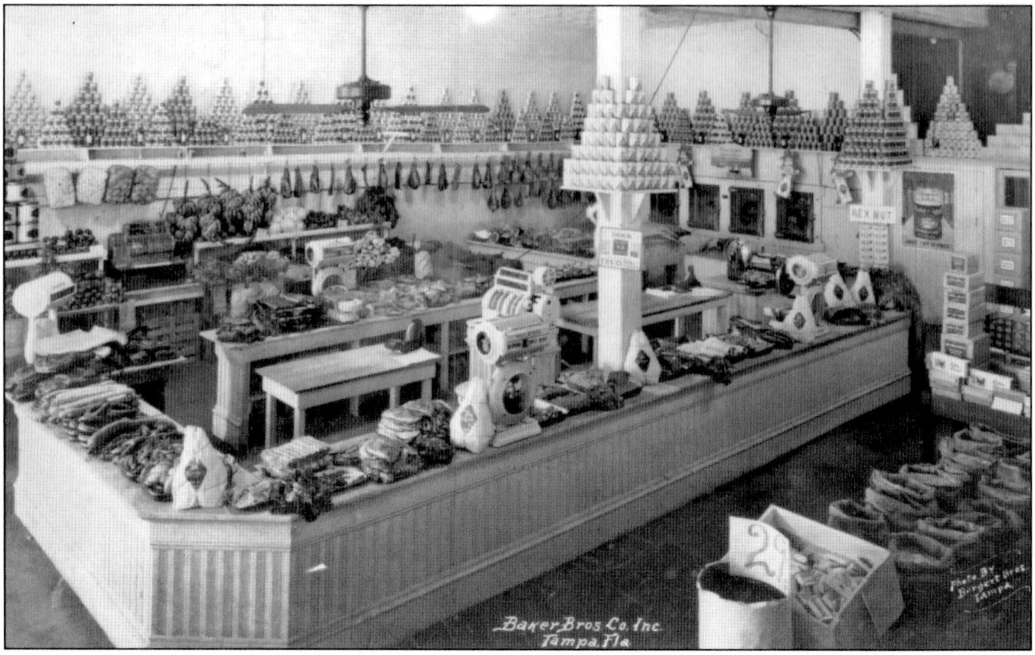

UNITED MARKETS, 1920. Nathan Rosenblatt's first job, in 1912, was as a bookkeeper. He then worked at Armour and Co., where he learned the food business. Shown here is a Baker Brothers store in 1920, when Nathan bought the business and started his own chain of retail grocery stores, United Markets. Known for quality meat, the chain expanded to locations in Central Florida. United Markets hosted many industry trade shows. (Courtesy of Dolly Williams.)

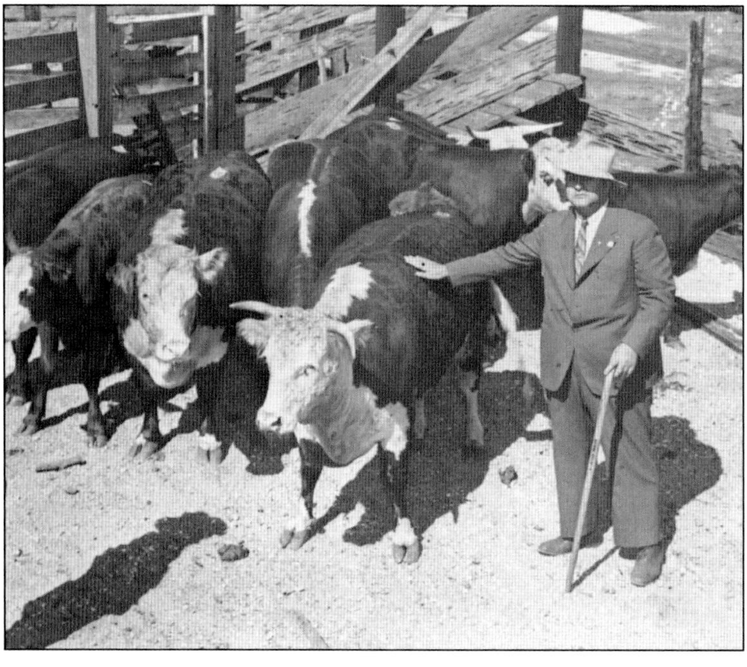

NATHAN ROSENBLATT AT CATTLE AUCTION, C. 1942. After many years in the wholesale and retail grocery business, which included the 50 stores of United Markets, Rosenblatt began National Meat Packers, Inc., in 1939. Nathan was known for assisting others in starting businesses and for his work with the Boy Scouts of America. He and Bess had seven children. (See page 26.)

Salha Bobo, 2000. "Mama" Salha Bobo is pictured here one year prior to her death. Syrian immigrant Salha Bobo (1907–2001) started in the grocery business in 1922 with her husband, Ralph, in Georgia. Moving to Tampa in 1946, they bought Blue Ribbon Market in Ybor City. Ralph died three years later, and Salha ran the tight-knit family and the business, later opening a second store and three mini-marts. At her 89th birthday in 1996, there were 101 family members in attendance. "Mama" Bobo valued hard work, Judaism, and her family, many members of which live in Tampa today. When this matriarch died in 2001, leaving 7 children, 26 grandchildren, and more than 50 great-grandchildren, her family said, "She memorized all our birthdays." (Courtesy of Bobo family.)

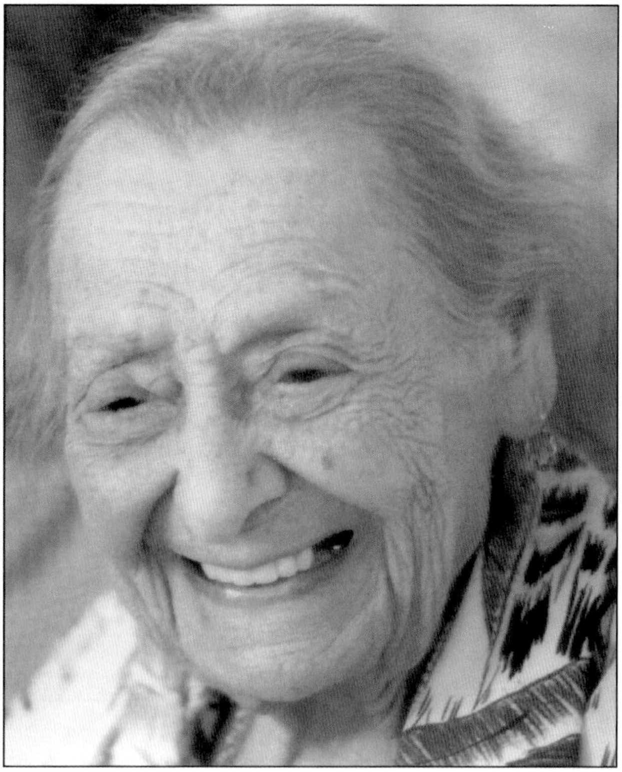

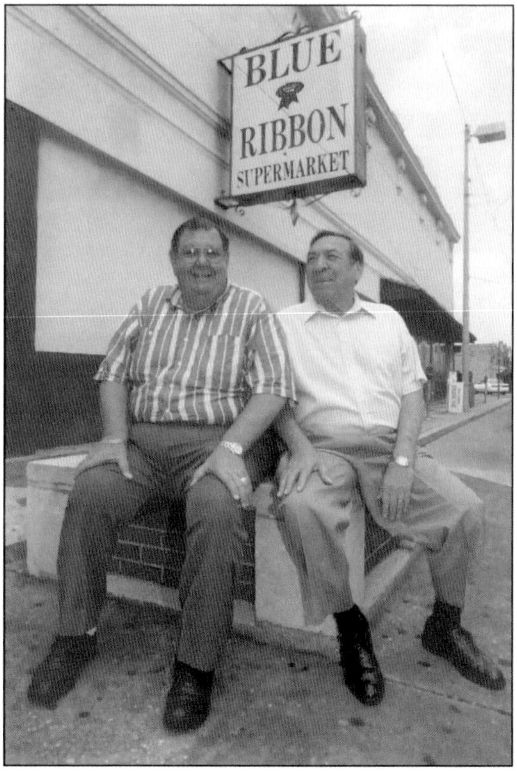

Sam and Eli Bobo, Blue Ribbon Market, 1999. Shown here are two of Salha Bobo's seven children. Sam (left) and Eli ran the market in later years and sold it in 2000. (Courtesy of *Tampa Tribune* and the Bobo family.)

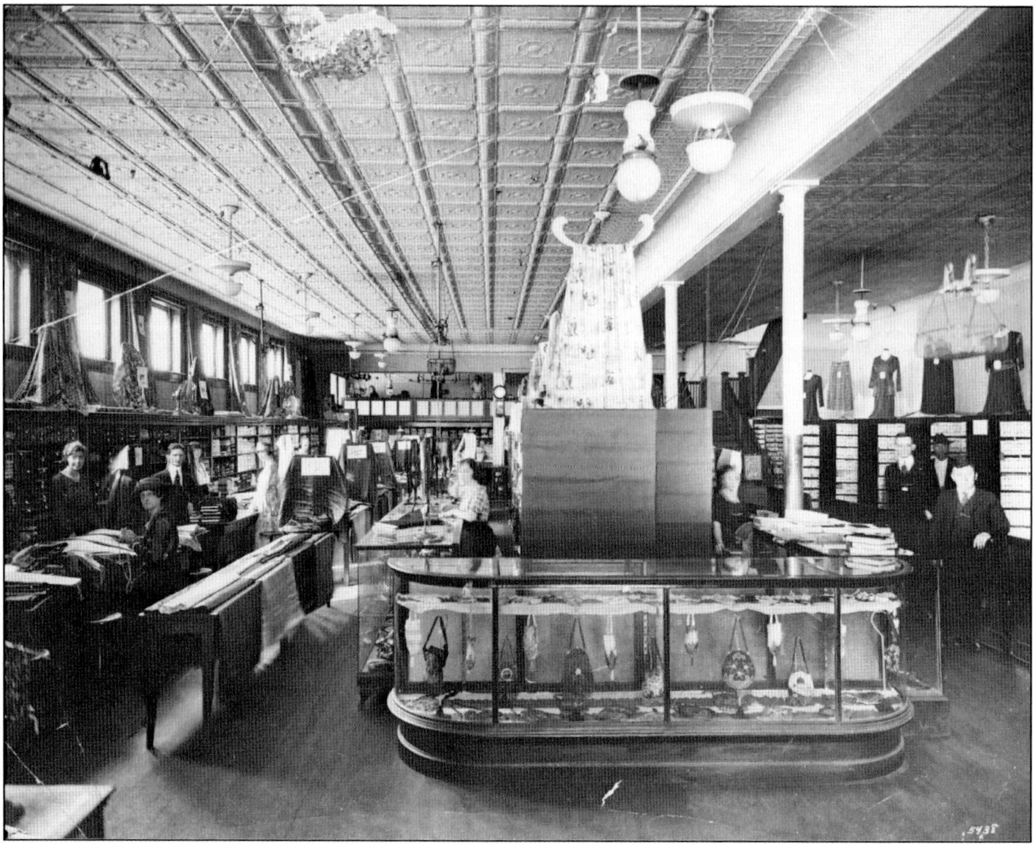

CRACOWANER'S DEPARTMENT STORE, 1918. In 1918, Daniel Cracowaner opened his store on the corner of Polk and Franklin Streets. He operated the store until 1929, using the motto, "Cracowaner's sells it for less—48 hours from Broadway."

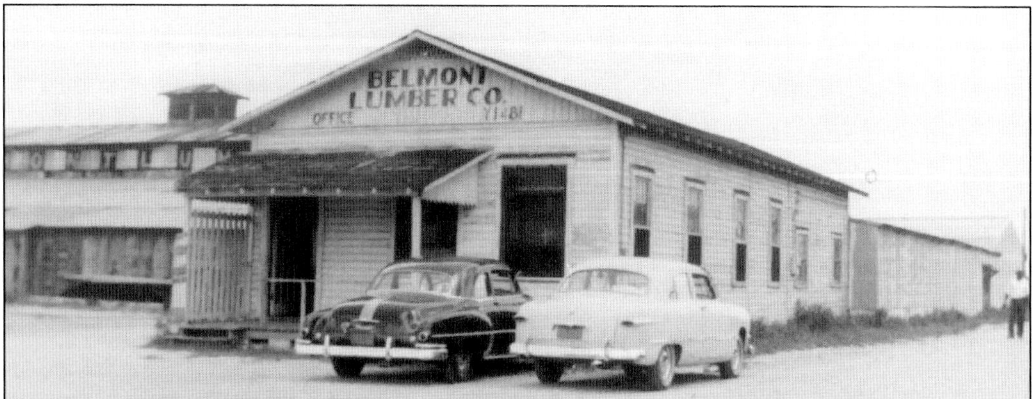

BELMONT LUMBER COMPANY, 1926. Ben Haimovitz came to America in 1908, married Lillian Solomon in 1913, and became the owner of this lumber company in 1926. Brothers Sam, Charles, and Aaron Haimovitz and sisters Annie Isaacs, Becky Golden, Rae Feiles, Fannie Bass, and Hannah Fisher came from Romania to join Ben in Tampa.

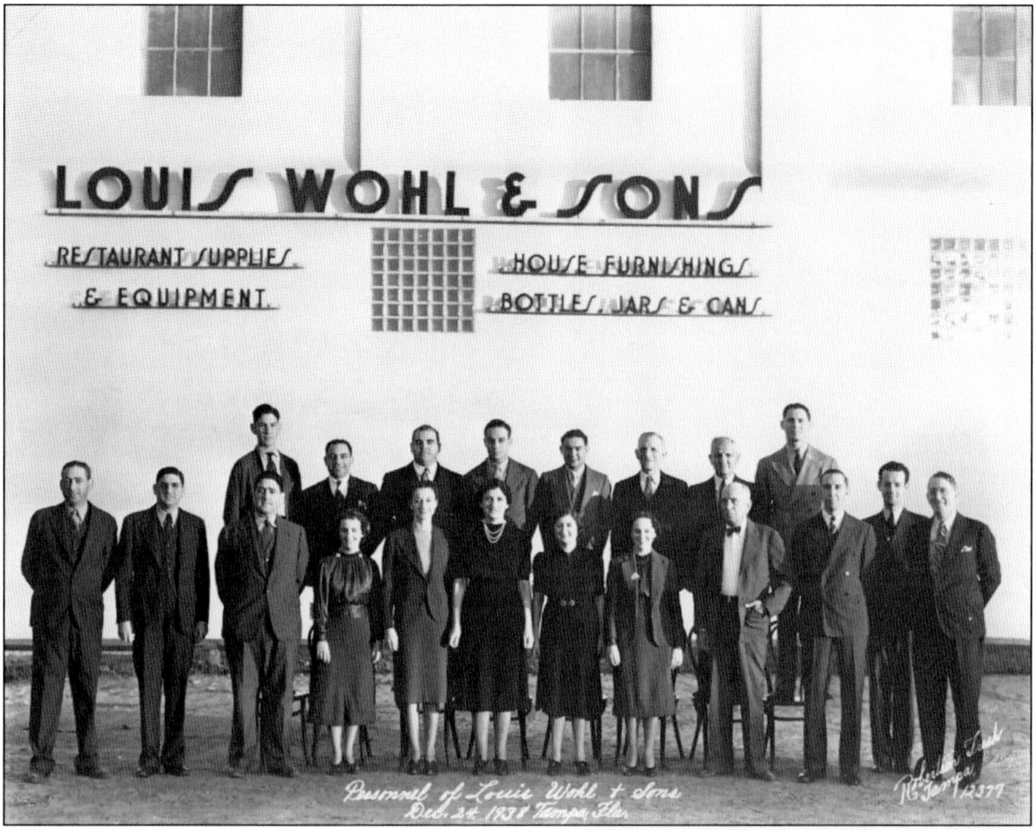

Staff of Louis Wohl & Sons, 1938. The Wohls served the community from 1897 to 1977, supplying myriad goods, from restaurant supplies and equipment to home furnishings. Shown in the first row are Charlie Wohl (far left), Isadore Wohl (second from left), Joseph Wohl (third from left), Clara Wohl (sixth from left) and Sarah Wohl Juster (seventh from left). The family members were very civic-minded. Ybor lost much of its character when Jewish merchants closed their shops during urban renewal.

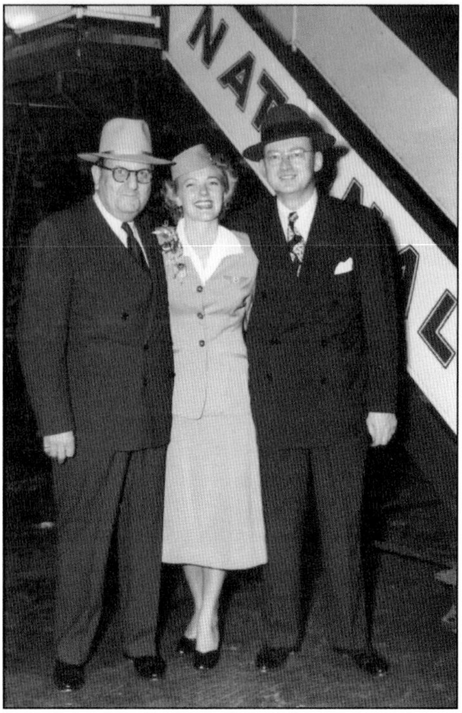

Jerome Waterman, 1949. Waterman (left) was one of the first businessmen in Florida to fly. His early lessons were taken at Drew Field, and Orville Wright signed his pilot's license. During National Air Mail Week in 1936, Waterman was commissioned to fly mail from Plant City to Tampa. He organized Gulf Airlines, which later merged with National Airlines, and he became the advisory director of National. (See page 89.) The gentleman and woman are unidentified. (Courtesy of Katherine Essrig.)

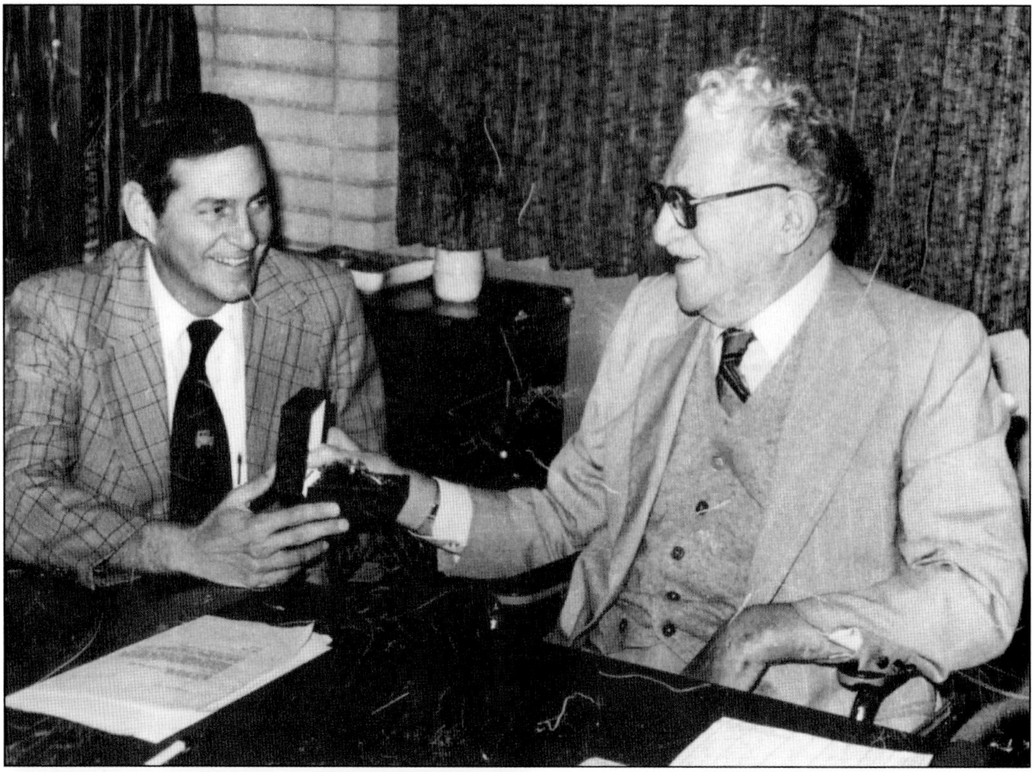

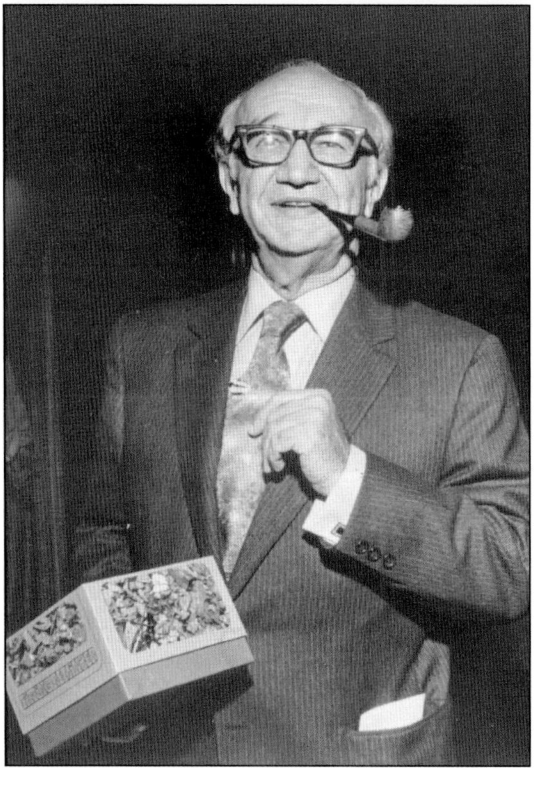

Samuel Louis Flom and Edward Flom, 1975. Sam Flom (right) came to Tampa in 1926 to work for Truscon Steel. In 1937, he and D.F. Taylor opened a company that became Florida Steel. Flom served as chairman of the board until his death in 1980. Very active in community affairs, he served as president of Schaarai Zedek and was named "Industrialist of the Year" in 1968 by the chamber of commerce. Sam, who was married to Julia Mittle, is seen here with his son Edward.

Charles Adler, 1969. Adler came to Tampa in 1936 and opened Bryn Alan Photography. He married Barbara Seckbach, who was active in Jewish organizations. Charles served as the chairman of the grand jury during the Tampa hearings for the Kefauver Crime Investigating Committee in 1950 and served as president of Schaarai Zedek from 1965 to 1967.

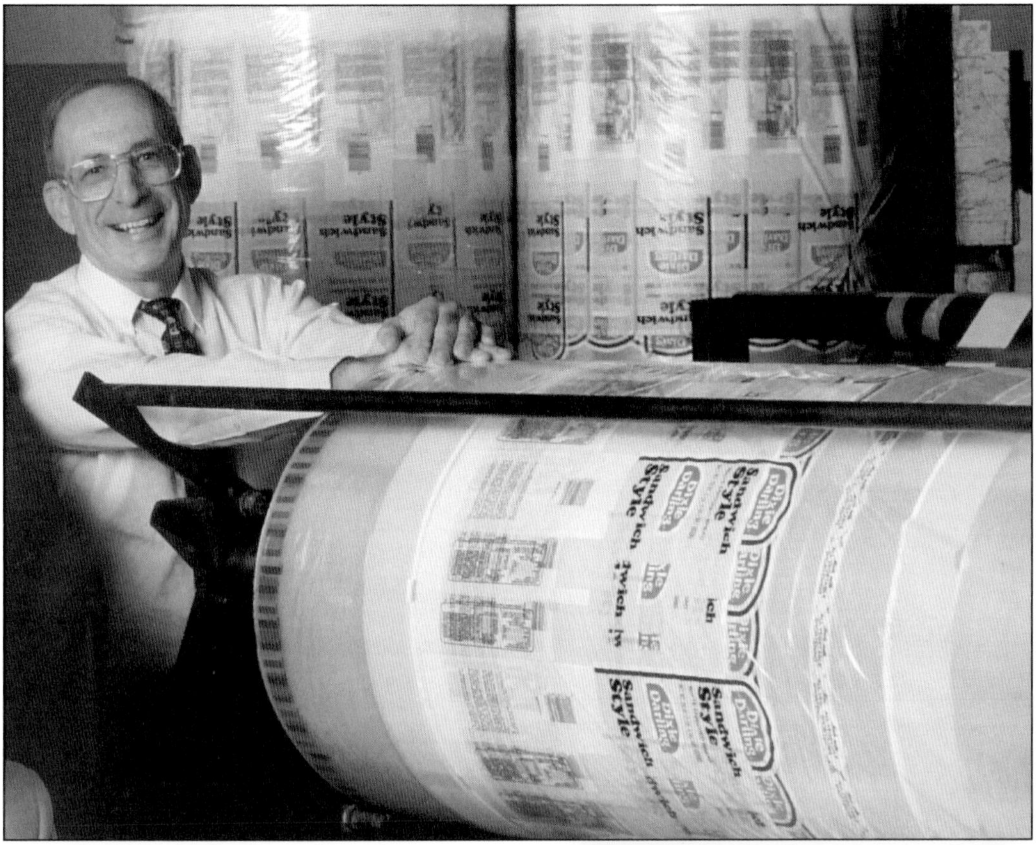

Dick Turkel, Chief Executive Officer and Owner, Master Packaging. Turkel came to Tampa in 1944. He first learned the food business when he ran a military mess hall in Germany in the 1950s. In 1958, he began working for Master Packaging Company. He grew this business, which made packaging for the food industry. Turkel bought it in 1972, sold it, and bought it back a few times. He was honored with a small business award in 1992. (Courtesy of Dick Turkel.)

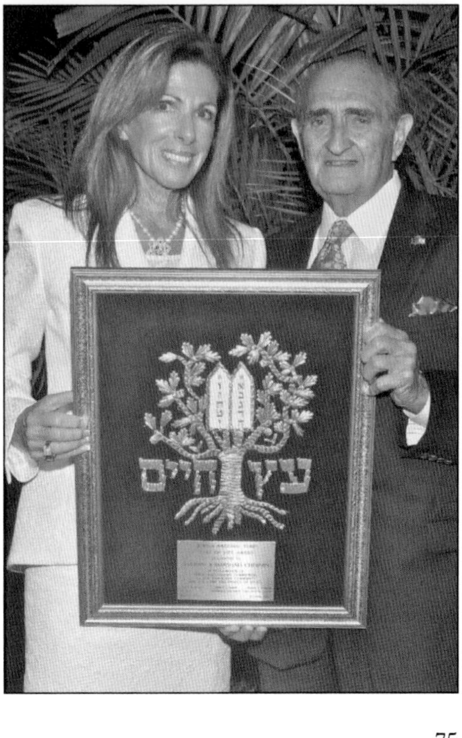

Ida Raye and Marshall Chernin, 2012. In 1970, Marshall Chernin began a meat-processing operation; by 1998, it had become the largest exporter of kosher meat to Israel. In 1999, the Chernins purchased Central Beef Industries, LLC., and, along with their two sons, built one of the most successful independently operated meat-processing operations in the Southeast. Ida Raye is active in the Jewish National Fund and the Hillel School of Tampa. The couple is shown here after being honored with the JNF Tree of Life Award.

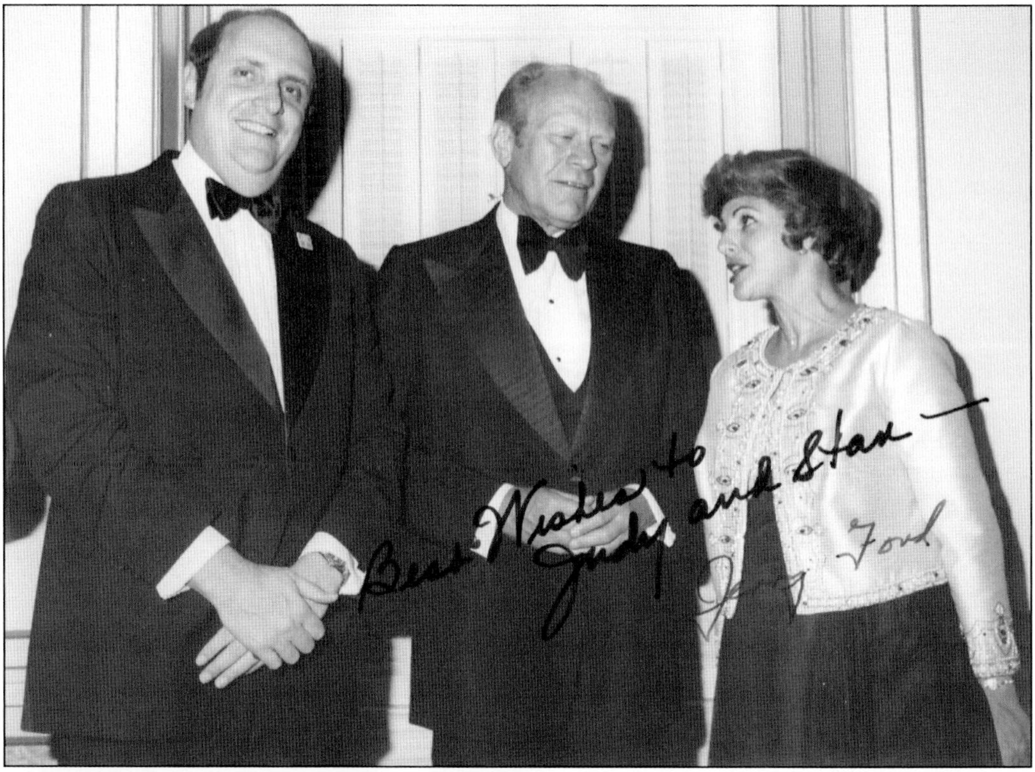

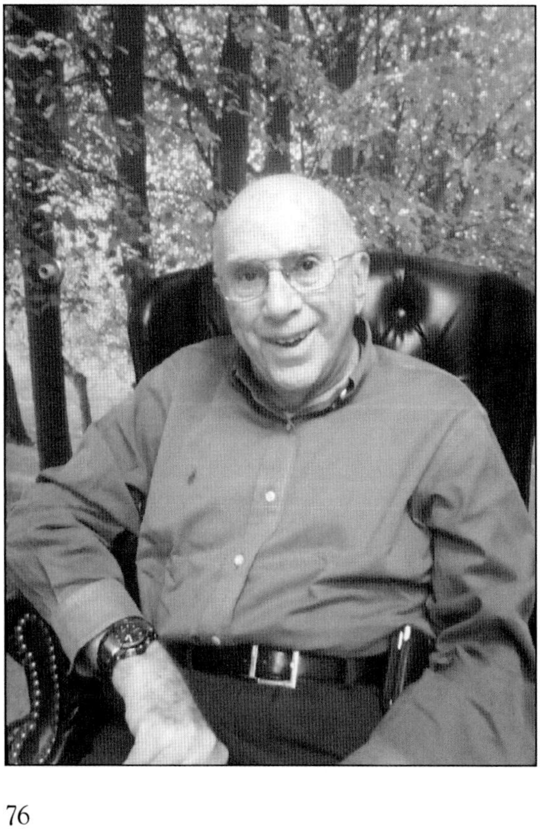

STANLEY ROSENKRANZ, 1974. Stanley Rosenkranz (left) is seen here serving as emcee for the Jewish Federation Dinner in 1974. With him are Pres. Gerald Ford and Judith Rosenkranz. Stanley Rosenkranz (1933–2004), a tax attorney, moved to Tampa in 1961. A major Gator fan and civic activist, he served as founding chairman of the health law section of the Florida Bar, chairman for the chamber of commerce's anti-drug task force, and president of both Congregation Schaarai Zedek and the Jewish Federation. (Courtesy of Judith Rosenkranz.)

DR. PHILIP ADLER, 1996. Adler was described by a television broadcaster as "An agent of change to provide equal medical care for people of all races," referring to Adler's championing of racial desegregation of a Tampa hospital in the 1960s. Dr. Adler arrived in Tampa in 1958 and practiced for more than 50 years. His first office, across from the original St. Joseph's Hospital, was also the referral center for unfunded children.

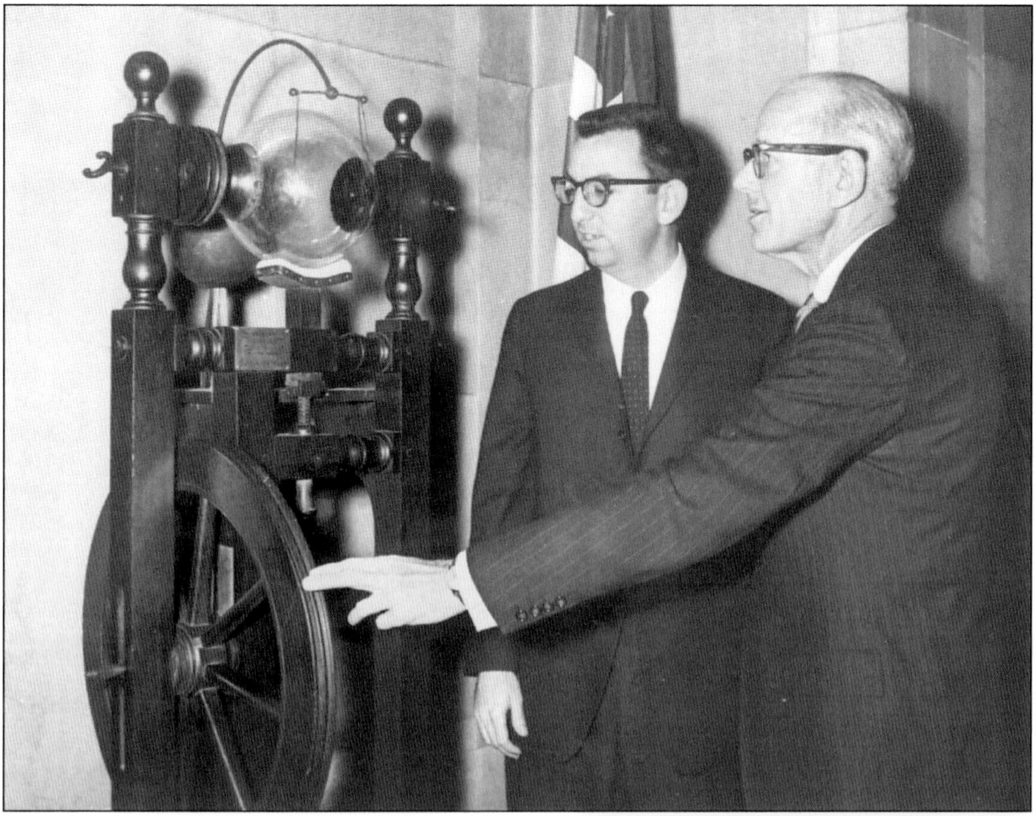

Martin Uman Shown with Ben Franklin's Equipment at Franklin Institute in Philadelphia, 1970s. Native Tampans, brothers Martin (left) and Myron Uman have made significant contributions in science. Martin is an internationally known expert in lightning research at the University of Florida. He was chosen "Teacher-Scholar of the Year" for 1988–1989 and was awarded the gold medal as Florida's "Scientist of the Year" in 1990. The gentleman on the right in this photograph is unidentified.

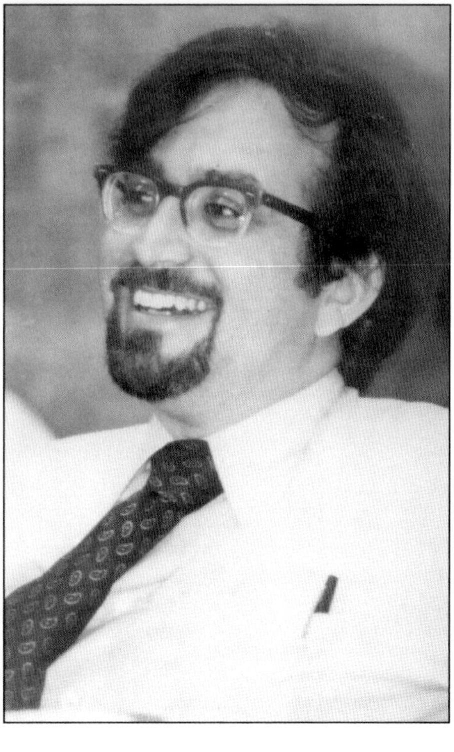

Myron Uman. Uman joined the National Research Council in 1975, and, in 1986, was appointed executive director of the research panel advising NASA on the redesign of the shuttle's booster rockets. He was given the NASA Public Service Medal for his work and, in 1989, the astronauts presented their own Silver Snoopy to Uman and the panel.

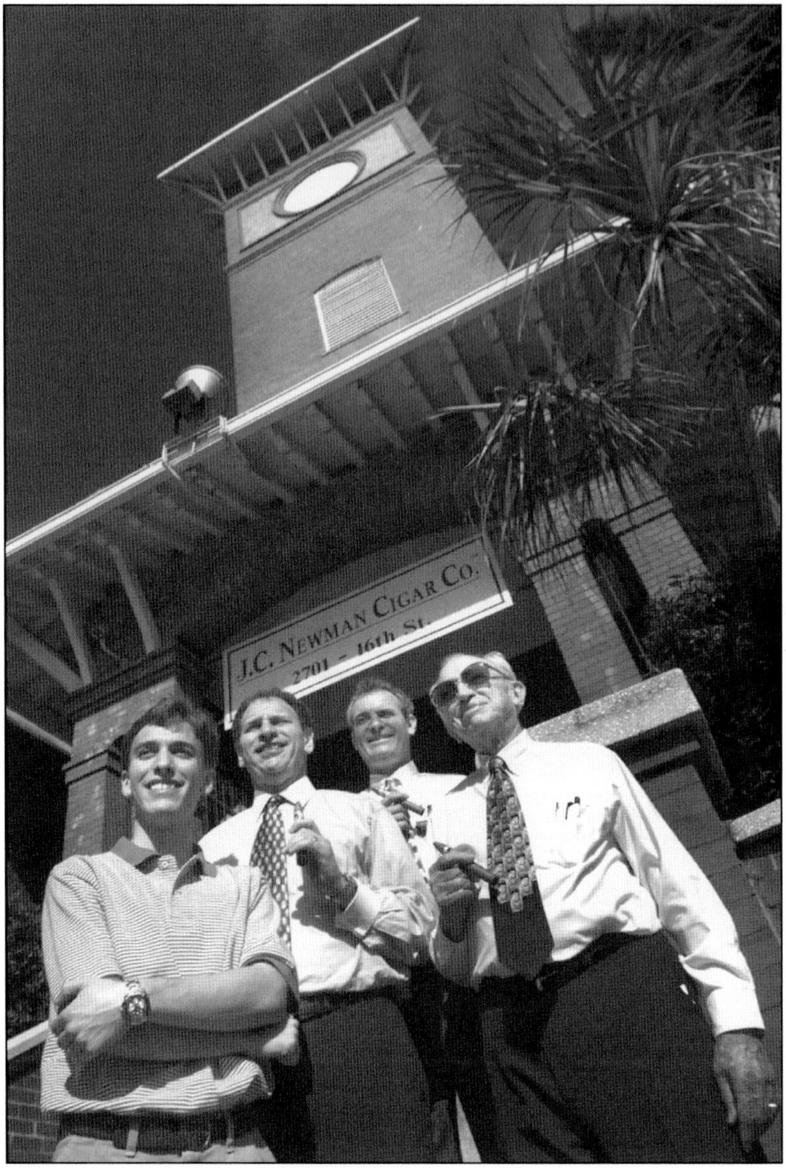

Three Generations of J.C. Newman Cigar Co., c. 2002. Shown here are, from left to right, Drew, brothers Eric and Bobby, and Stanford Newman, a son of founder Julius Caesar Newman (1875–1958). Stanford Newman (1916–2006) was president of the Tampa Cigar Manufacturer's Association for 30 years. Beginning as a 14-year-old cigar maker apprentice in Cleveland and then starting his own business in 1895 in a barn, Hungarian immigrant J.C. Newman grew his company until, by 1916, it had 700 employees. After World War II, sons Stanford and Millard joined him. In 1954, J.C. Newman moved his operation to Ybor City. He found his ideal manufacturing location at a landmark structure. Built in 1910, the Regensburg factory was one of the last and largest cigar factories ever built in Tampa. The Regensburg had a nickname: El Reloj, Spanish for "the Clock." For generations, residents had risen and retired to the hourly chimes from its brick clock tower. After decades of silence, the landmark El Reloj rings again, thanks to a restoration by the Newman family in 2002. J.C. Newman is the only operating cigar factory in Ybor City. (Courtesy of the Newman family.)

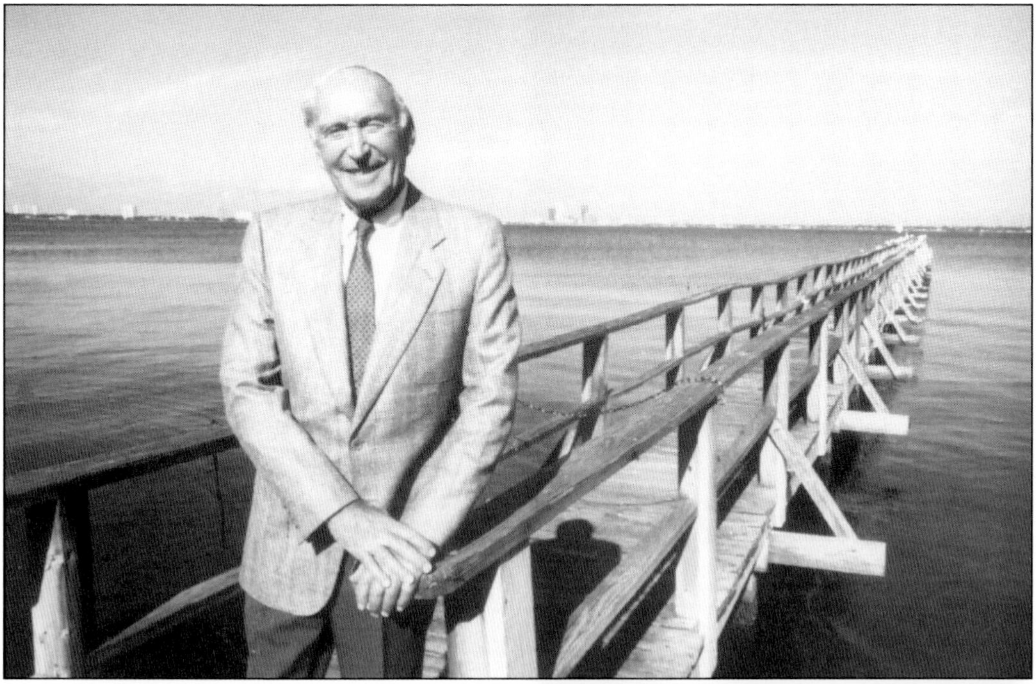

Stuart Golding, c. 1981. In 1959, encouraged by relatives already here, Golding moved to Tampa and became a leading shopping center developer. His projects included Seminole, Park Plaza, Sunset Square, Gateway, Brandon, Town 'N' Country, Twelve Oaks Plaza, and the one-million-square-foot Countryside Mall. His "obsession" was the 1986 restoration of Washington, DC's, fabled Willard Hotel to its former elegance and prestige. There is a Stuart S. Golding Endowed Chair of Contemporary Art at USF.

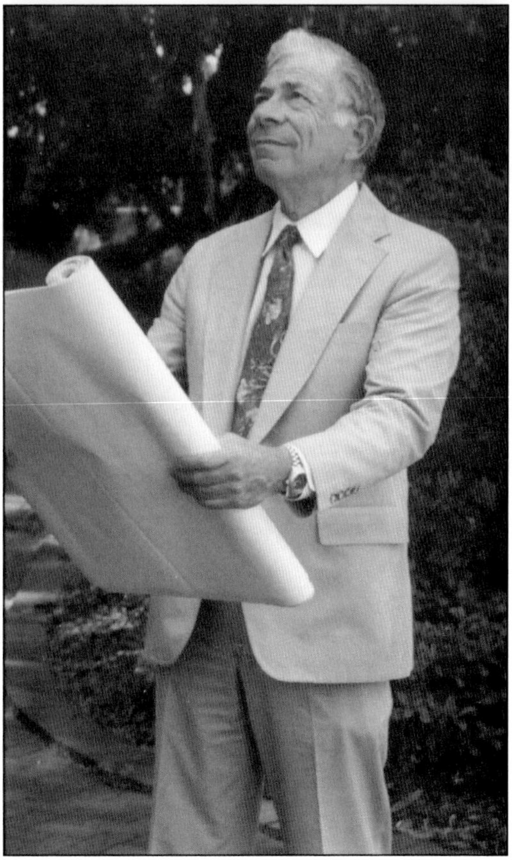

George Karpay. Karpay began building large-tract home developments in Tampa in 1959 and went on to construct 7,000 units by the early 1990s. One of his most prominent developments was Timberlane, created in the 1970s. Most of the customers for this project were first-time homeowners and service personnel stationed at MacDill Air Force Base. Karpay conceived the widely recognized theory of "Valued Engineering." He was active in the community and was a Federation president.

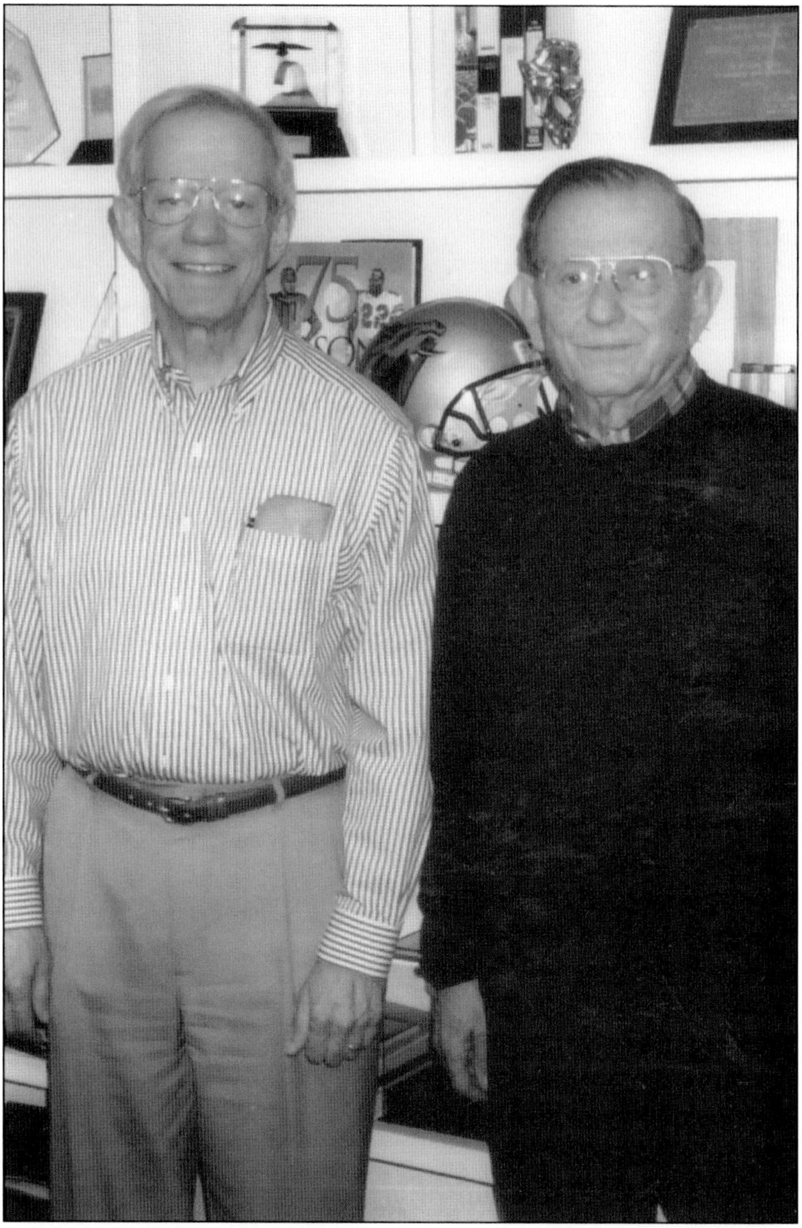

MANDELL AND JAMES SHIMBERG, 2004. Brothers James "Jim" (right) and Mandell "Hinks" Shimberg built more than 8,000 homes in the Tampa area. They are best known for Town 'N' Country, a massive residential community with many commercial and retail services, schools, medical facilities, and recreational complexes. Hinks was Civitan Club's Citizen of the Year in 1998 and was noted for keeping the Tampa Bay Buccaneers in Tampa and promoting a new stadium. He served as chairman of the Downtown Development Authority for the City of Tampa and as vice chairman of the Tampa Bay Performing Arts Center. Jim donated $1 million for the Center for Affordable Housing at the University of Florida. He served on two governors' task forces to develop state policies on growth management and to assess its effect on housing, and he was the first chairman of the board of trustees of University Community Hospital of Tampa. (Courtesy of Elaine Shimberg.)

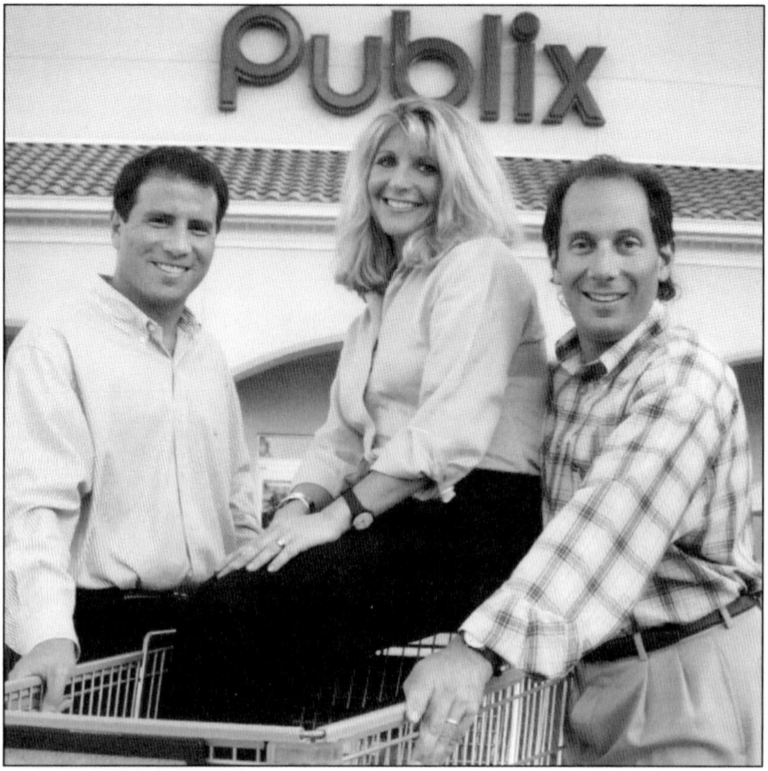

RMC Property Group, 2006. Mitchell and Susie Levin Rice have a portfolio of more than four million square feet of retail and office properties, including more than 140 freestanding drugstores and 25 grocery-anchored shopping centers. Shown here in front of a Publix grocery store are, from left to right, Michael J. Leeds, president of RMC Property Group; Susie Levin Rice, vice chairman; and Mitchell F. Rice, chief executive officer.

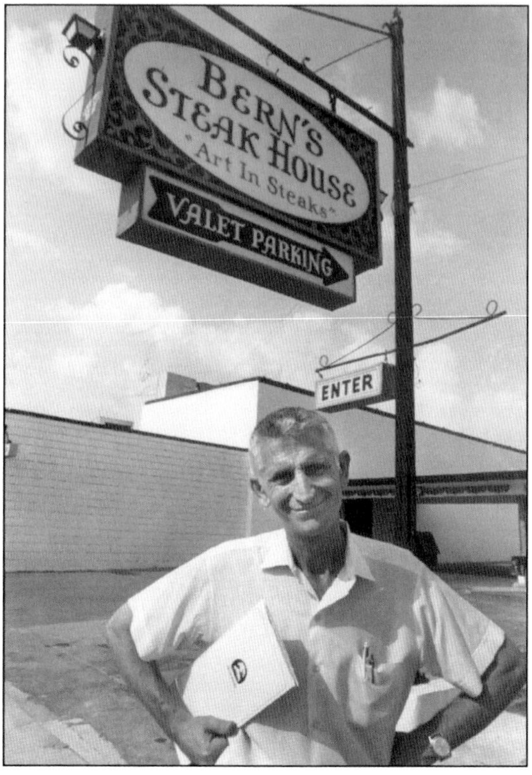

Bern Laxer, Bern's Steak House. Bern Laxer and his wife, Gert, owned the Beer Haven Bar. When they started a steak house in 1956, they salvaged letters from their original sign and bought an "s" to create the name Bern's. They gradually expanded, buying adjoining buildings on South Howard Avenue. The Harry Waugh Dessert Room was built in 1985, using redwood wine casks to create 48 private rooms. Their son, David, runs the business today.

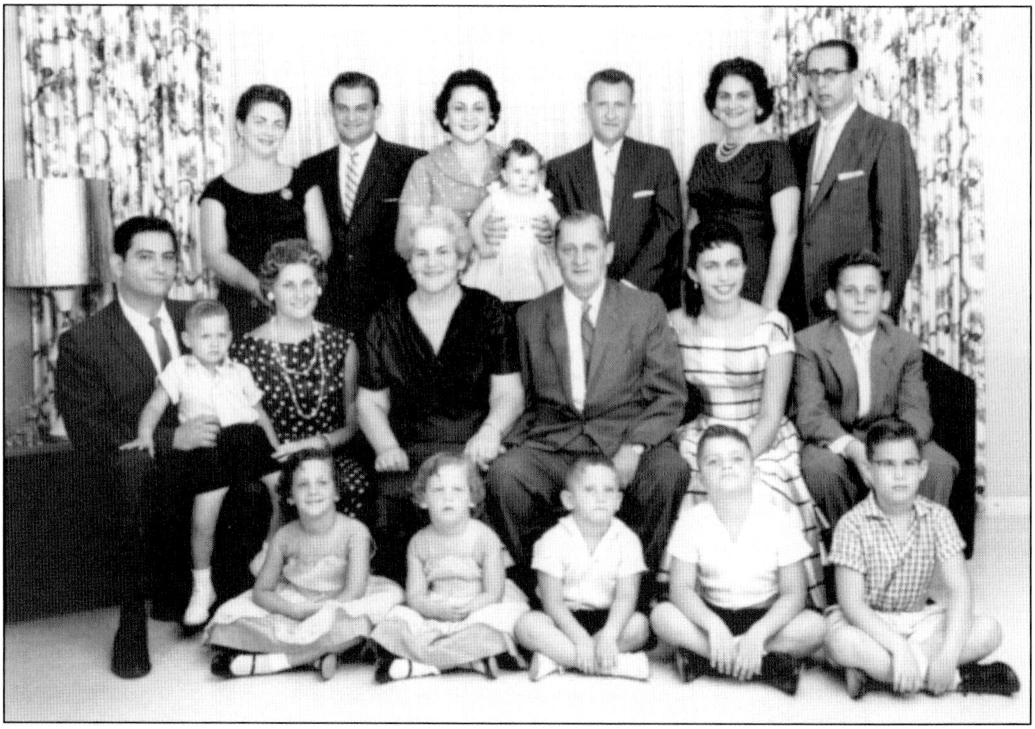

Waksman Family, Cuba, 1958. The story of Corona Brushes, Inc., spans thousands of miles and eight decades. In a small village amid the turmoil of post–World War I Russia, Jude Waksman learned the trade of processing hog bristles for paintbrush manufacturing. After the Bolsheviks seized power, Waksman left Russia. Although he wanted to come to America, immigration quotas prohibited him from doing so. He settled in Havana, Cuba, found work as a laborer, and sent for his wife and daughter, still in Russia. After the family reunited in Cuba, two boys and another daughter were born.

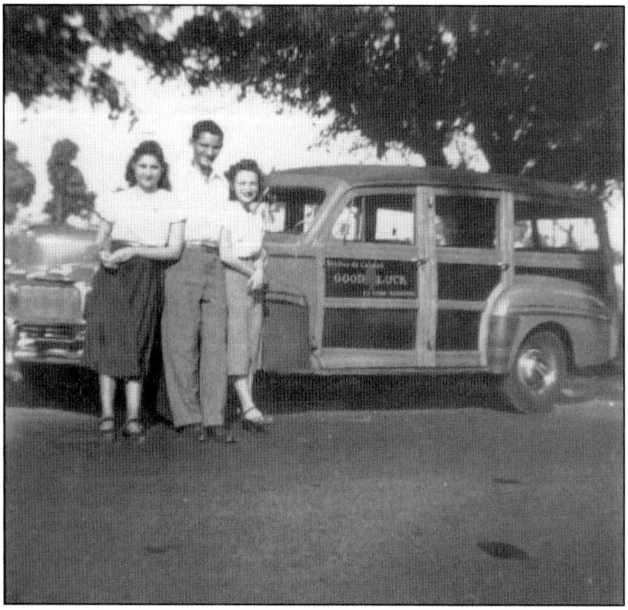

Gregory and Maria Waksman and Company Truck, Cuba, 1948. The original name of Corona Brushes was Good Luck. The name was changed when people in Cuba could not pronounce it. World War II disrupted the supply of Chinese and Russian bristle to US paintbrush manufacturers. Jude Waksman seized the opportunity and built a processing facility outside Havana to supply bristle from Cuban hogs. He eventually started producing paintbrushes after the war, when US companies stopped buying the Cuban hog bristle. Shown here are Gregory and Maria Waksman (left) and an unidentified friend in 1948.

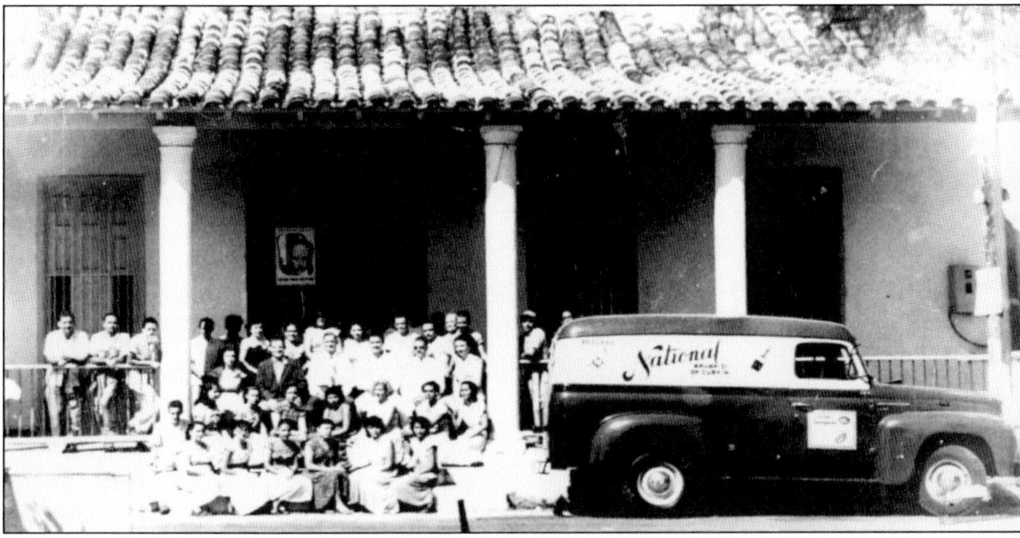

EMPLOYEES OF NATIONAL BRUSH COMPANY, 1959. Jude Waksman can be seen in the third row, center, wearing a tie. Gregory Waksman is to the right of Jude, and David Waksman is to Jude's left. The National Brush Company was a forebear of today's Corona Brushes.

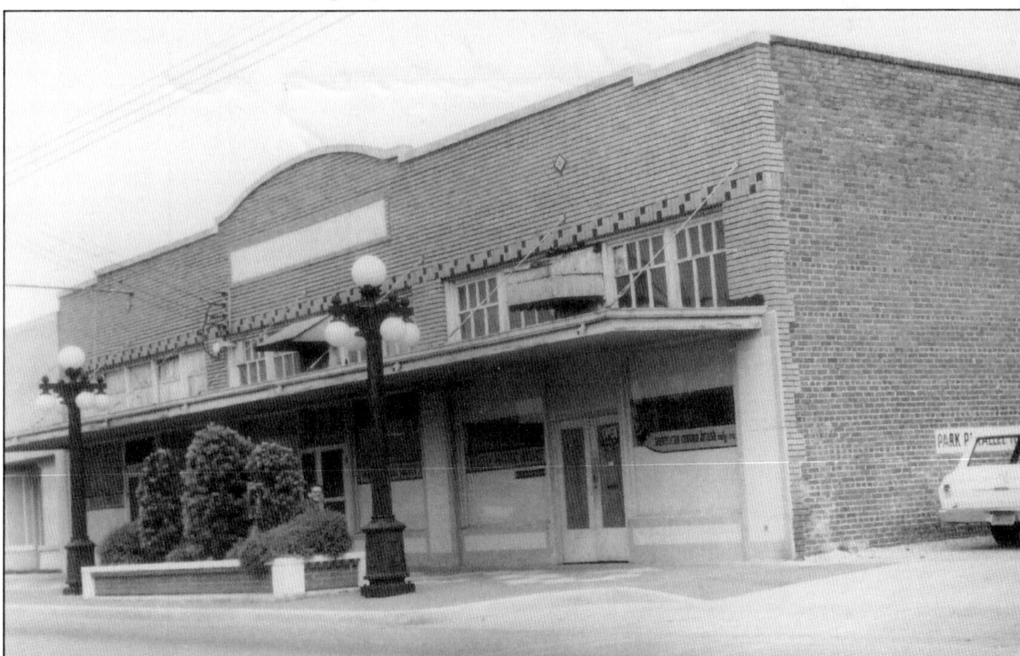

CORONA BRUSHES, YBOR CITY, 1962. In 1959, Fidel Castro came to power in Cuba, ushering in a repressive communist regime. The Waksman family left behind a thriving business and fled to Miami. After deciding not to stay in Miami, the family moved to Tampa and started another paintbrush factory. Jude and his sons, David and Gregory, adapted their paintbrushes to a new market and slowly earned the loyalty of independent dealers. The successful company began marketing outside of Florida with the motto "Corona—It's what paint needs." Gregory's sons, Benjamin and Albert, continued in the family business and have taken over the leadership of Corona Brushes. In 2011, the company celebrated 50 years in business in America.

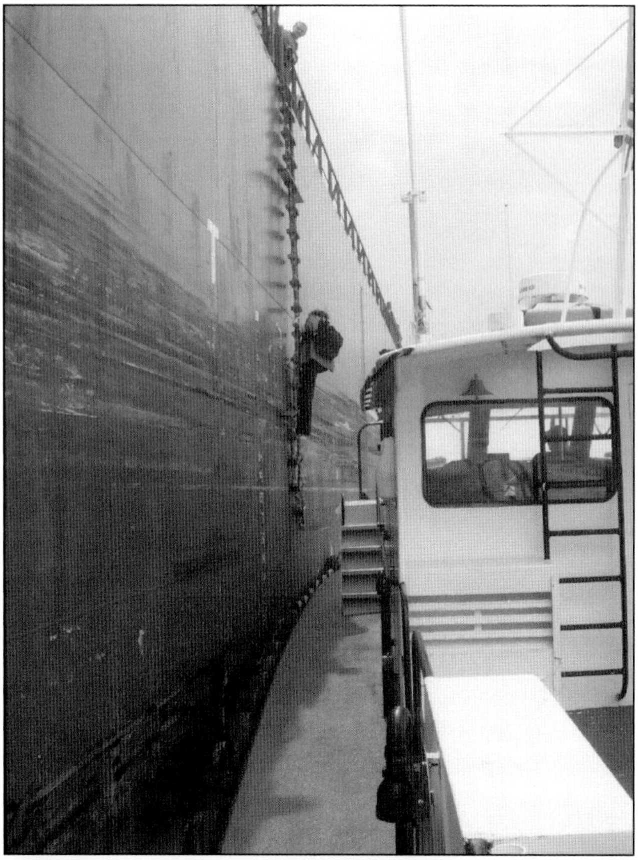

Carolyn Kurtz, Florida's First Female Harbor Pilot, 2010. For 18 years, Kurtz has brought ships into the Port of Tampa. From the pilot boat, she snugs up to an incoming vessel, jumps to the ship's dangling rope ladder, and climbs 30 feet (left). Kurtz then takes control of the ship from the captain, telling the crew how to make it safely through Tampa Bay's 42-mile channel, the state's longest. Kurtz graduated from the US Merchant Marine Academy in 1986 and is one of 23 pilots—the only woman—working for the Tampa Bay Pilots Association. Preventing collisions and groundings requires familiarity with the coastline, weather, and tides, as well as various ships' propulsion systems, rudders, radar, GPS systems, and hull designs. Kurtz sings in the choir for Congregation Schaarai Zedek and is preparing for her son's Bar Mitzvah this year. (Both, courtesy of Jorge Viso.)

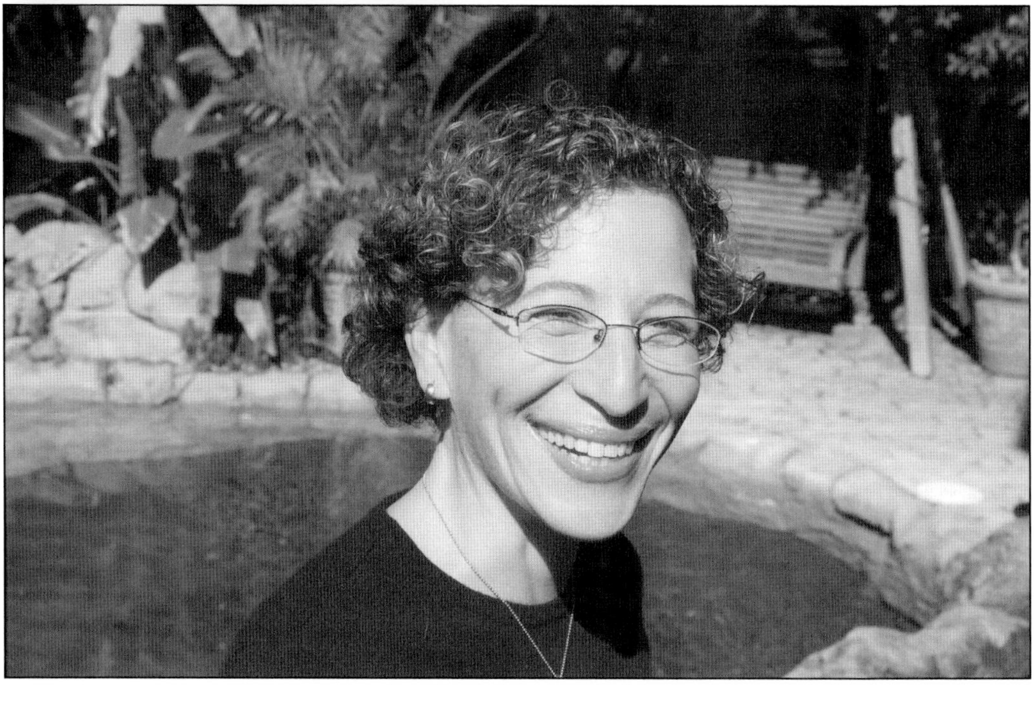

Four

In the Community

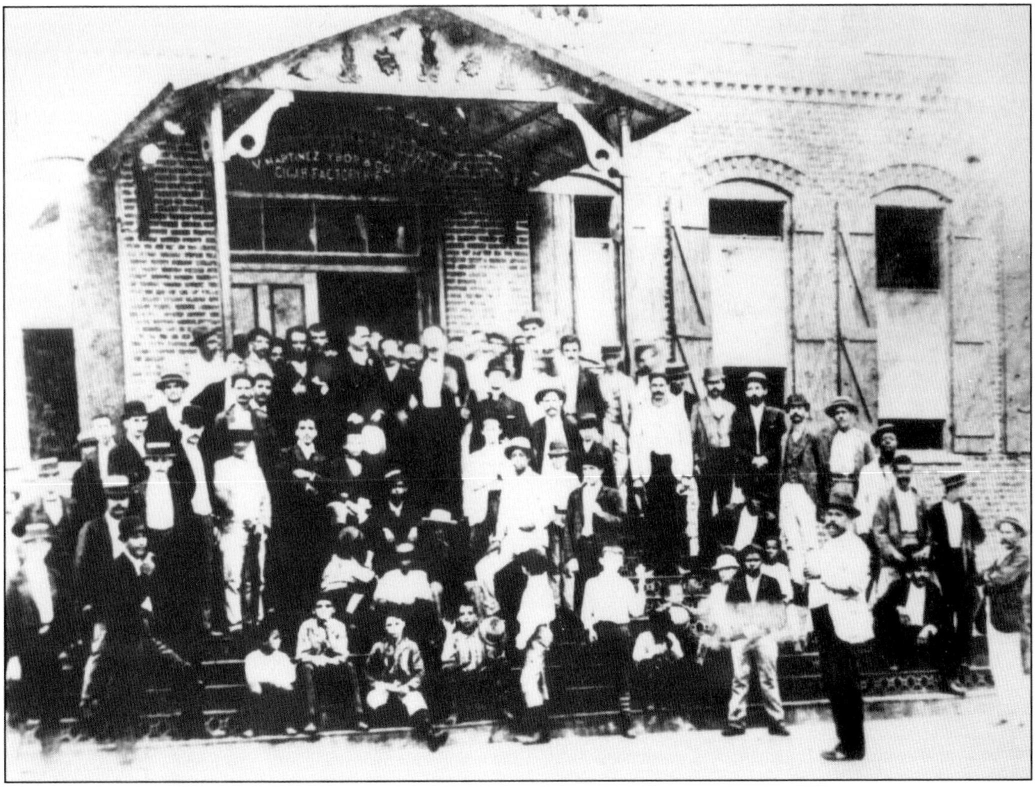

Jose Marti in Ybor City, 1893. Marti led the struggle for Cuban independence. Romanian Jews working in the tobacco industry and as merchants in Ybor City joined in support of the Cuban activists. The Jews could relate to repressive regimes and the desire for independence from Spanish colonial rule, as Spain had instituted the Inquisition and expelled the Jews in the 15th century. Marti is pictured in the center of the top steps with his jacket open and his hands in his pockets.

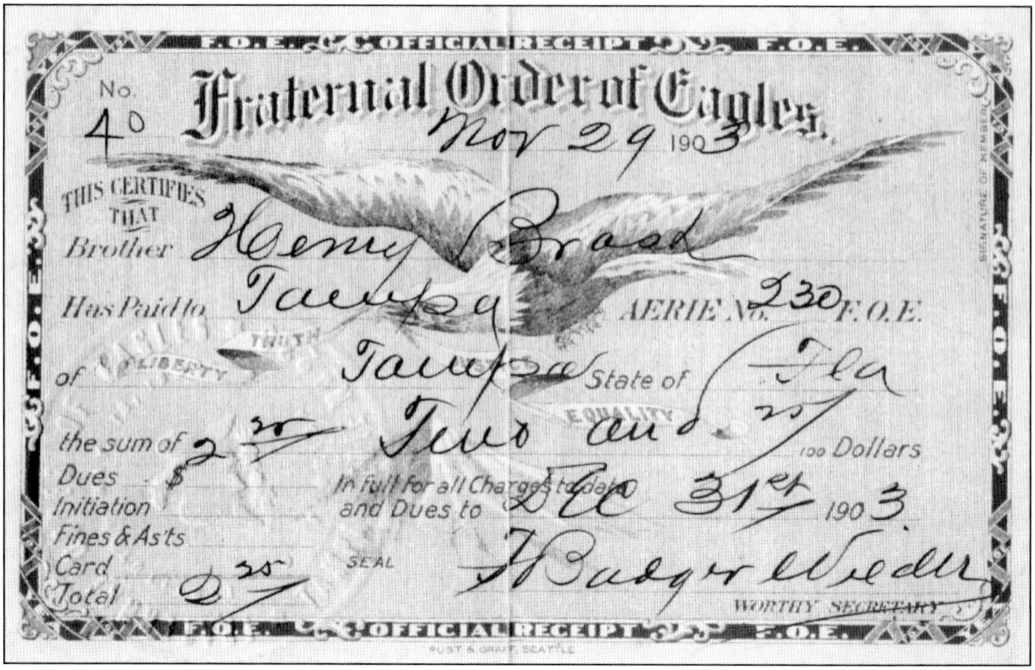
F.O.E. OFFICIAL RECEIPT F.O.E.

No. 4O **Fraternal Order of Eagles**

Nov 29 1903

THIS CERTIFIES THAT Brother Henry Brash

Has Paid to Tampa AERIE No. 230 F.O.E.

of Tampa State of Fla

the sum of 2 50/— Two and 50/100 Dollars

Dues $

Initiation

Fines & As'ts

Card

Total 2 50/—

In full for all Charges to date and Dues to Dec 31st 1903

SEAL

WORTHY SECRETARY

F.O.E. OFFICIAL RECEIPT F.O.E.

Fraternal Order of Eagles Membership Receipt, 1903. The Fraternal Order of Eagles was founded in 1898 by a group of six theater owners. Originally made up of those engaged in one way or another in the performing arts, the Eagles grew and claimed credit for establishing the Mother's Day holiday in the United States as well as providing the impetus for Social Security. This receipt belonged to Henry Brash.

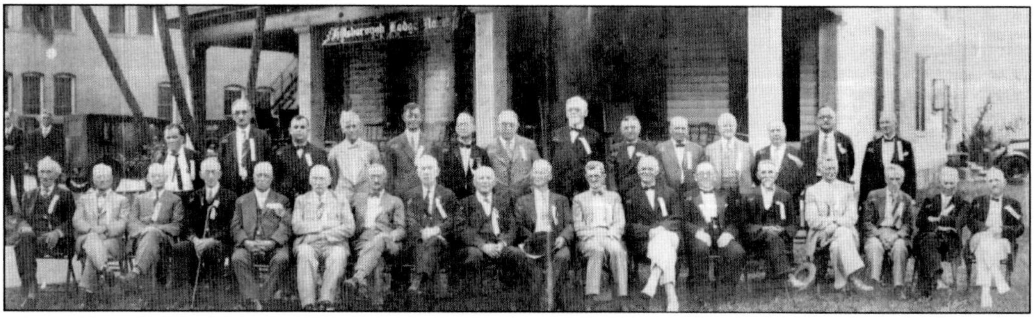

Masons Hillsborough Lodge No. 25, 1928. Included in this *Tampa Tribune* photograph of the Hillsborough lodge, founded in 1850, are Henry Brash (first row, fourth from left), Abe Maas (first row, sixth from right), and Isaac Maas (second row, sixth from right). This was Tampa's oldest Masonic lodge. Freemasonry is a fraternal organization, with meetings at lodges, that promotes separation of church and state and the discussion of politics. Masonry's emphasis on universal brotherhood and tolerance significantly paved the way for Jews in the community. Members are involved in charities and community service activities. Many Jews participated in fraternal organizations, which allowed them to express their civic responsibility.

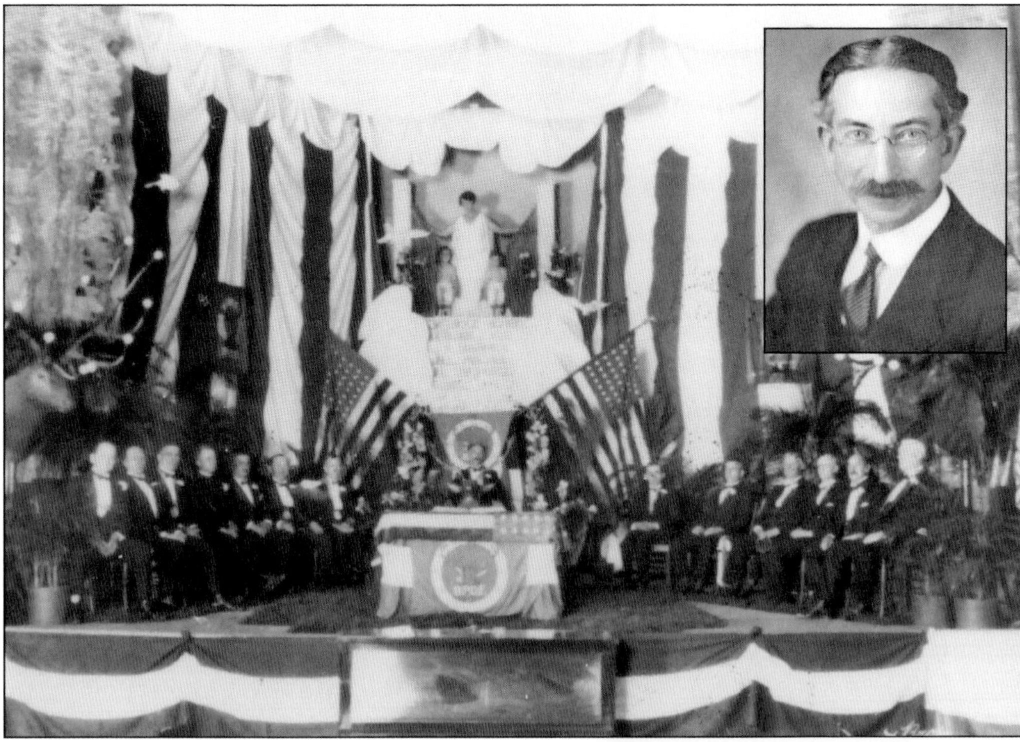

Moses Henry Cohen, Elks President, 1926. Moses Henry Cohen (1872–1943) was admitted to the practice of law in Florida in 1894, the same year he became the first secretary of Schaarai Zedek, where he served for 28 years. He married Julia Wolf, whose family owned Wolf Brothers. Cohen served in the Spanish-American War, then was a municipal judge and assistant city attorney. He was very active in Tampa's civic and fraternal organizations. He is seen at the podium in this photograph.

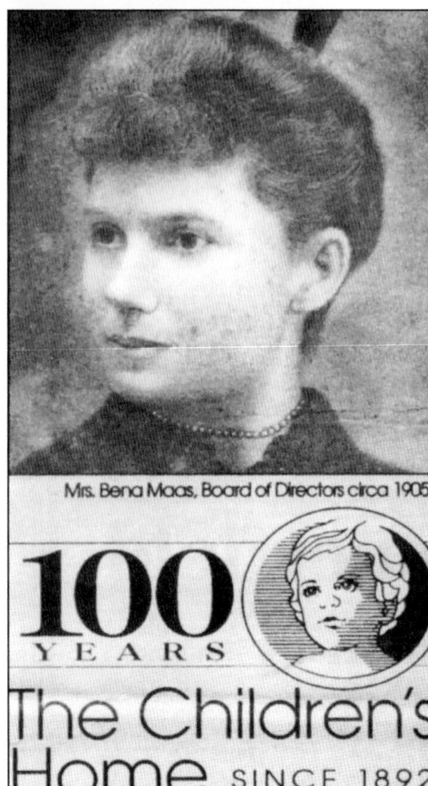

Bena Maas, Founder, The Children's Home, 1905. Philabena Wolf (1863–1947) and Abe Maas were childhood sweethearts in their native Germany. They married in 1883. Bena worked alongside Abe at Maas Brothers until the business stabilized. She was president of The Children's Home for 25 years and was engaged, for the most part anonymously, in many other charitable and welfare projects, especially for orphans. Bena Maas was the last surviving charter member of the Order of Eastern Star in Tampa.

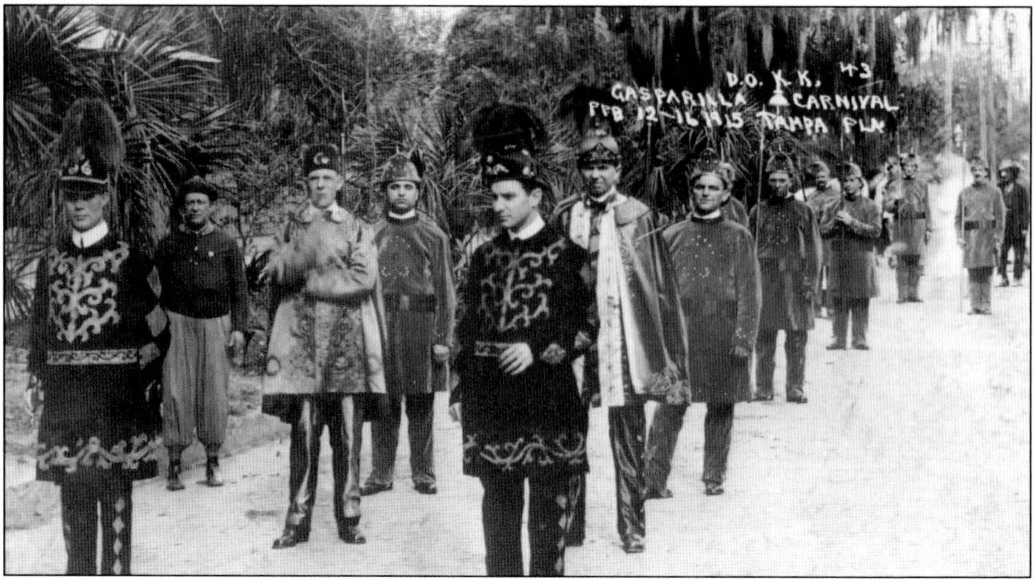

MAX ARGINTAR IN GASPARILLA, 1915. Since 1904, Tampa's social and civic leaders have adopted the legendary pirate Jose Gaspar, "last of the Buccaneers," who terrorized the coastal waters of West Florida during the late 18th and early 19th centuries. A citywide annual celebration includes the traditional invasion, with a fully rigged pirate ship, a colorful parade, and a week's worth of activities. Max Argintar is seen here at center participating in the event.

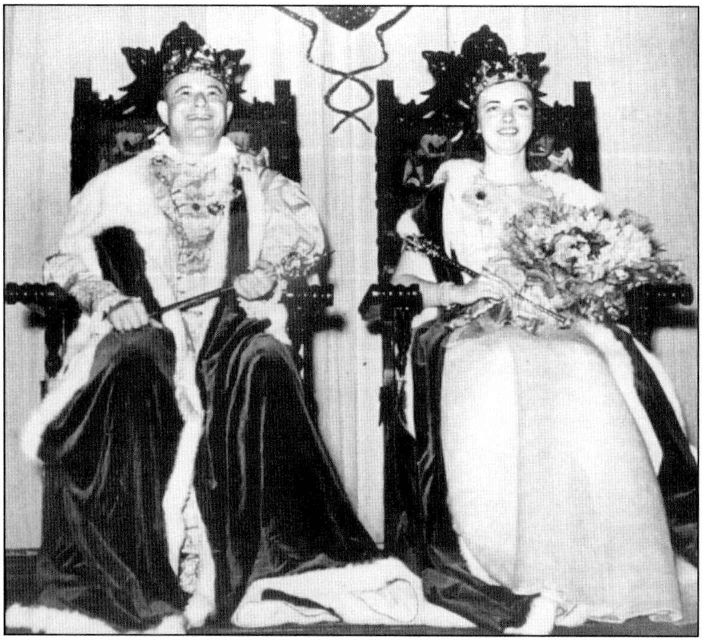

DAVID A. FALK, GASPARILLA KING XXX, 1938. David Falk, born in Tampa in 1896, was the son of Offim and Emma Falk. He joined his father in the family business, O. Falk's Department Store, and served on the University of Tampa's board of trustees from 1948 until his death in 1960. The 1,000-seat Park Theater on Lafayette Street (West Kennedy Boulevard), built in 1928 and renamed in his honor in 1962 as the Falk Theater, hosts UT student productions. The queen pictured is Mary Frances Swann.

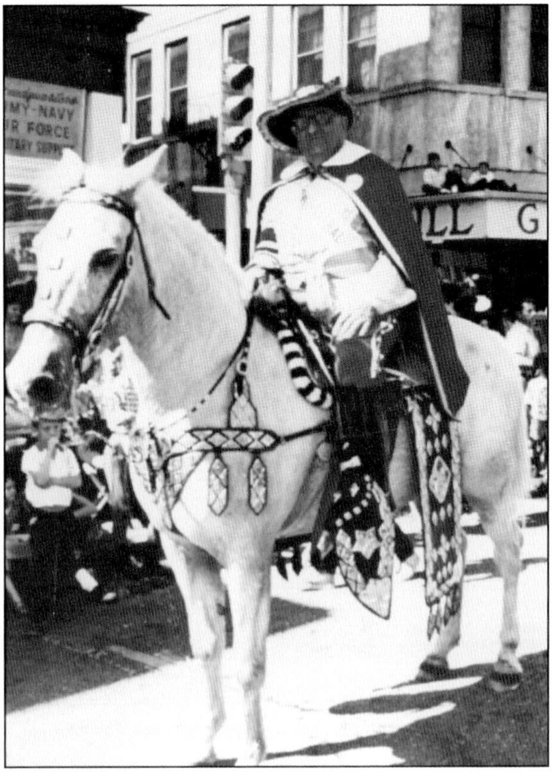

JEROME WATERMAN, GRAND MARSHAL OF GASPARILLA, 1964. A Maas nephew, Jerome Waterman arrived in 1907 and made his way from bookkeeper to chief executive at Maas Brothers. He made lasting contributions to the community, including opening Tampa's early movie theaters. He played a major part in the growth of aviation in Tampa, wrote books and newspaper columns, and enjoyed the outdoors. He is seen here at the age of 80. Waterman is remembered at MacDill Air Force Base where a room in the officers' club is named for him.

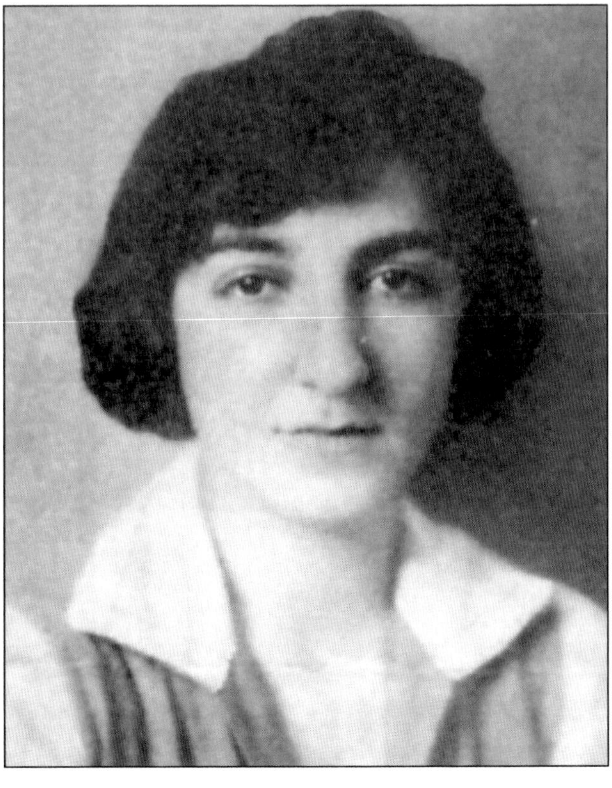

DAISY GUGGENHEIMER WATERMAN, C. 1930S. Jerome Waterman's wife, Daisy, led the Tampa chapter of the National Council of Jewish Women in 1935 to establish the Lighthouse for the Blind, which was named for her after she died of cancer at age 45. The Lighthouse is a United Way recipient; its building, erected at 1106 West Platt Street in 1955, still bears Waterman's name. (See her daughter and granddaughter on page 104.)

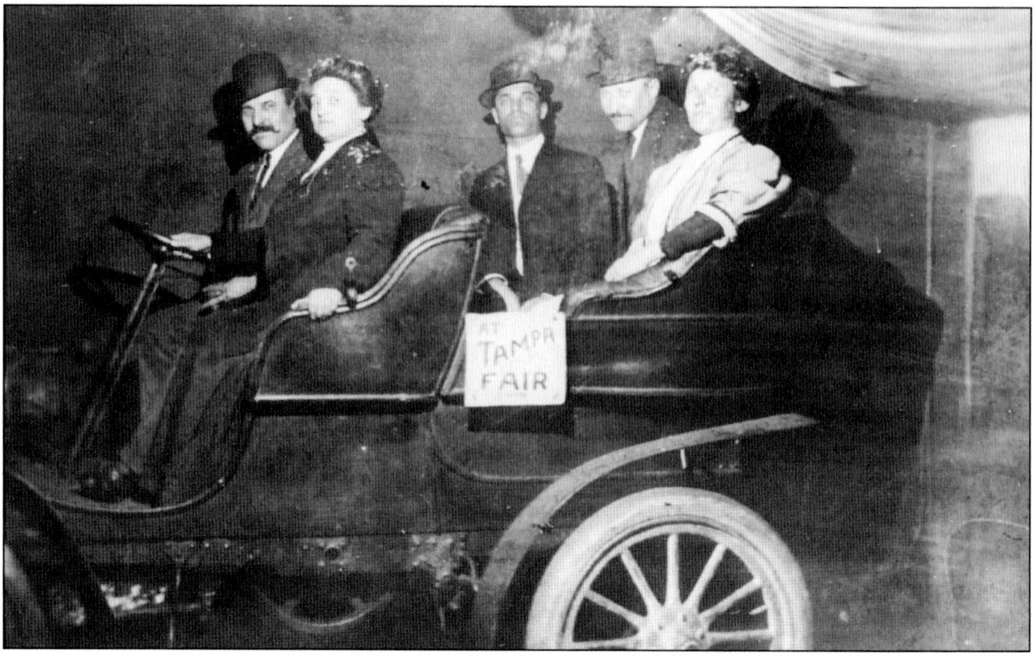

Florida State Fair, February 22, 1909. Every February since 1904, Tampa hosts the Florida State Fair, a 12-day salute to the state's best in agriculture. Shown here in the front seat are Mr. and Mrs. Morris (Celia) Aronovitz. Seated in the back seat are, from left to right, Max Argintar and Mr. and Mrs. (Rosie) Fishman.

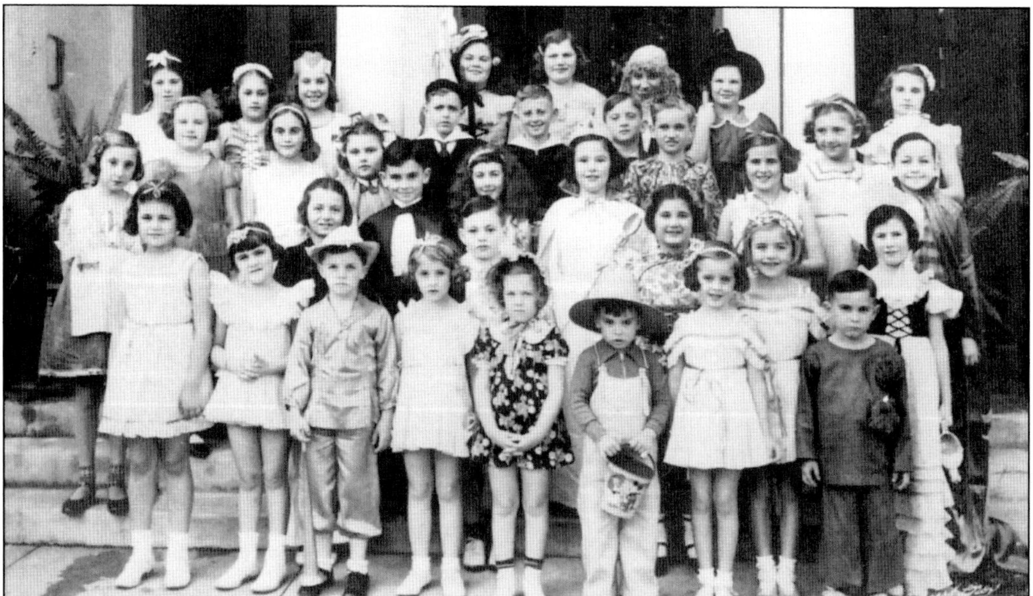

Children Performing at Friday Morning Musicale, 1939. Formed in 1902, the Musicale acquired the land at 809 West Horatio Street in Hyde Park North with war bonds purchased during World War I. It hearkens back to an era when the arts and local theater were ingrained in Tampa's culture. The Musicale was at the roots of the Florida Orchestra and at the forefront of music education in Florida schools. These children are from Congregation Rodeph Sholom.

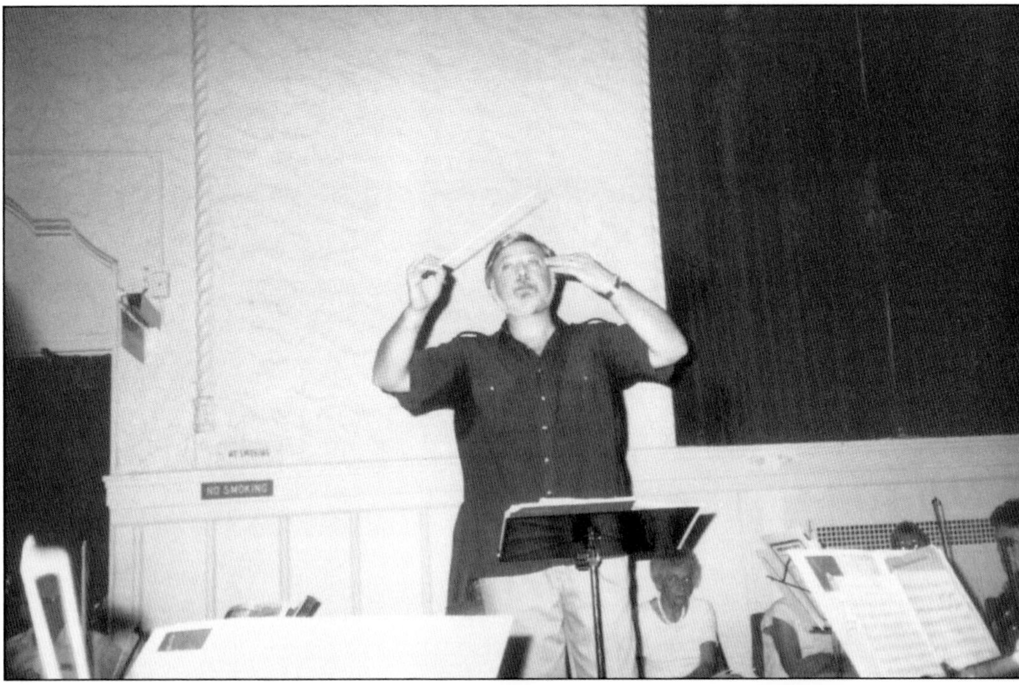

MUSICAL DIRECTOR JACK HELLER, 1985. A violin player since the age of five, Heller retired in 2011 after 25 years as music director of the Tampa Bay Symphony. He joined the USF faculty as director of the school of music in 1985 and is still teaching there. In 1991, Jack was invited to Prague, Czechoslovakia, to direct the National Radio Symphony Orchestra, one of the most respected ensembles in Europe.

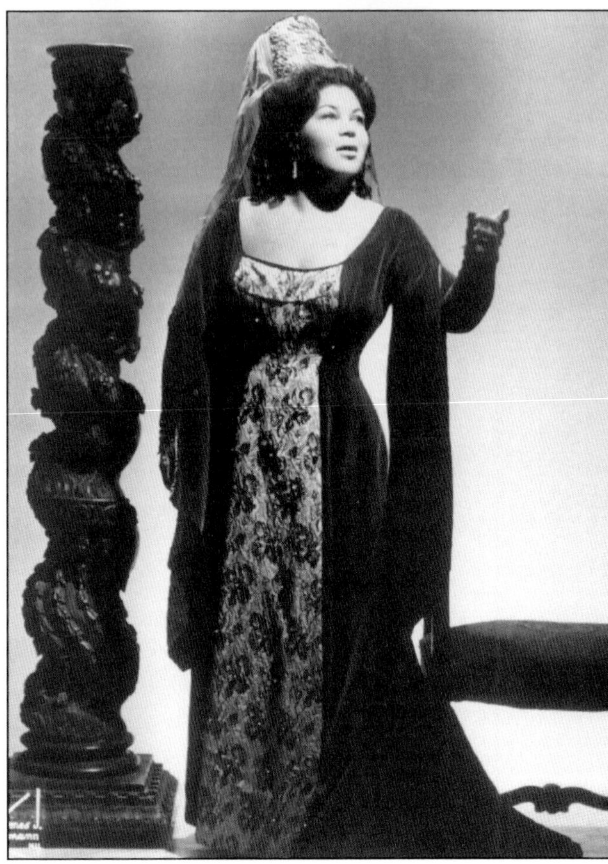

ELINOR ROSENTHAL ROSS, c. 1968. Born in Tampa in 1932, Elinor Ross used her gift of a dramatic soprano voice to advance to stardom at the Metropolitan Opera in New York. Ross enjoyed a successful national and international career. Her repertoire included roles such as Abigail, Lady Macbeth, Amelia, Leonora, Elisabetta, Aida, Gioconda, Santuzza, Maddalena, Tosca, Donna Anna, Medea, and Norma. She was forced into retirement in 1979 due to illness.

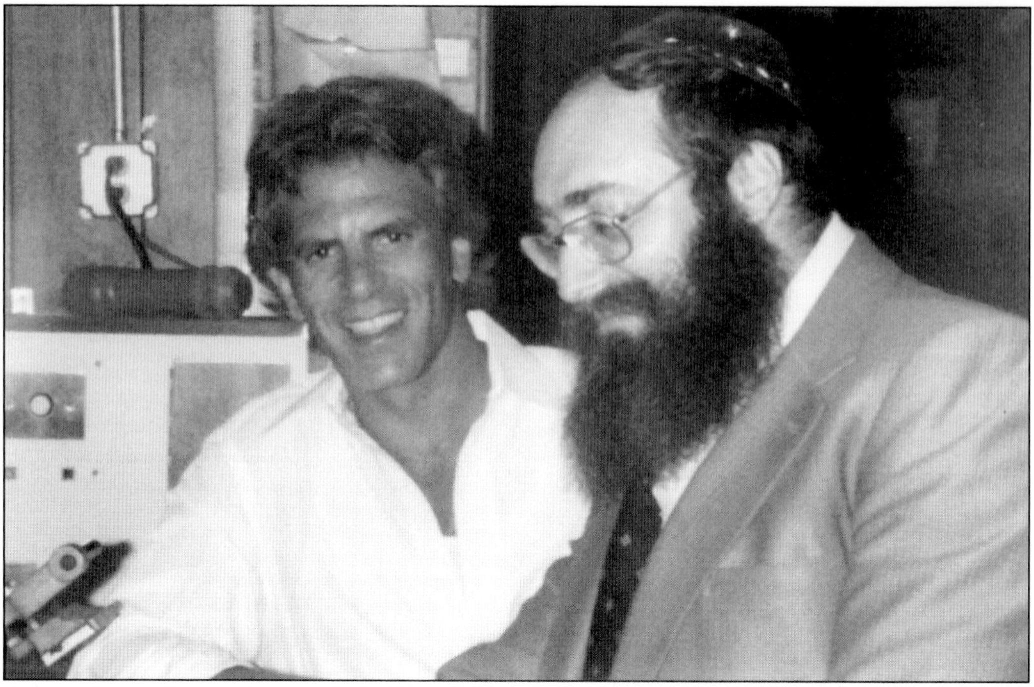

JEWISH SOUND RADIO SHOW, 1979. Ben Linsky (left) and Rabbi Lazer Rivkin, creator and host, respectively, of *Jewish Sound* at WMNF 88.5, are seen here in the old Hyde Park studio. The broadcast was the first Jewish radio show in the Tampa Bay area. It became *Sunday Simcha* in 1981 with a new host, Mike Eisenstadt. The show continues to be heard every Sunday from noon to 2:00 p.m.

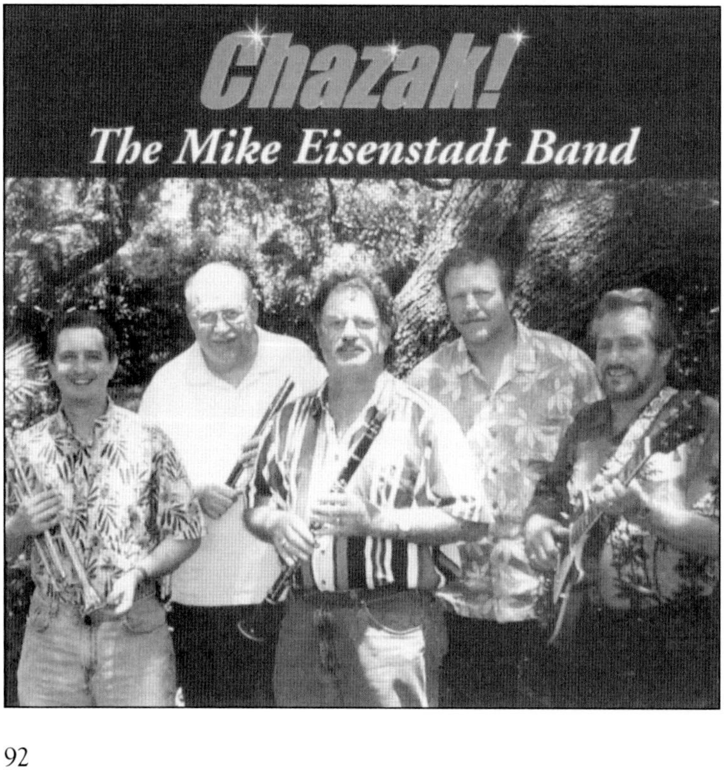

MIKE EISENSTADT BAND, 2005. Shown here on the cover of the Mike Eisenstadt Band's CD are, from left to right, Kevin Frye, Lenny Balistreri, Mike Eisenstadt, John Healy, and Tony King. Eisenstadt had a Klezmer band, was volunteer host of *Sunday Simcha*, and was the first paid staff director of the Jewish Community Relations Council. He led tours to Israel and rallies for Israel. This album was released at Kol Ami, where his funeral was held; Eisenstadt was the official shofar blower there. His mother and her family were known as the Buckler Family Band.

Donated Home for Elderly Blacks, 1963. Ben Haimovitz of Belmont Lumber donated 31 lots to the Lily White Security Benefit Association to build a home for the aged in Tampa's black community. The home was completed in 1963 and dedicated as a memorial to the Haimovitzes.

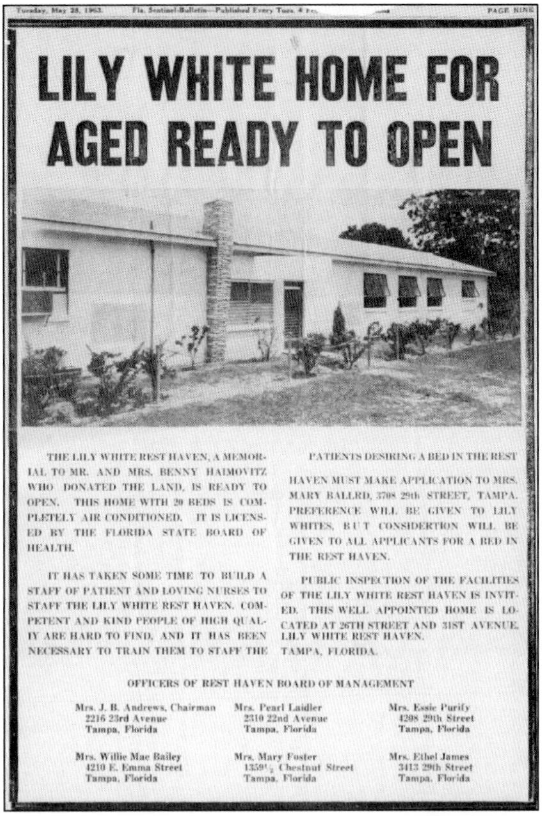
Tuesday, May 28, 1963. Fla. Sentinel-Bulletin—Published Every Tues. & Fri. PAGE NINE

LILY WHITE HOME FOR AGED READY TO OPEN

THE LILY WHITE REST HAVEN, A MEMORIAL TO MR. AND MRS. BENNY HAIMOVITZ WHO DONATED THE LAND, IS READY TO OPEN. THIS HOME WITH 20 BEDS IS COMPLETELY AIR CONDITIONED. IT IS LICENSED BY THE FLORIDA STATE BOARD OF HEALTH.

IT HAS TAKEN SOME TIME TO BUILD A STAFF OF PATIENT AND LOVING NURSES TO STAFF THE LILY WHITE REST HAVEN. COMPETENT AND KIND PEOPLE OF HIGH QUALIY ARE HARD TO FIND, AND IT HAS BEEN NECESSARY TO TRAIN THEM TO STAFF THE

PATIENTS DESIRING A BED IN THE REST

HAVEN MUST MAKE APPLICATION TO MRS. MARY BALLRD, 3708 29th STREET, TAMPA. PREFERENCE WILL BE GIVEN TO LILY WHITES, BUT CONSIDERTION WILL BE GIVEN TO ALL APPLICANTS FOR A BED IN THE REST HAVEN.

PUBLIC INSPECTION OF THE FACILITIES OF THE LILY WHITE REST HAVEN IS INVITED. THIS WELL APPOINTED HOME IS LOCATED AT 26TH STREET AND 31ST AVENUE.
LILY WHITE REST HAVEN.
TAMPA, FLORIDA.

OFFICERS OF REST HAVEN BOARD OF MANAGEMENT

Mrs. J. B. Andrews, Chairman
2216 23rd Avenue
Tampa, Florida

Mrs. Pearl Laidler
2310 22nd Avenue
Tampa, Florida

Mrs. Essie Purify
4208 29th Street
Tampa, Florida

Mrs. Willie Mae Bailey
4210 E. Emma Street
Tampa, Florida

Mrs. Mary Foster
1359½ Chestnut Street
Tampa, Florida

Mrs. Ethel James
3413 29th Street
Tampa, Florida

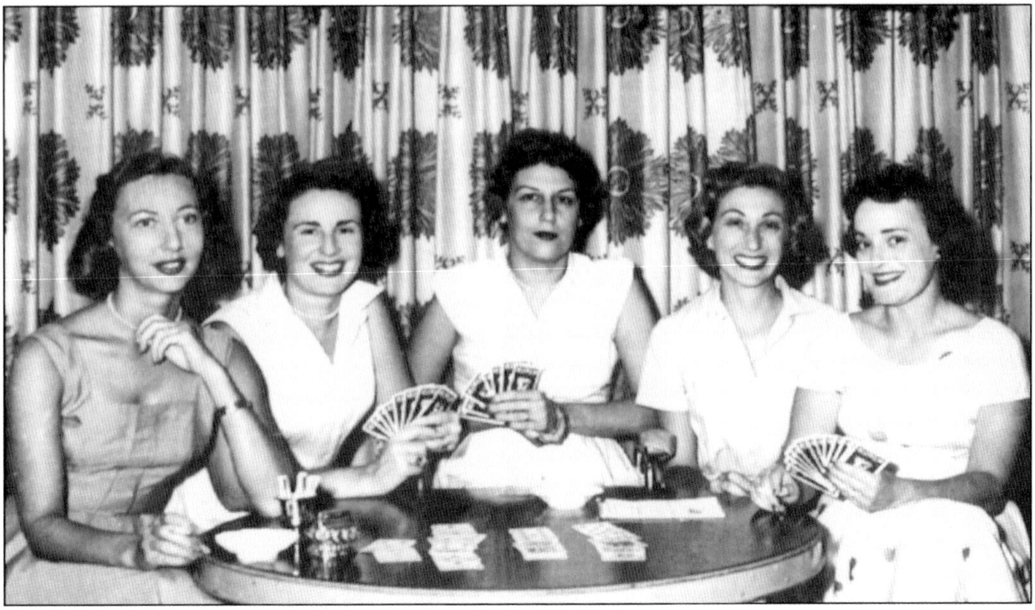

Ladies Taking Time Out, 1950s. This group kept very busy volunteering in the community and also took time to play bridge, canasta, or mah-jongg. Shown here are, from left to right, Marge Hodes, Barbara Garrett, Jane Goldman, Joan Saul, and Phyllis Stone. (Courtesy of Barbara Shine Hicks.)

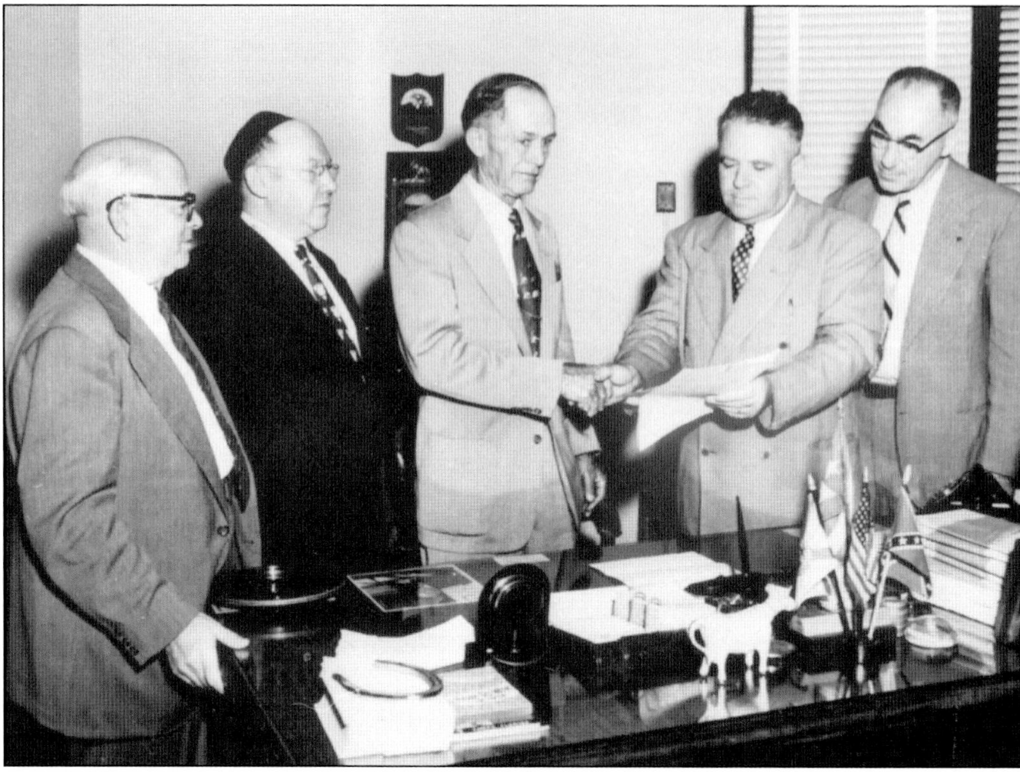

ZIONIST WEEK DECLARED BY MAYOR CURTIS HIXON, 1952. The Tampa community and its leadership have demonstrated support for Israel since its birth in 1948 and have encouraged collaborations. Pictured at the ceremony are (from left to right) Jacob Fuch, Rabbi Theodore Brod, Mayor Hixon, Israel Zack, and David Cowen.

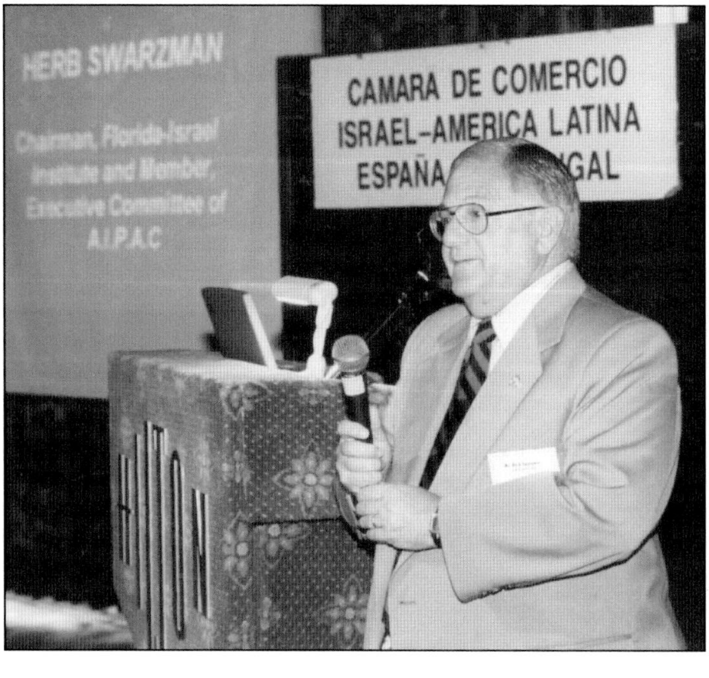

HERB SWARZMAN AT ENTERPRISE FLORIDA TRADE MISSION, TEL AVIV, 1990S. In 1988, Swarzman founded the Florida-Israel Institute (FII), which was established by the Florida Legislature to enhance economic, research, cultural, and educational exchanges between Florida and Israel. FII cooperates with Enterprise Florida to bring trade to Florida from Israel. Swarzman has also been the Tampa Bay area chairman of the American Israel Public Affairs Committee for 30 years and serves on the National Council.

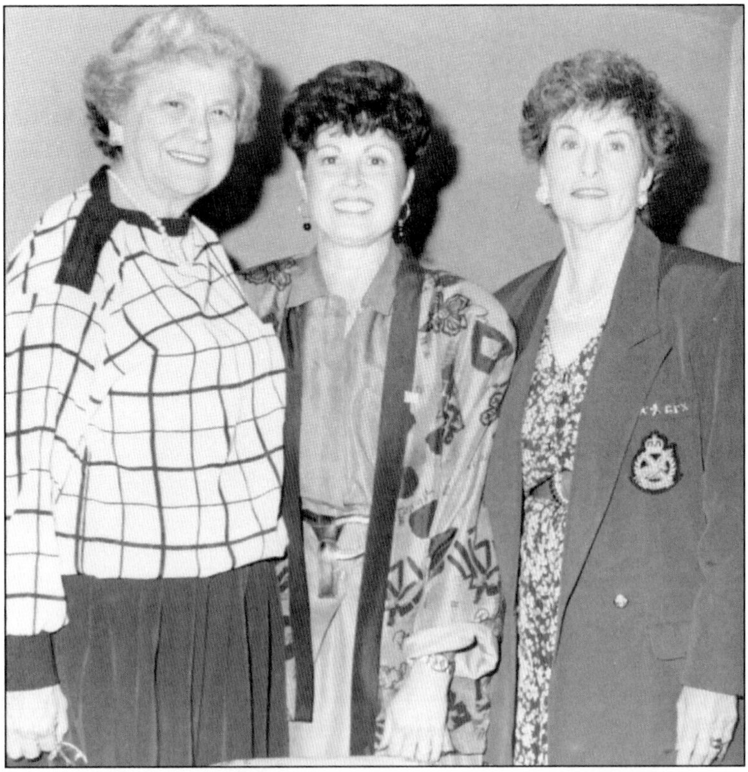

MOSAIC: Jewish Life in Florida Tampa Task Force, 1990. Shown here are cochairs Nellye Friedman (left) and Doris Rosenblatt (right) with MOSAIC state coordinator Marcia Jo Zerivitz. During the 1980s, Zerivitz traveled around the state, working with volunteers to retrieve material evidence of Jewish life in Florida since 1763, when Jews were first allowed to settle. An exhibit was created that traveled to 13 cities, including to the University of Tampa in 1992. This project evolved into the Jewish Museum of Florida in 1995.

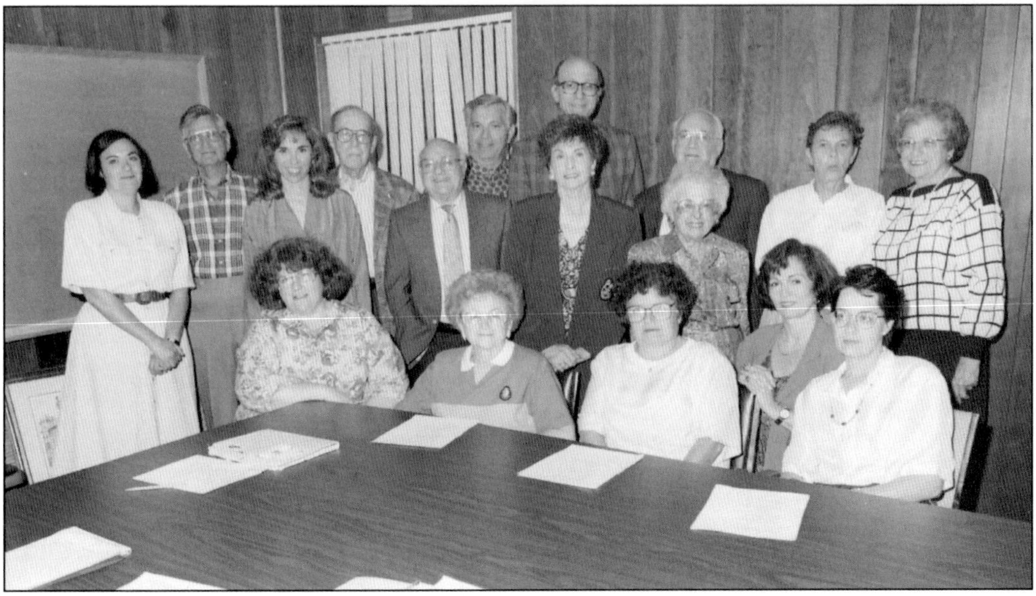

MOSAIC Tampa Task Force, 1990. This group worked to collect and document the Jewish history of Tampa in order to create a Tampa module for the MOSAIC traveling exhibit. Shown here are, from left to right, (seated) Dolly Williams, Dorothy Skop, Myrna Everson, Johanna Barat, and unidentified; (standing) Sherry Stein, Frank Rosenblatt, Erica Mandelbaum, Herman Rosenberg, Art Skop, Jacob Gottfried, Doris Rosenblatt, Edward Stein (behind Rosenblatt), Florence Rosenberg, Herbert Friedman (behind Rosenberg), Lucille Falk, and Nellye Friedman.

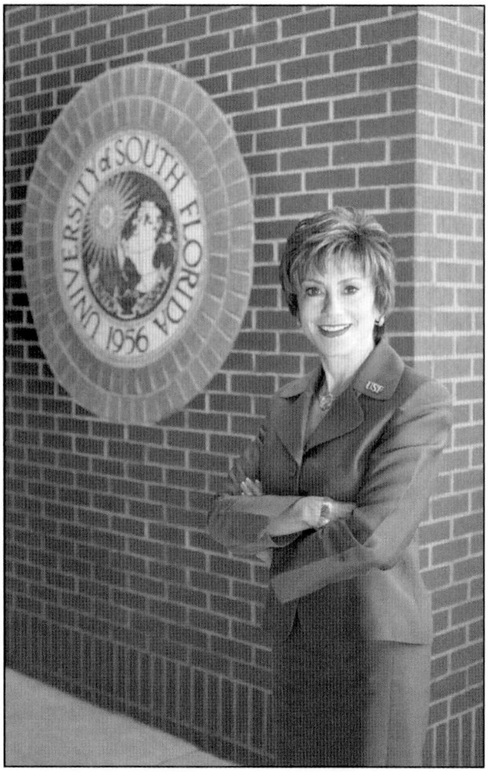

Judy Genshaft, President and Chief Executive Officer, University of South Florida. Genshaft's family teachings of strong Jewish values set the direction for her life. Since her appointment in 2000, she has created a synergy of academia, business, and community that strengthens the Tampa Bay area. USF has campuses in Tampa, St. Petersburg, Sarasota-Manatee, and Lakeland, serving more than 47,000 students in more than 232 degree programs. Genshaft is past chair of the National Collegiate Athletic Association, Division One.

Katrina Hurricane Relief, Congregation Beth Am, 2005. The Jewish community responds to many national crises. Following Hurricane Katrina in New Orleans, congregation members donated and collected items to take to the victims. Bruce Silverman, Cantor Vikki's husband, donated a truck and a driver for delivery. The truck departed Tampa on September 25, 2005. Congregant Mary Young rode in the passenger's seat to supervise. Rabbi Brian Zimmerman is at front left. (Courtesy of Vikki Silverman.)

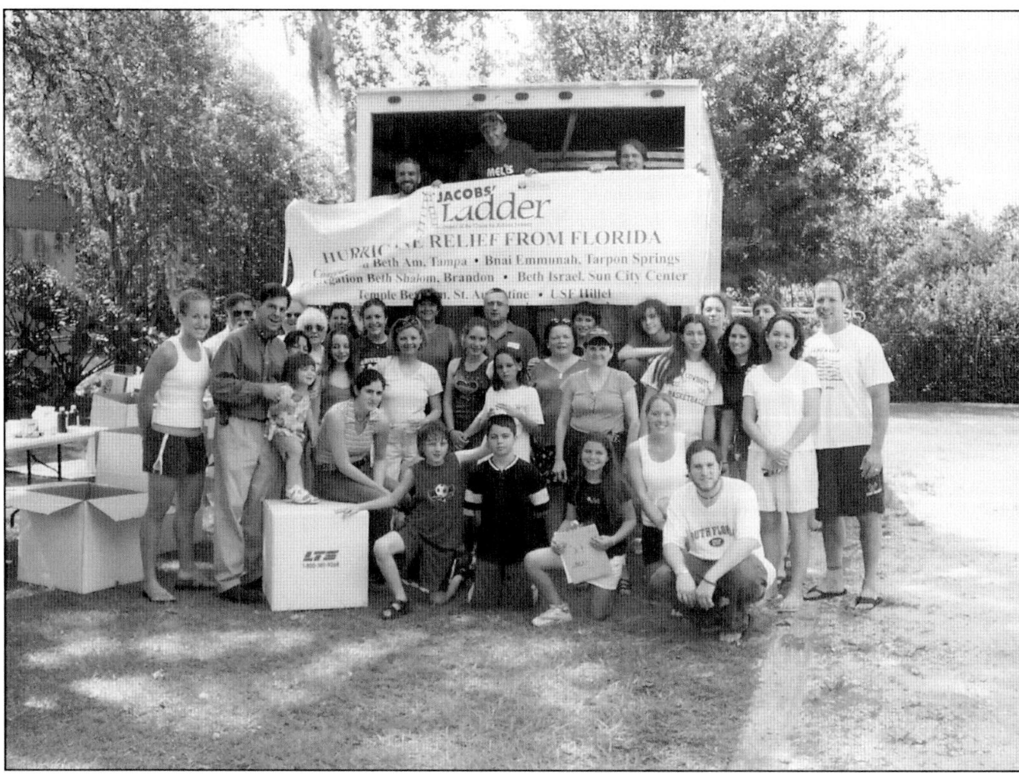

Five

In Politics

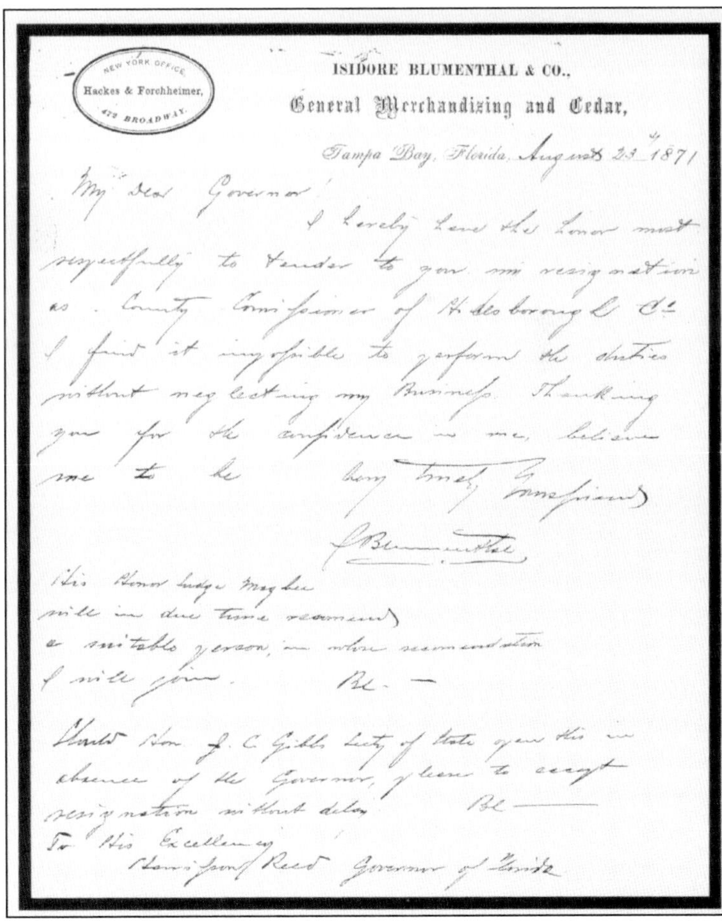

NEW YORK OFFICE
Hackes & Forchheimer,
472 BROADWAY.

ISIDORE BLUMENTHAL & CO.,
General Merchandizing and Cedar,
Tampa Bay, Florida, August 23 1871

My dear Governor!
I hereby have the honor most respectfully to tender to you my resignation as County Commissioner of Hillsborough Co. I find it impossible to perform the duties without neglecting my Business. Thanking you for the confidence in me, believe me to be
Very truly Your friend
I Blumenthal

His Honor Judge Magbee will in due time recommend a suitable person, in whose recommendation I will join. Bl. —

Should Hon. J. C. Gibbs Secty of State open this in absence of the Governor, please to accept resignation without delay Bl —

To His Excellency
Harrison Reed Governor of Florida

Letter of Resignation from Isidore Blumenthal, Hillsborough County Commissioner. Blumenthal was the first Jewish commissioner on what was then a five-member board. During his tenure, from 1871 to 1873, he worked to improve local conditions and raise the standards for public service. He resigned due to an injury and business challenges, but was persuaded to stay on to enact needed reforms. Another Jew, Charles Slager, was serving as county sheriff, and the minutes reflect that he cooperated with Blumenthal. (Courtesy of FSA.)

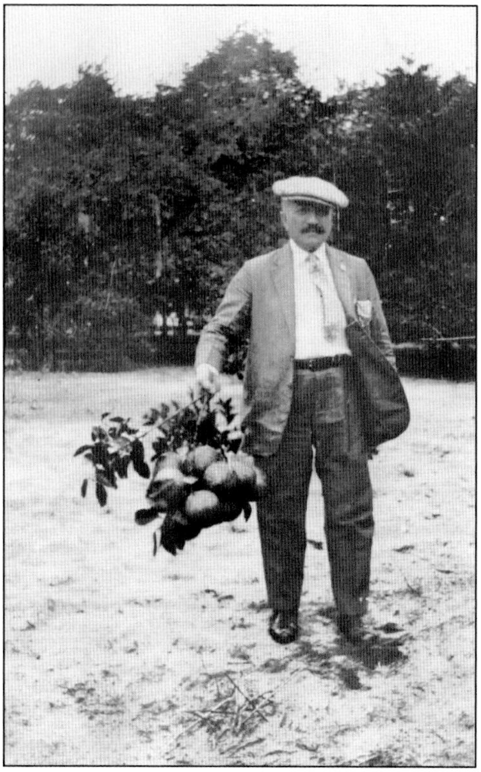

Morris Lewy, Founder of Jeffersonian Democratic Society of Florida, c. 1920. Dr. Morris Lewy, a podiatrist, founded the Jeffersonian Democratic Society in honor of the nation's third president. Jefferson strengthened the powers of the executive branch and was the first president to lead a political party. Through this position, he exercised control over the Congress of the United States. Jefferson had great faith in popular rule, and it is this optimism that is the essence of what came to be called Jeffersonian democracy.

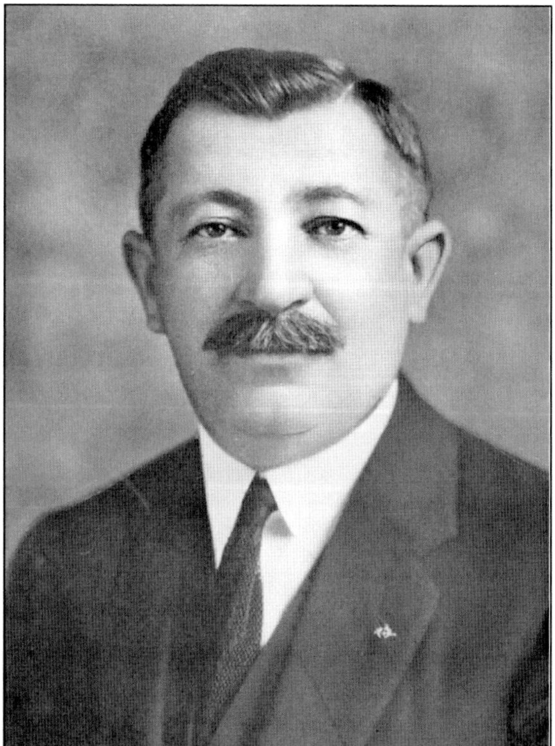

Adolph Goldstein, Tampa City Council. Romanian immigrant Adolph Goldstein was the next Jew to serve on the city council after Offim Falk (1910–1914). Goldstein, like other Jewish citizens, became deeply patriotic and involved in politics to demonstrate admiration and enthusiasm for democracy, which provided the freedoms and opportunities that brought his family and fellow Jewish immigrants to Tampa. He served on the city council from 1920 to 1921 and again from 1928 to 1929.

HARRY SANDLER. Harry Sandler (1889–1965), a Florida legislator and judge, arrived in Tampa in 1911 with a law degree. His father, a tailor, had earlier relocated in Ybor City, and Harry was an inveterate cigar smoker. He began his practice and acquired a reputation for integrity. Sandler served in the Florida Legislature from 1932 to 1935, was Speaker of the House, and sponsor of the Homestead Exemption Amendment. Appointed to the 13th Judicial Circuit Court in 1935, he served until 1964. He and his wife, Hannah, had three children.

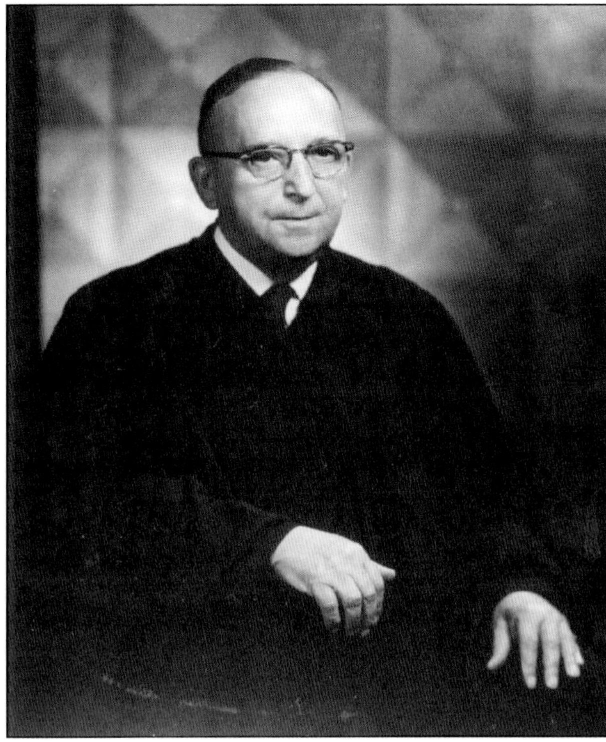

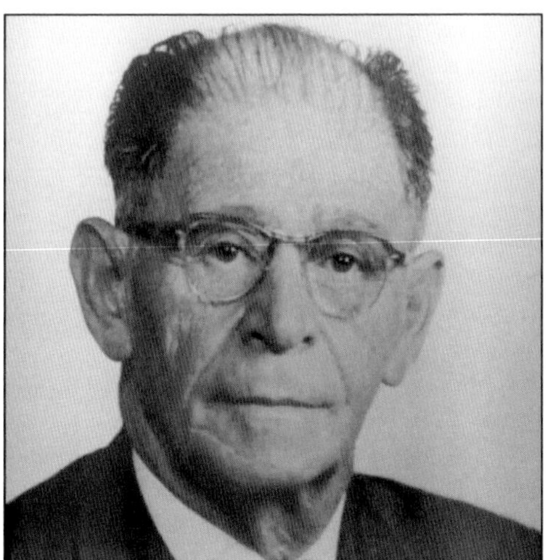

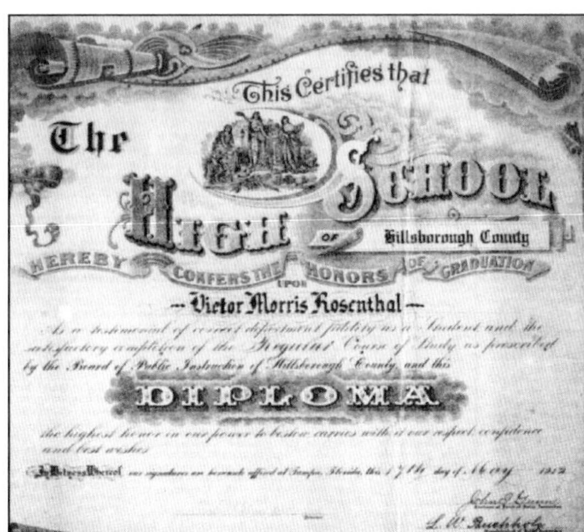

VICTOR MORRIS ROSENTHAL. A native of Tampa, Dr. Rosenthal (1895–1981) was a son of Tillie and Isaac Rosenthal, who arrived in 1885. Victor became a dentist in Ybor City in 1920 and got involved in politics. He was elected alderman in 1925, to the Tampa City Council (1929–1941), and he chaired the city council (1941–1945). His 1912 high school diploma is seen here. (Left, courtesy of Debbie Rosenthal.)

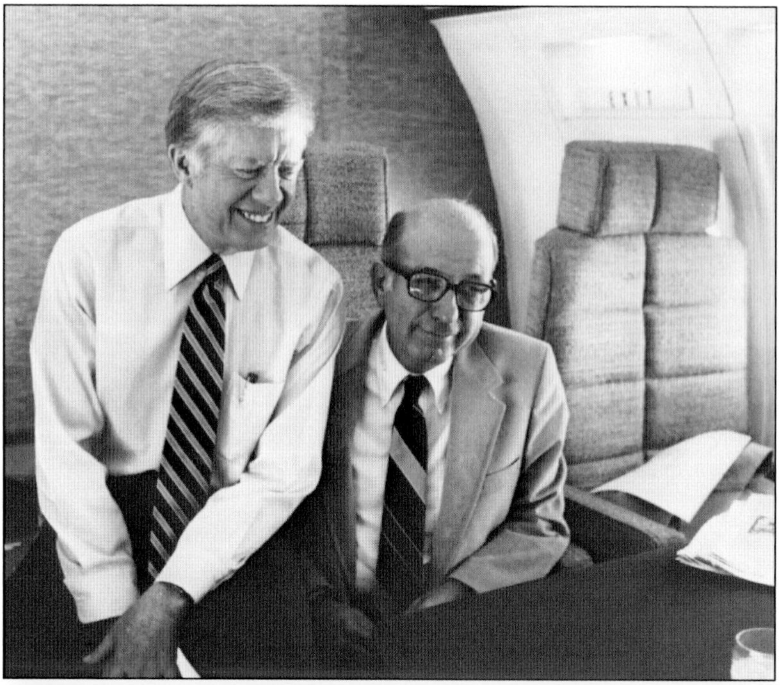

Dr. Richard Hodes on Air Force One with Pres. Jimmy Carter, 1980. Dr. Hodes (right) was elected to the Florida House of Representatives in 1966, where he served for 16 years. He gave the nominating speech for Jimmy Carter at the Florida Democratic Convention in 1975. Hodes became the first chairman of the University of South Florida's anesthesiology department in 1982.

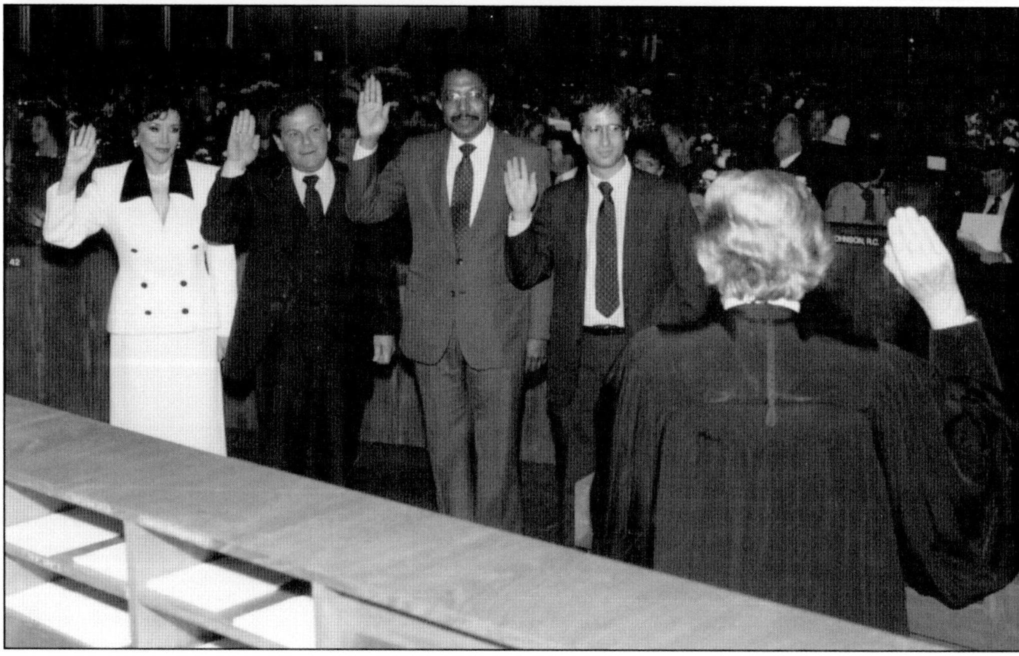

Helen Gordon Davis and Ron Glickman Being Sworn In to Florida Legislature, 1986. Helen (far left) came to Tampa after World War II and worked as a model, actress, teacher, and homemaker. She entered politics in 1974, was the first Tampa female elected to a state office, served in the Florida House of Representatives for seven terms, and served in the Florida Senate in 1988. She is known for her work on social, women's, and family issues and her interest in Florida's justice system. Ron Glickman (far right) won his first election in 1984 as a Hillsborough County Commissioner. He was elected to the Florida House of Representatives in 1986.

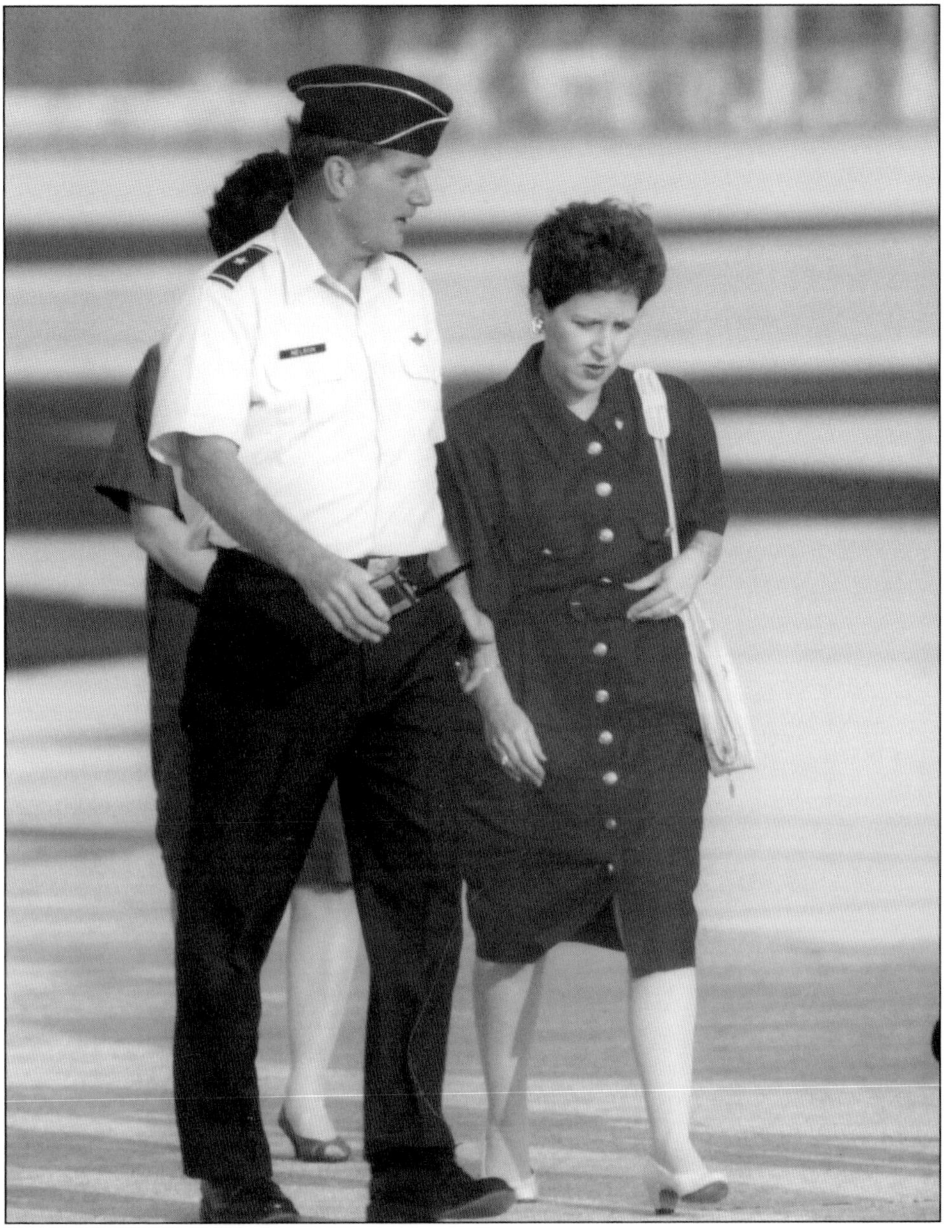

Mayor Sandra Warshaw Freedman at MacDill Air Force Base, 1992. In this photograph, Gen. Ben Nelson Jr. accompanies Mayor Freedman as they welcomed home troops from Operation Desert Storm. Tampa's first female mayor and second Jewish mayor, Freedman served from 1986 to 1995. She had wanted to be mayor since sixth grade, and she first served on the Tampa City Council in 1974. Freedman started task forces to halt the escalating crime rate caused by drugs. She increased the size of the police department by more than 20 percent, organized Tampa's first march against hate crimes, and appointed a substantial number of minorities and women in city government. During her terms, Tampa opened a new convention center and the Florida Aquarium, and instituted recycling and water conservation programs. In 1990, Tampa was designated as the "All-American City." Freedman, now retired, is active in civic affairs. (See page 117.) (Courtesy of TBHC.)

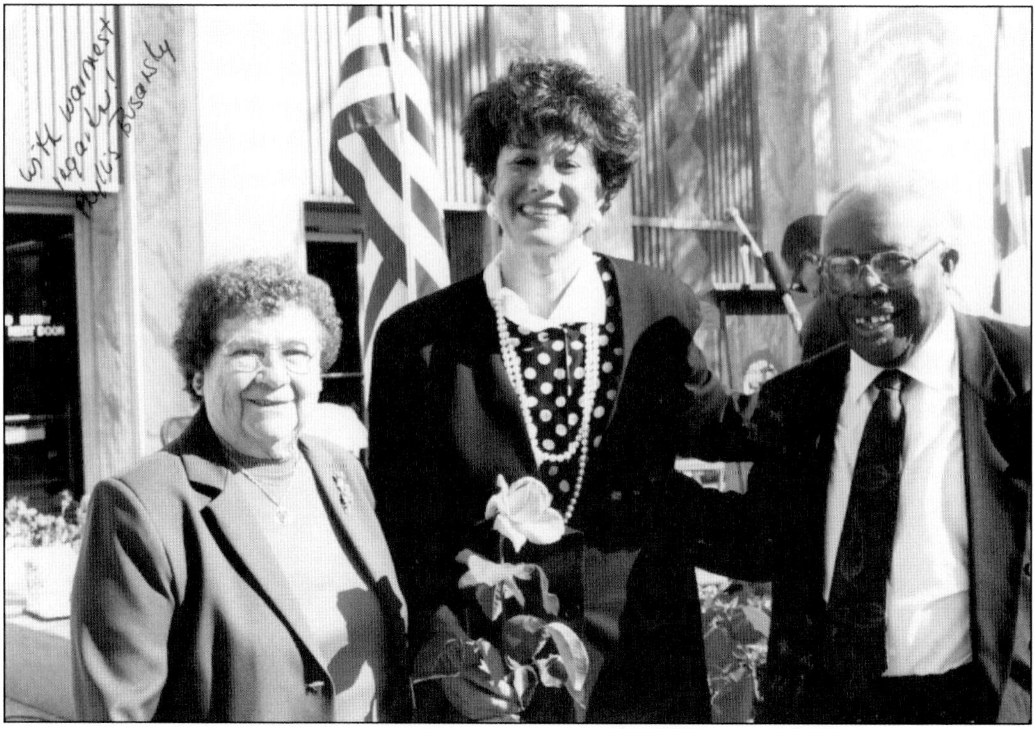

Phyllis Hendler Busansky, 1988. In 1962, Phyllis (1937–2009) and Sheldon Busansky moved to Tampa, where she served as a Hillsborough County commissioner from 1988 to 1997. She was the first executive director of Florida's welfare-to-work agency under Governors Lawton Chiles and Jeb Bush. In 2008, she was elected Hillsborough County supervisor of elections. In 2012, she was posthumously inducted into the Hillsborough County Women's Hall of Fame. In this photograph, Busansky (center) takes part in a ceremony honoring workers at the Lee Davis Service Center.

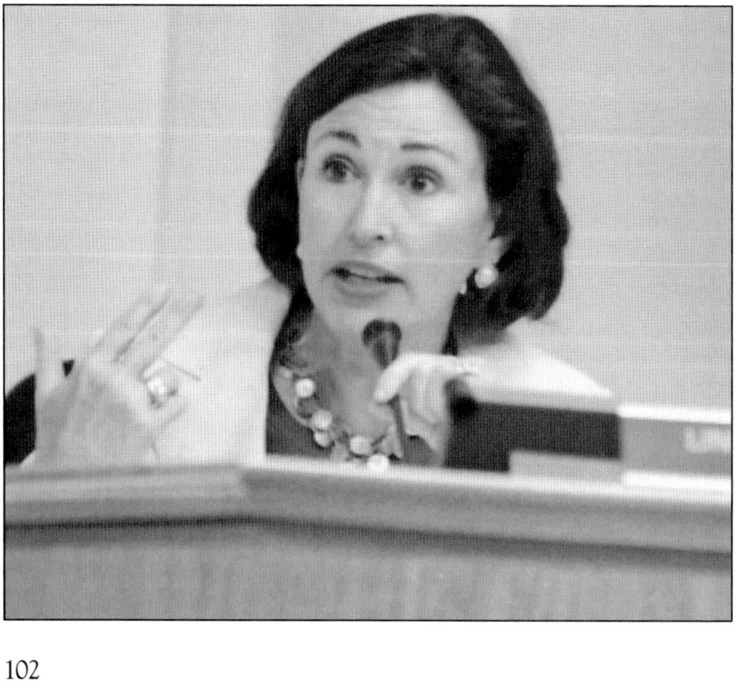

Linda Saul-Sena on Tampa City Council. As a city council member for five terms (1987–1995; 1999–2003–2010), Saul-Sena was an advocate for the environment, the arts, historic preservation, and urban redevelopment. In 2011, she was appointed to the board of the Community Foundation of Tampa Bay. She also serves on the board of directors for the Florida Trust for Historic Preservation and the Tampa Theatre Foundation.

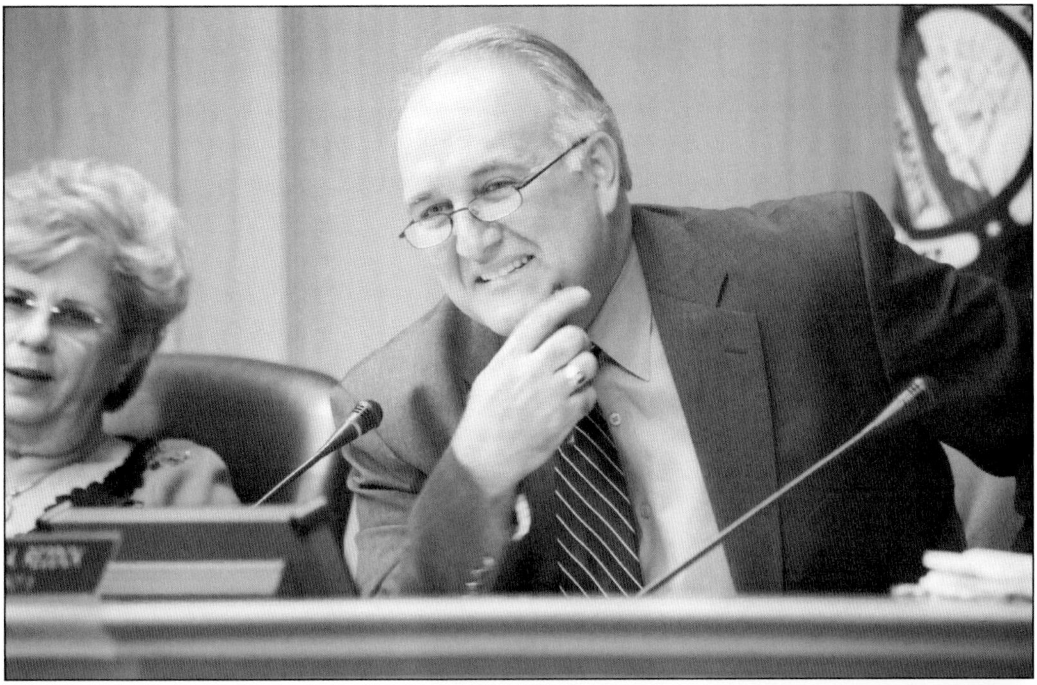

JOHN DINGFELDER, TAMPA CITY COUNCIL. A Tampa native, Dingfelder was elected in 2003 to serve District 4, and he held that position until 2010. A lawyer by profession, he is part of the Scarritt Dingfelder Law Group. He was assistant public defender and served as Hillsborough County's assistant county attorney. He has done environmental and construction litigation for Carlton Fields Law Firm. (Courtesy of Lynn Dingfelder.)

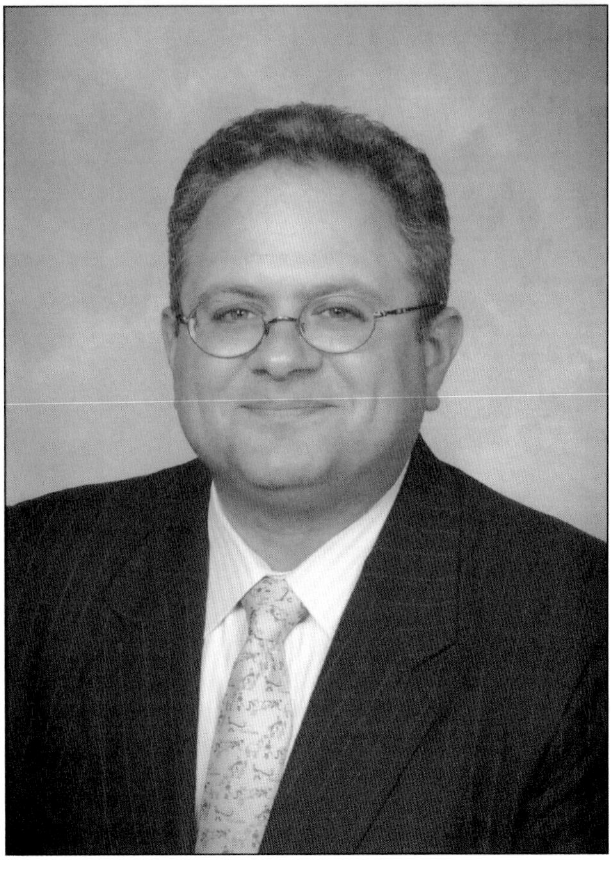

HARRY COHEN, TAMPA CITY COUNCIL. In 2011, Tampa native Cohen, an attorney who has worked in private and public practice, won the District 4 council seat that covers South Tampa. He chairs the council's finance committee and was elected chair pro tem of the council in 2012.

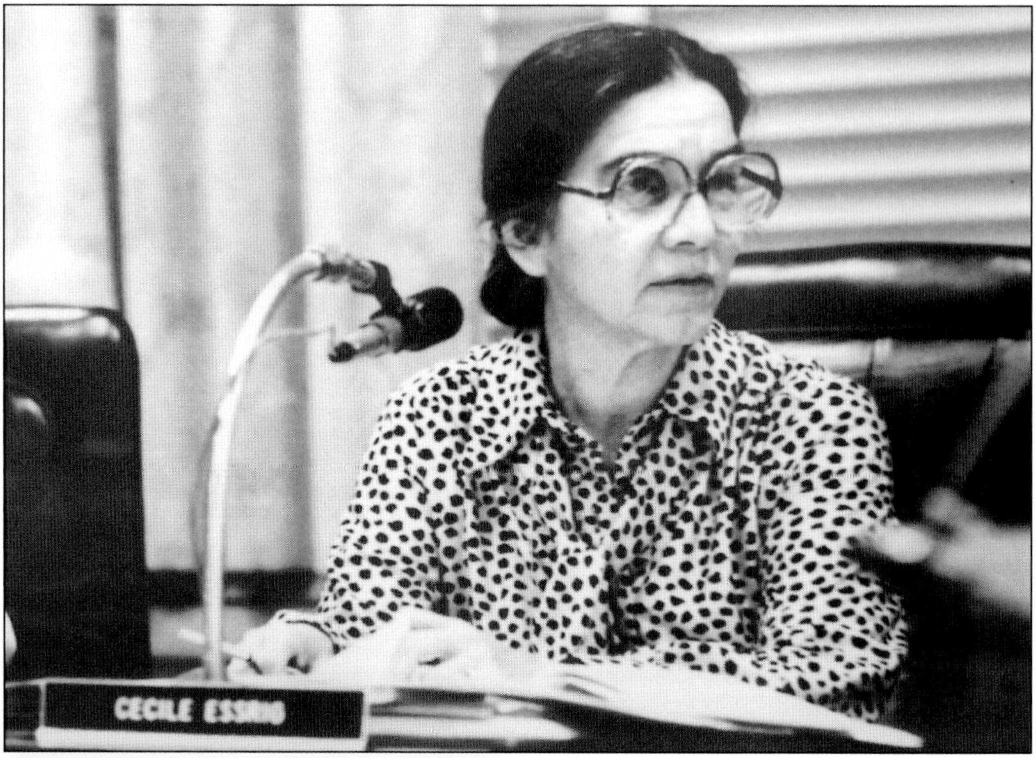

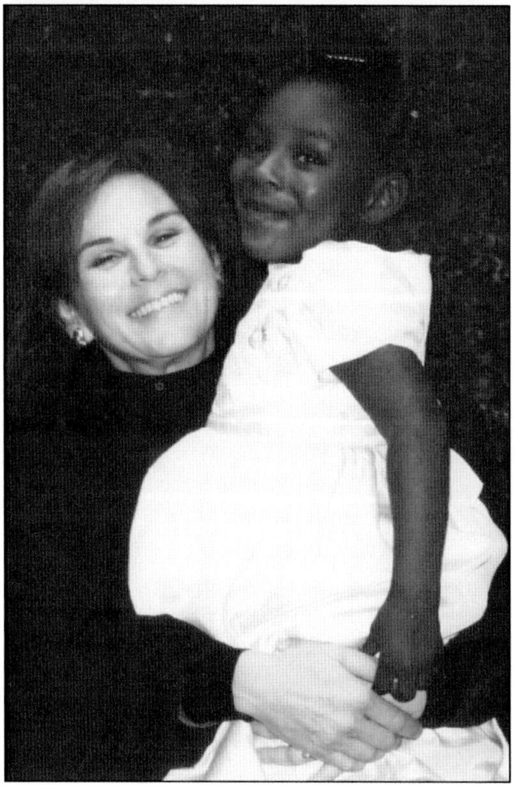

Cecile Waterman Essrig. Essrig, the daughter of Daisy and Jerome Waterman, became the first woman elected to the Hillsborough School Board in 1967 and served 21 years. Focused on inclusion and civil rights, she helped lead the school system and community through many turbulent periods. Essrig created the Youth Council to give students a direct voice to the school board. A Carrollwood elementary school was named for her in 1987.

Circuit Court Judge Katherine Essrig, 2012. This photograph was taken immediately subsequent to an adoption hearing on National Adoption Day. Judge Essrig, born in Tampa and the daughter of Cecile Essrig and granddaughter of Daisy Waterman, has served as a Unified Family Court and Juvenile Dependency Division judge of the 13th Judicial Circuit Court since 1997. In 2008, she was elected to another six-year term. Essrig worked as an assistant state attorney prior to joining the Hillsborough County Court in 1991. (Courtesy of Judge Essrig.)

Six

In the Military

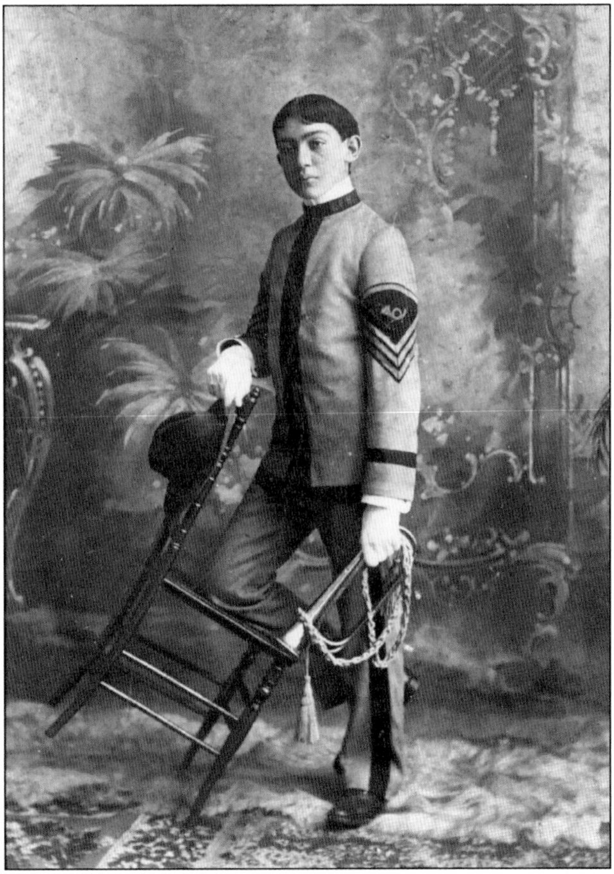

Sol Maas, at East Florida Military Seminary, Gainesville, 1895. After graduating from the University of Florida, Sol Maas, son of Abe and Bena Maas, became affiliated with Maas Brothers. He took an active part in Tampa civic life as a member of Schaarai Zedek, the Elks, Masons, and Shriners. Sol (1884–1944) married Julia Cahn (1888–1978), whose nickname was "Blizzard," because she was born during a snowstorm. The couple had two children, Frances and Joseph Morton Maas.

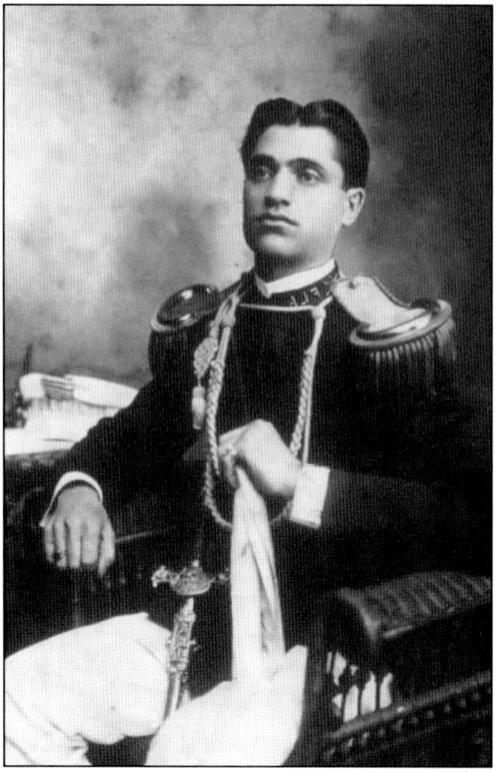

Max Argintar in Home Guard Uniform, 1917. On April 6, 1917, the United States declared war on Germany. Tampa citizens sprang into action to do their part for the war effort. Argintar is one example of the immigrant Jews who were deeply patriotic and eager to express their appreciation for and defend the freedoms and opportunities of democracy.

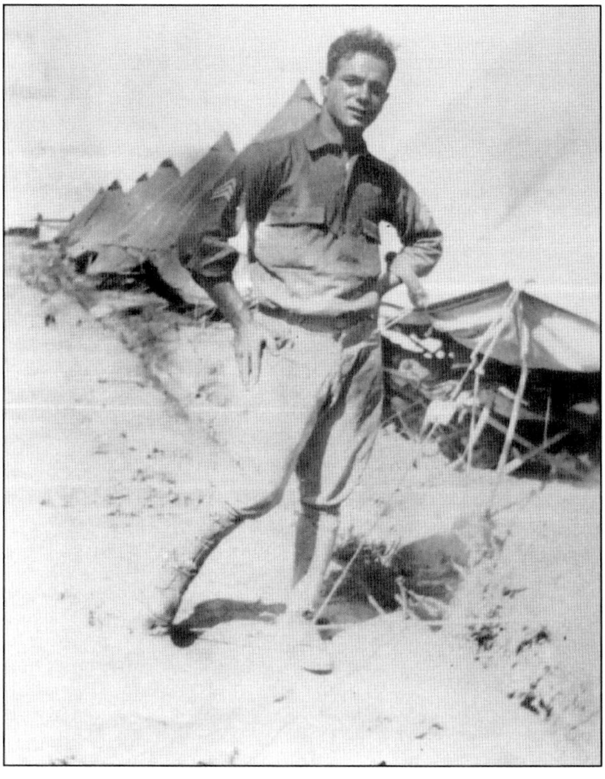

US Army Sergeant Asher Frank, c. 1916. Asher was the son of Julia and Julius Frank, who settled in Miami in 1896. From Tampa, Asher served in the 2nd Florida Regiment, Infantry, a unit of the National Guard. Prior to the American entry into World War I, the 2nd Florida was mobilized for service on the Mexican border of Texas in June 1916. Frank is remembered for starting the Florida Safety Council.

JOSEPH ABRAMOWITZ, HOME GUARD, 1917. Tampa was a bustling city with large shipyards, and during World War I, it became a major shipbuilding center. Jews joined others in enlisting to defend their nation, whether for the Home Guard or on active duty. Abramowitz came from Romania, married Hilda Daniels in Jacksonville, and spent more than 40 years at Met Life in the Tampa office.

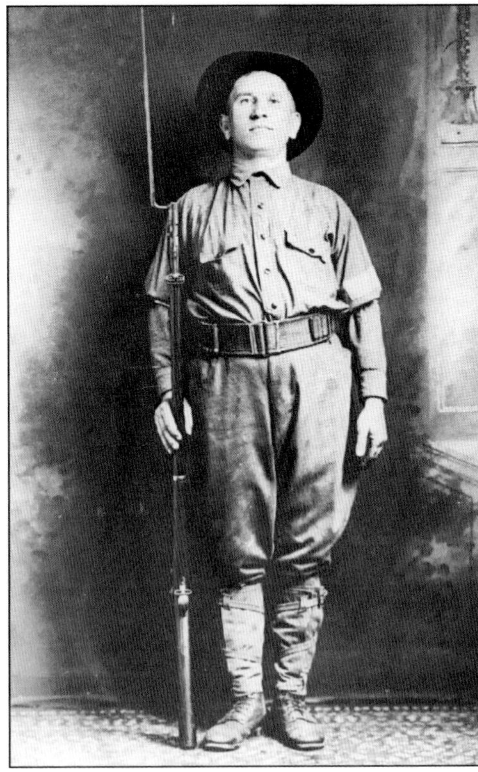

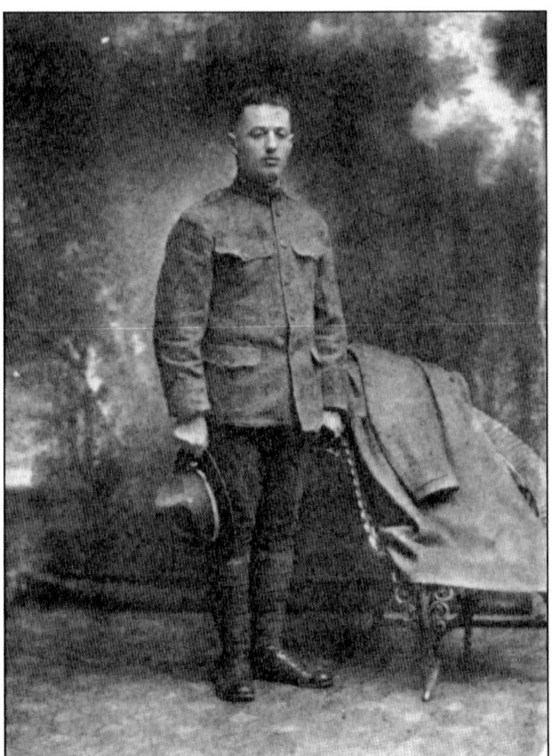

US ARMY PRIVATE JOSEPH WEISSMAN, C. 1917. In 1917, Romanian immigrant Weissman was appointed first cook in Company G, 324th Infantry Regiment, 81st Division, and shipped to France the next year. He participated in the assault on German positions. The troops advanced through heavy fog and German shelling and machine gun fire, then the firing abruptly stopped. The war was over. In 1920, Weissman opened the Red Globe Department Store in Ybor City.

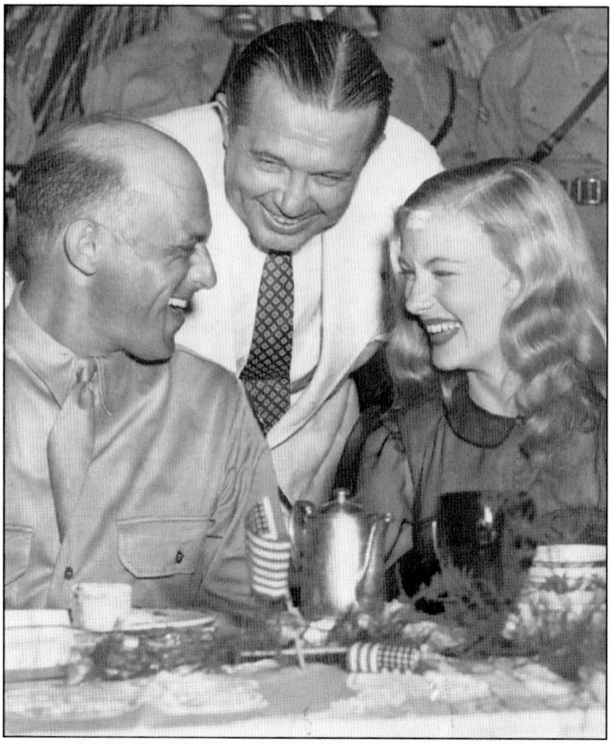

Pvt. Abraham Verkauf, 1942. This photograph appeared on the front page of the *Tampa Daily Times* on September 26, 1942. Verkauf (left), stationed with the medical department at Plant Field, bought $3,000 worth of war bonds to attend an event. He was welcomed by actress Veronica Lake and the president of the Tampa Shipbuilding Co., George Howell, who said, "There's a man in this room who is fighting for what we want but is helping to pay for it."

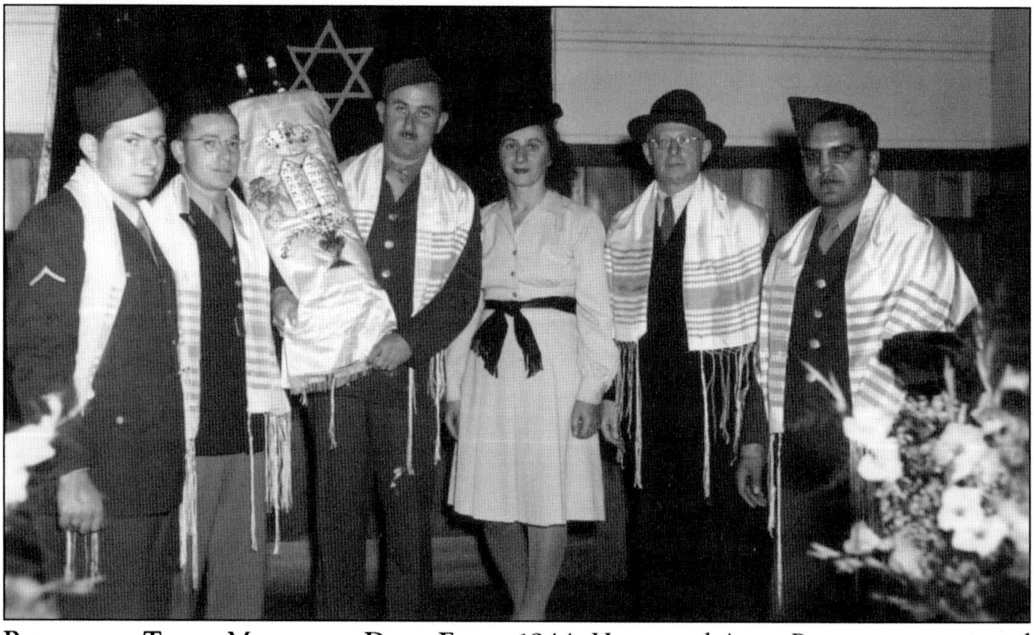

Presenting Torah Mantel at Drew Field, 1944. Henry and Anna Parnes were stationed at Drew Army Air Field in Tampa. When Henry was shipped overseas, Anna remained on the base. The Torah shown here was a gift from Anna Parnes and Lottye Grossman in honor of Pfc. Henry Parnes, Capt. Sidney Grossman, and Sgt. Howard Grossman. Shown here are, from left to right, Pfc. Morris Resnick, Chaplain Pinchos Chazin, Pfc. Henry Parnes, Anna Parnes, Lawrence Lavine, and Pfc. David Negin.

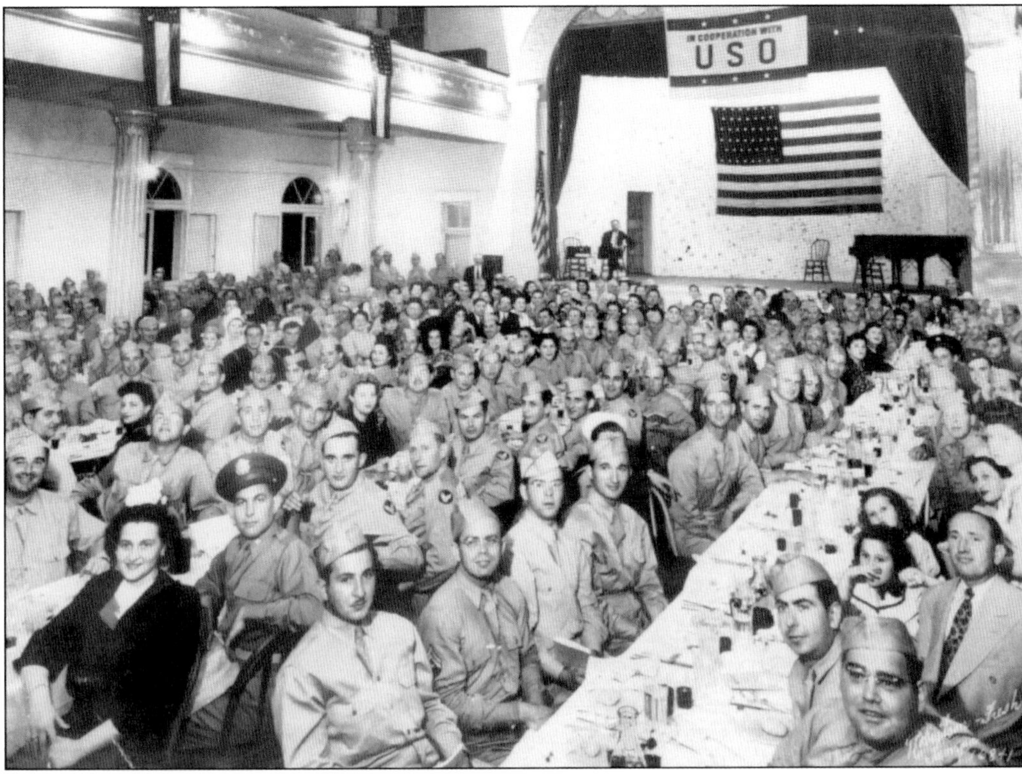

Passover Seders with Soldiers, 1943. Passover is a Jewish holiday in the spring to celebrate the delivery of the Israelites from slavery in Egypt more than 3,300 years ago. A Seder is held in the home with the family to tell the story, eat ritual foods, and sing songs of freedom. To create a family environment for Jewish military personnel and their families serving in Tampa and away from their homes for the holiday, the local Jewish community sponsored traditional Seders at both Congregation Schaarai Zedek and the Hillsboro Hotel in Tampa. This was an occurrence in most communities around the United States during World War II. In Florida, this warm, welcoming hospitality, along with the favorable weather, were factors in decisions by many military personnel to return following the war. Some of the Jews who met at these events later married.

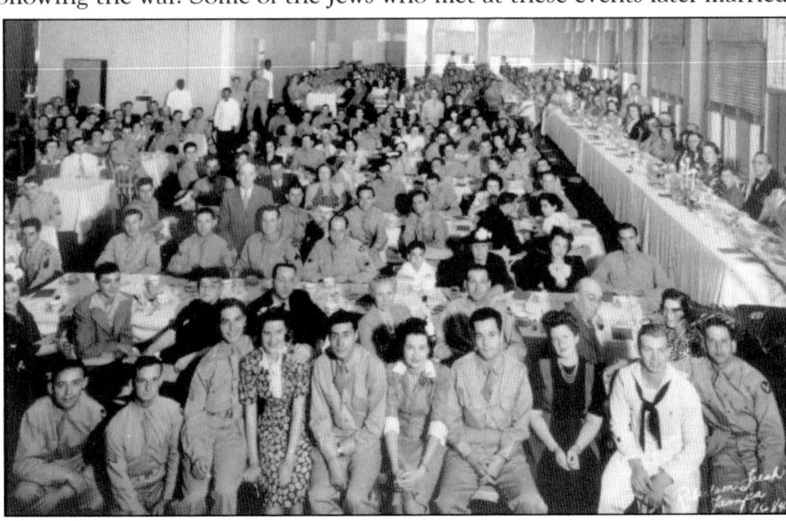

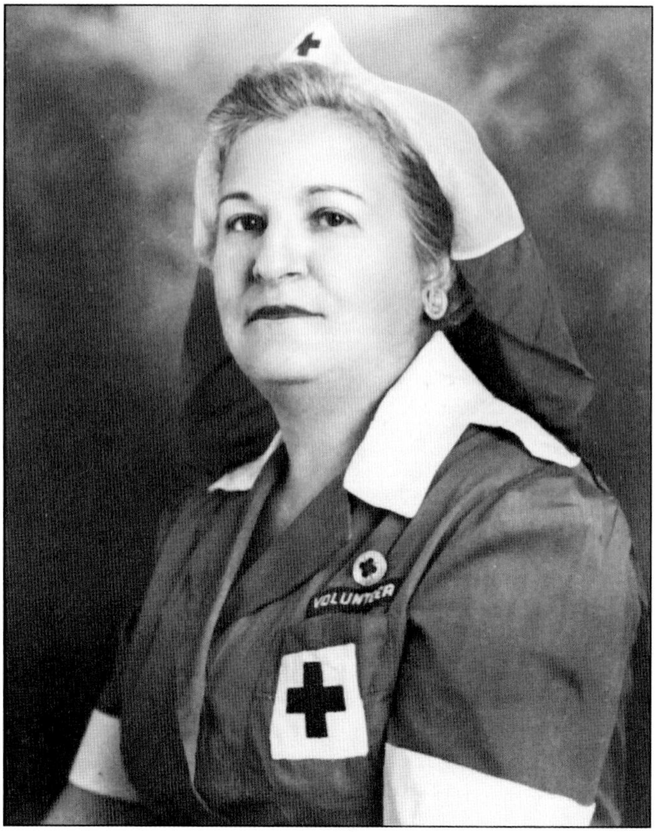

Bess Rosenblatt, Red Cross Volunteer, 1943. Bess was the matriarch of the Rosenblatt family of Tampa. Her three sons, Charles, Frank, and Nathan, served in the armed forces during World War II. On the home front, Bess volunteered to prepare packages and collect blood for American troops overseas and for prisoners of war.

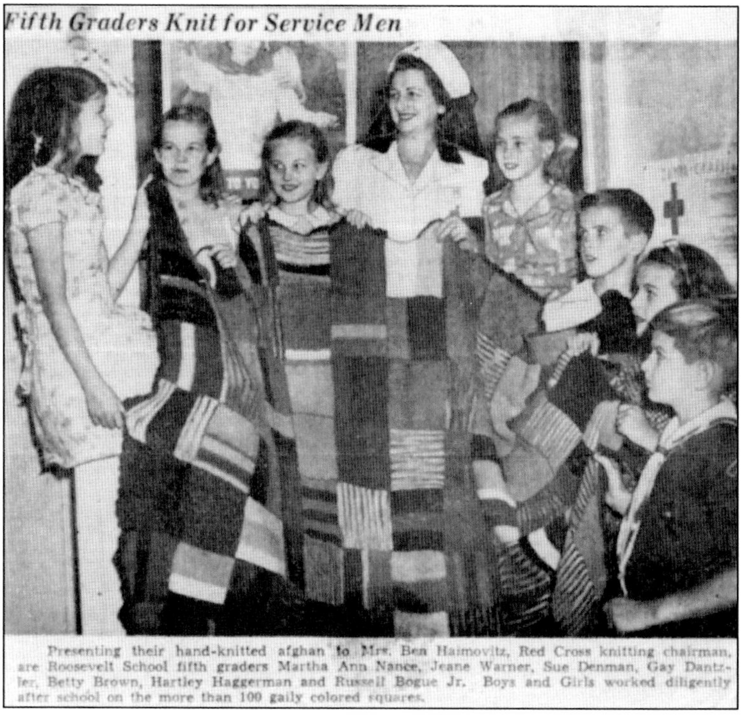

Lillian Haimovitz, Red Cross Knitting Chair, 1942. Fifth graders at Roosevelt School made more than 100 squares to create an afghan for the Red Cross to send to a military hospital. This project was organized by Lillian Solomon Haimovitz, who moved to Tampa when she married Ben. The students shown here with Haimovitz are, from left to right, Martha Ann Nance, Jeane Warner, Sue Denman, Gay Dantzler, Betty Brown, Hartley Haggerman, and Russell Bogue Jr.

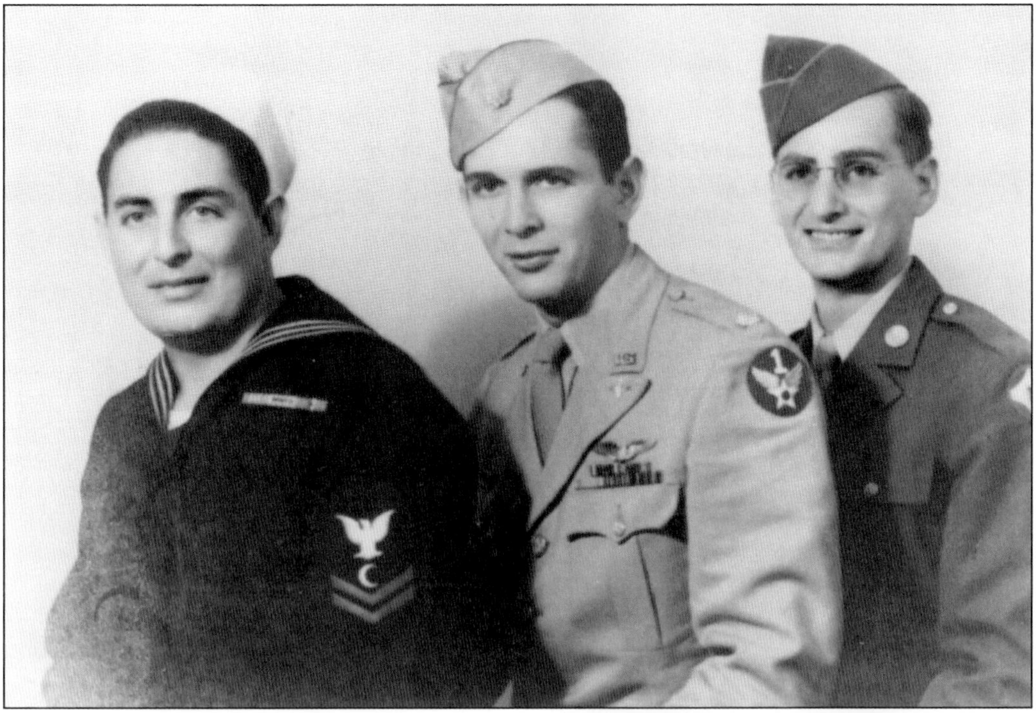

Rosenblatt Brothers, 1946. All three brothers survived the war and made it safely home to Florida. Shown here are PO2 Nathan Rosenblatt Jr., USN (left); Maj. Charles Rosenblatt, USAAF (center); and Cpl. Frank Rosenblatt, USA. In 1943, Frank left the University of Florida to join the Army Medical Corps. He was stationed at Camp Blanding for 14 months before being sent to other bases to research tropical diseases.

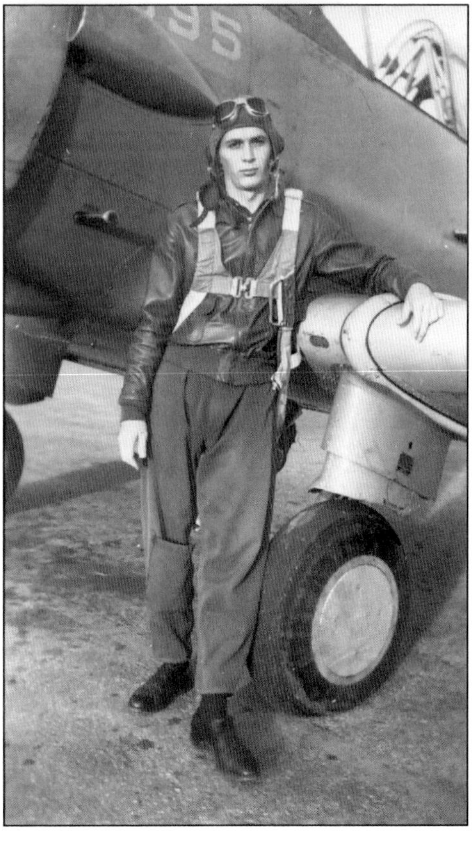

Maj. Charles Rosenblatt, USAAF, c. 1944. Major Rosenblatt is next to his P-47 Thunderbolt fighter aircraft. He flew 102 combat missions during World War II and was twice awarded the Distinguished Flying Cross and four times the Air Medal. He served as a fighter pilot during the Korean War and retired as a colonel after 22 years of service.

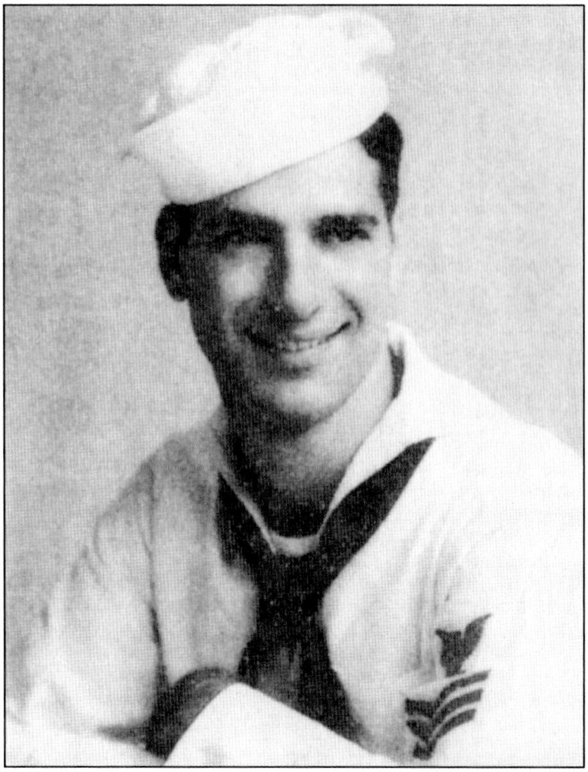

PO1 Sammie Argintar, USN, c. 1943. A Tampa native, Argintar enlisted on December 24, 1941, at age 21. In 1943, he was assigned to the USS *Cates* and then to the USS *Slater*, both in Tampa. After the war, Sammie returned to his father's menswear store in Ybor City, eventually taking over operations.

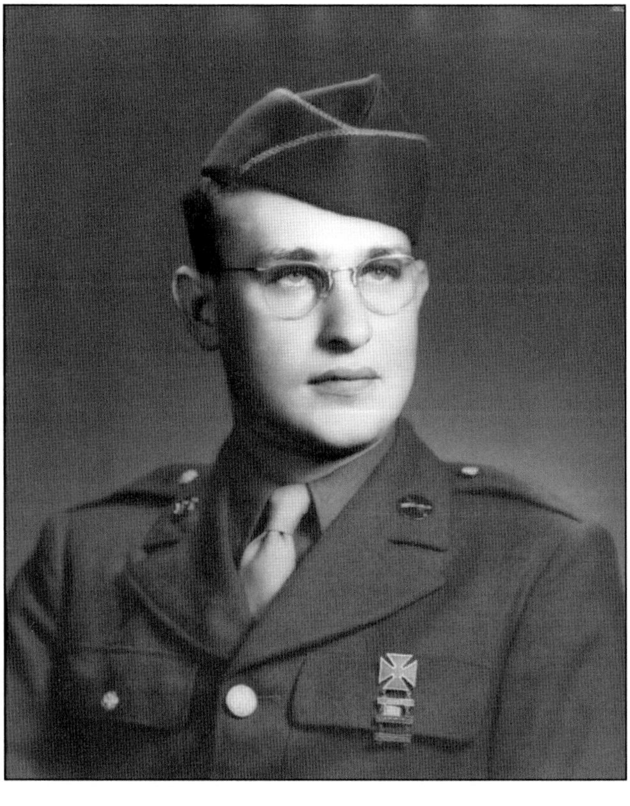

S.Sgt. Harvey Wittner, USA, c. 1945. Tampa native Wittner graduated from Hillsborough High School in 1942 and the Northern Illinois College of Optometry. He served with the 158th Regimental Combat Team, Bushmasters, fighting in the Philippines at Luzon and Leyte and earning the Combat Infantryman's Badge and the Bronze Star.

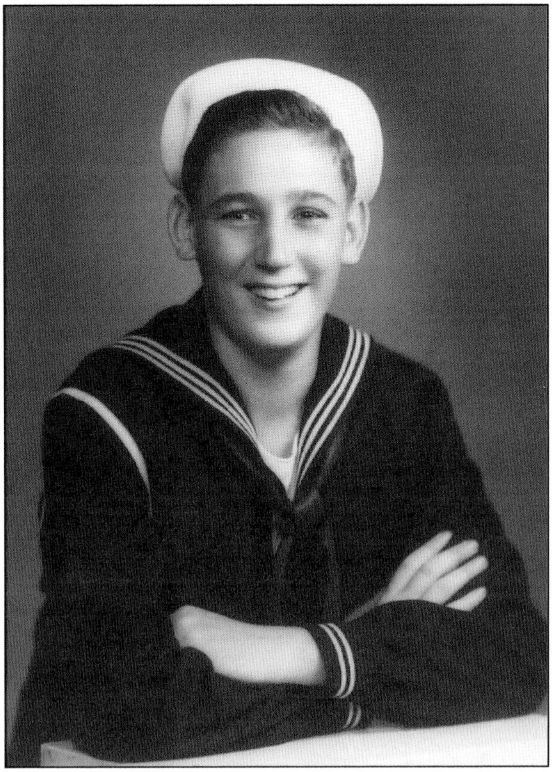

Pharmacist's Mate 3rd Class Sorrell Wolfson, USN, 1946. This Tampa-born son of Mildred and Abe Wolfson enlisted in the Navy, where he was assigned as a corpsman on an aircraft carrier. This spurred his interest in medicine, and after being discharged, he used his GI Bill to attend college and medical school. He opened his practice in Tampa and went on to become a nationally known researcher in pediatric hematology and oncology.

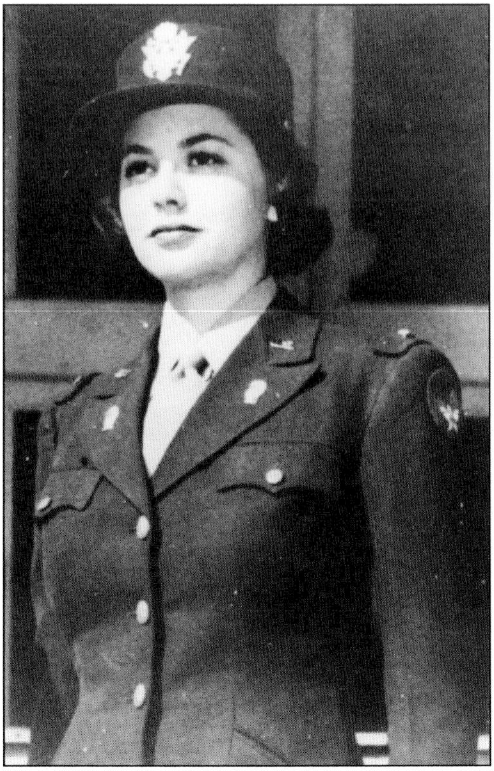

Capt. Nellye Israelson, USA, 1943. A Florida native and one of the first women to enlist in the Women's Army Corps (WAC), Israelson became an officer and, after the war, married another soldier, Herbert Friedman. She served for three years as the Special Services officer at Napier Field in Dothan, Alabama, where she organized recreational social programs. Israelson raised a family in Tampa and is deeply involved in Schaarai Zedek and the community.

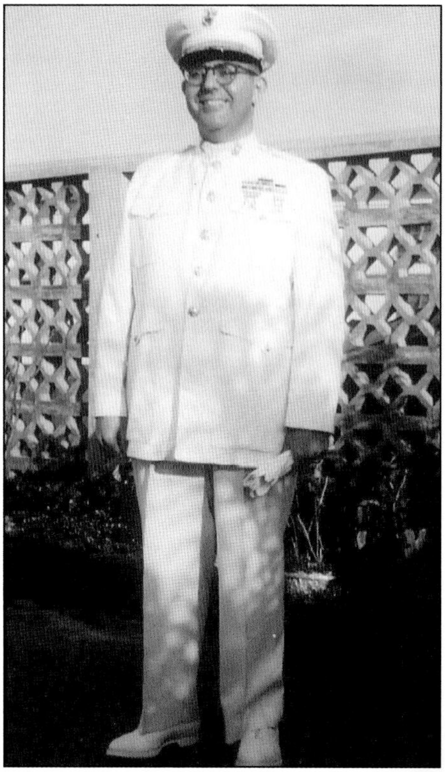

Maj. Morris Jenkins, USMC, c. 1963. Jenkins (1925–2008) was born in Tampa. After graduation from Jefferson High in 1943, he enlisted in the Marine Corps. His 25-year career included service during World War II, the Korean War, and the Vietnam War. When he retired in Tampa, he had been awarded the Good Conduct, World War II Victory, Korean Service, and UN Service for Korea and Korean War Service medals.

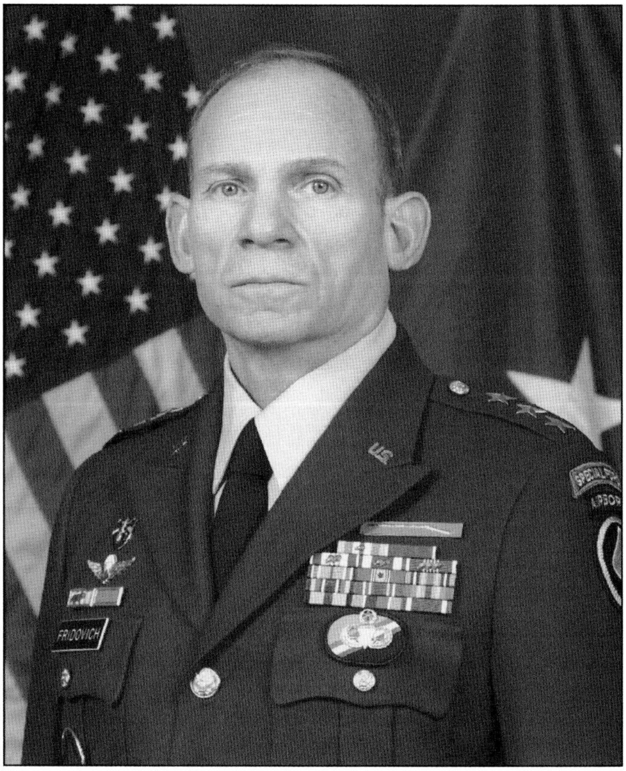

Lt. Gen. David P. Fridovich, USA, 2009. Fridovich retired in 2011 after 37 years in the Army and as the senior Green Beret. The ceremony was held at MacDill Air Force Base, where, from 2007 to 2009, he was director of the Center for Special Operations. He served as commander at every level in the Army and commanded counterterrorism forces throughout the world. In 2012, he joined the Jewish Institute for National Security Affairs as director for defense and strategies.

Seven

In Sports

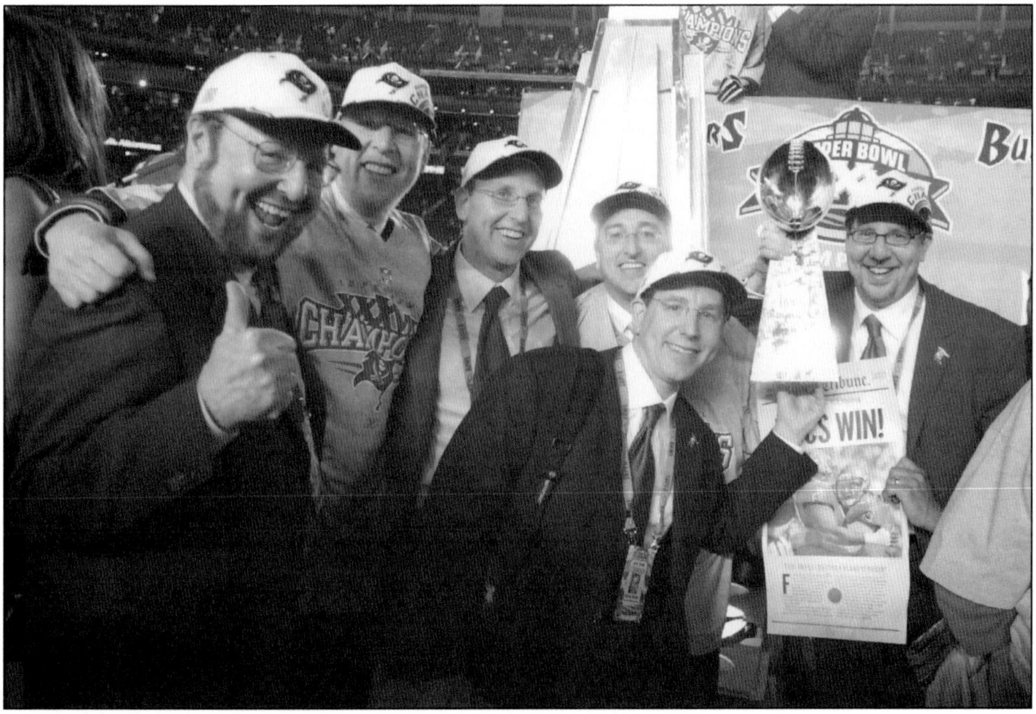

Tampa Bay Buccaneers Owners with Vince Lombardi Super Bowl XXXVII Trophy. Malcolm Glazer, the owner and president of the Tampa Bay Buccaneers, is seen here celebrating the team's victory in Super Bowl XXXVII at Qualcomm Stadium in San Diego, California, on January 26, 2003. Shown here posing with the Vince Lombardi Trophy after the game are, from left to right, Malcolm Glazer, Avie Glazer, cochairman Joel Glazer, cochairman Edward Glazer, and cochairman Bryan Glazer helping hold the trophy. Kevin Glazer is in front. Malcolm Glazer, who has worked since age eight, purchased the Buccaneers in 1995. In 2005, he purchased Manchester United, the world's most popular and valuable sports team. (Courtesy of Tampa Bay Buccaneers.)

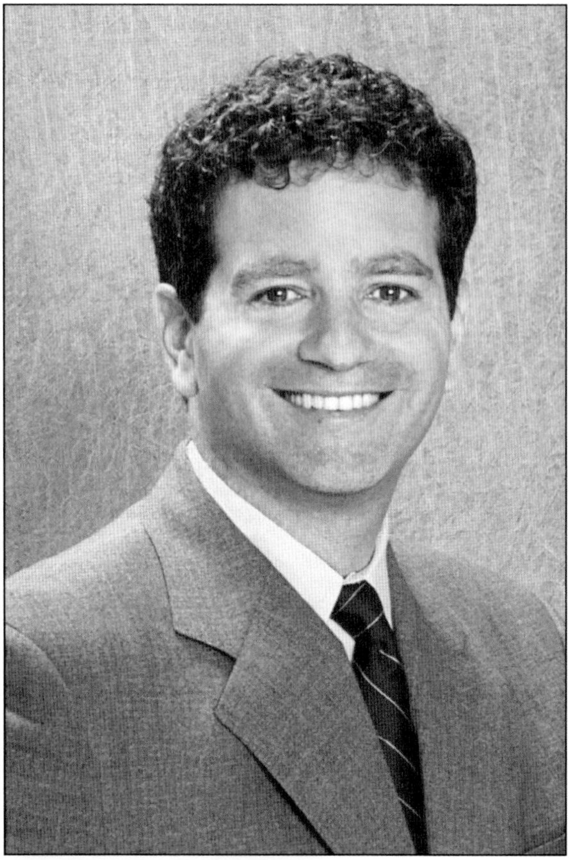

Stuart L. Sternberg, Principal Owner of the Tampa Bay Rays. Sternberg assumed control in 2005 and believes the Rays should play an important role in the Tampa Bay community. In 2006, the team established the Rays Baseball Foundation, which focuses primarily on youth and education programs. Sternberg's passion for baseball developed in childhood. He has played in organized baseball leagues and has especially enjoyed coaching his two sons' Little League teams.

Jeffrey Vinik, Chairman and Governor of the Tampa Bay Lightning. In 2010, Vinik bought Tampa's hockey team. Vinik and his wife, Penny, made an impact in the Tampa community by pledging $10 million to the Lightning Community Heroes program, which honors a local hero and a representative charity with $50,000 at each of the team's 41 home games during the season. Vinik is involved with real estate ventures in downtown Tampa. (Courtesy of Lightning.)

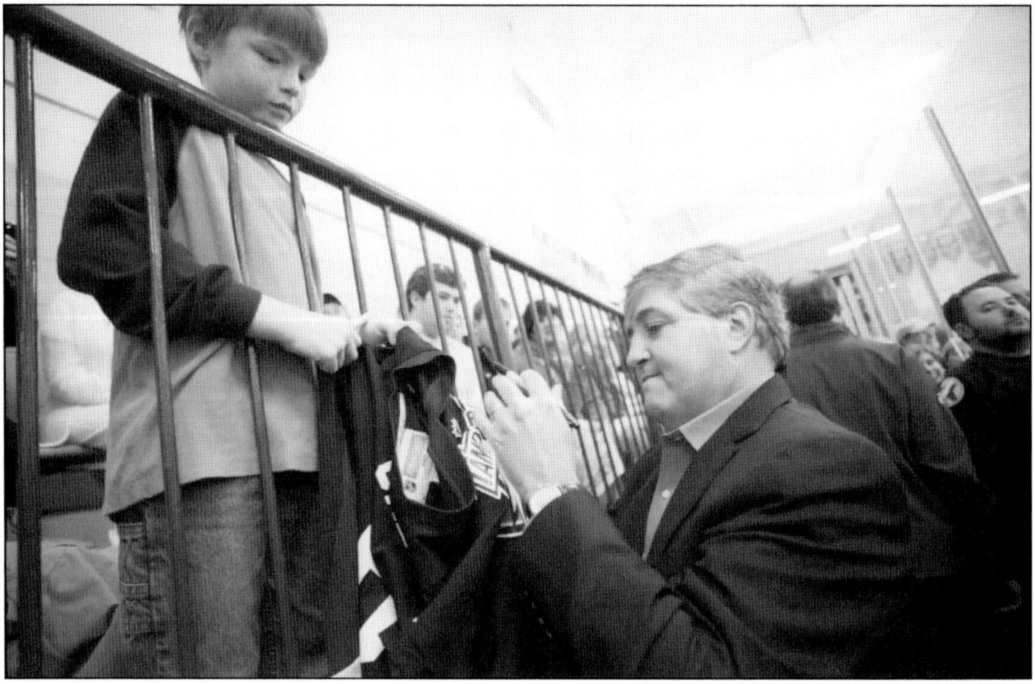

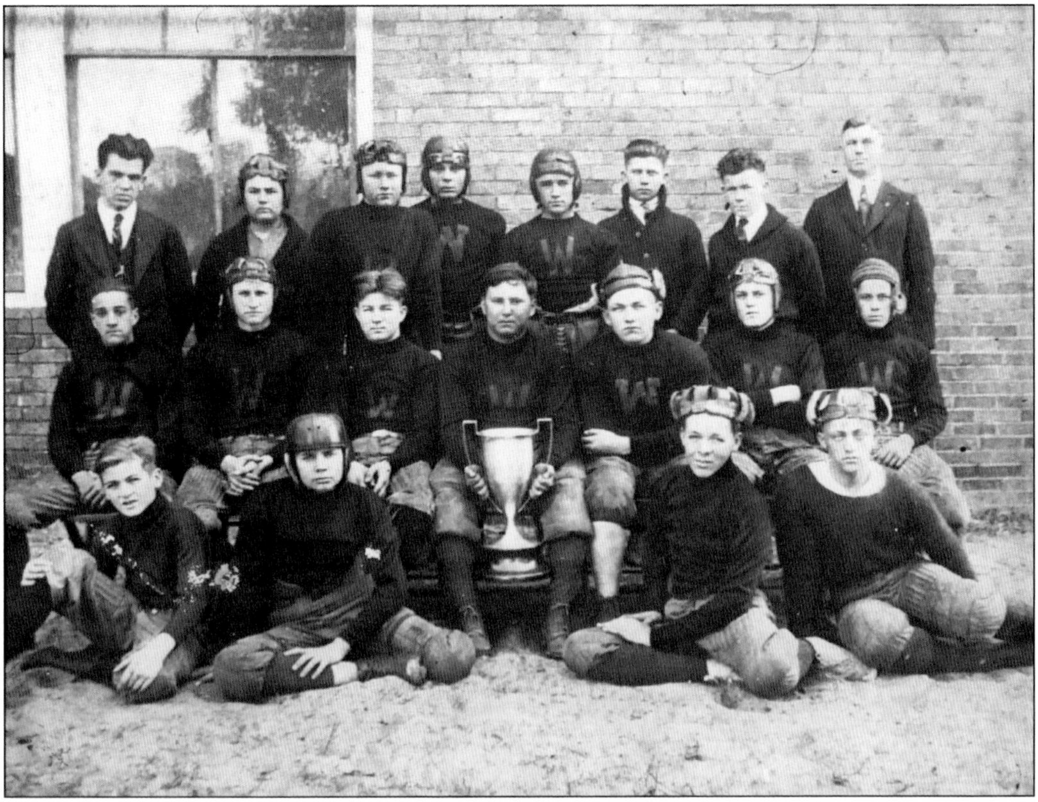

Abe Verkauf, Morty Juster, Junior High Football, 1919. Two Jewish boys played varsity football at George Washington Junior High.

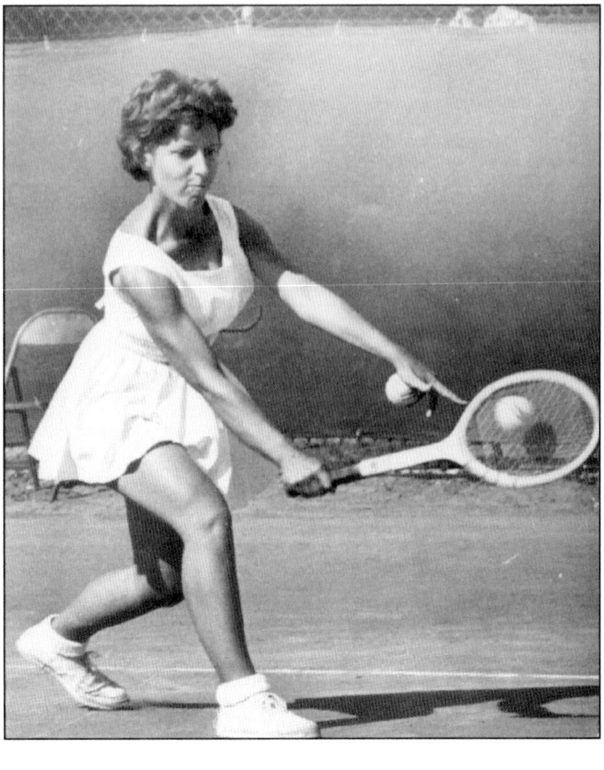

Sandy (Warshaw) Freedman, c. 1960. A Tampan since age two, Freedman was a city, state, and Florida intercollegiate tennis champion. At one time, she was ranked fifth in the nation as an amateur before knee injuries ended her career in college. Freedman was the mayor of Tampa from 1986 to 1995. The Sandra W. Freedman Tennis Complex is a public tennis facility on Davis Islands, named after the former mayor. It is owned and operated by the City of Tampa.

"SALTY" SOL FLEISCHMAN, DEAN OF FLORIDA'S SPORTSCASTERS, 1972. Radio, television, and newspaper personality Fleischman (1910–2000) reigned for 53 years, broadcasting almost every sports event in the Tampa Bay area. His association with fishing and saltwater is where his nickname originated. Larger than life and full of personality, Sol was named Florida's No. 1 Conservationist, and the Tampa City Council renamed the Gandy Boulevard boat ramp in his honor.

GEORGE AND LEONARD LEVY, 1984. Tampa natives George (left) and Leonard Levy are known for their promotion of sports in Tampa. Leonard was instrumental in bringing the Buccaneers to Tampa, and he was vice chair of the Super Bowl Task Force. In 1995, Leonard was Civitan's Outstanding Citizen of the Year. George was named to the Tampa Swimming Hall of Fame, was a member of the Sports Authority from 1978 to 1985, and was a member of the Super Bowl XVIII Task Force. (Courtesy of George Levy.)

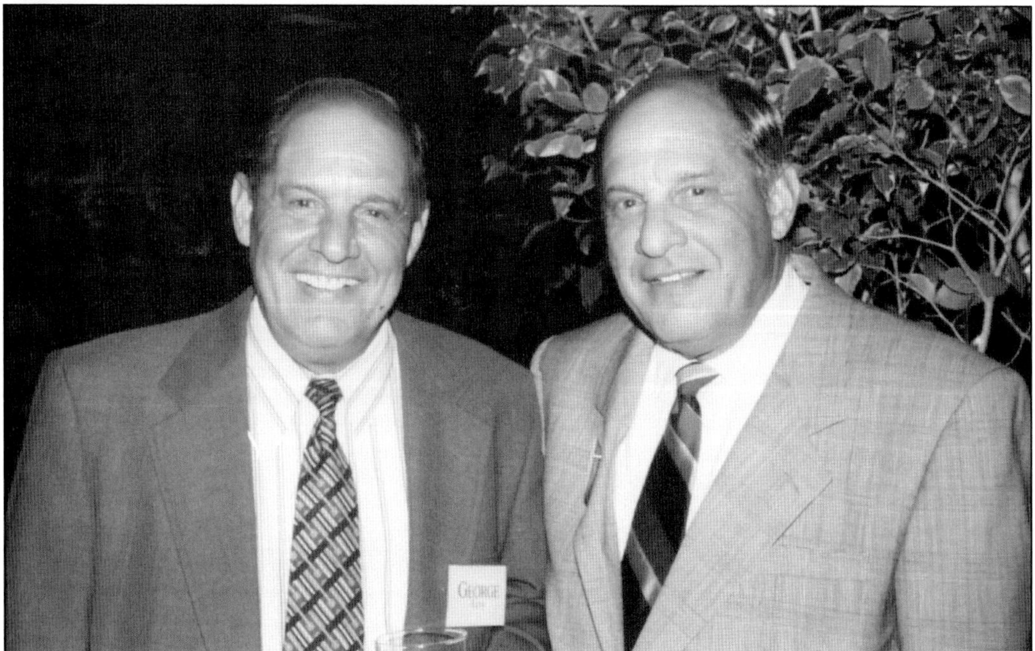

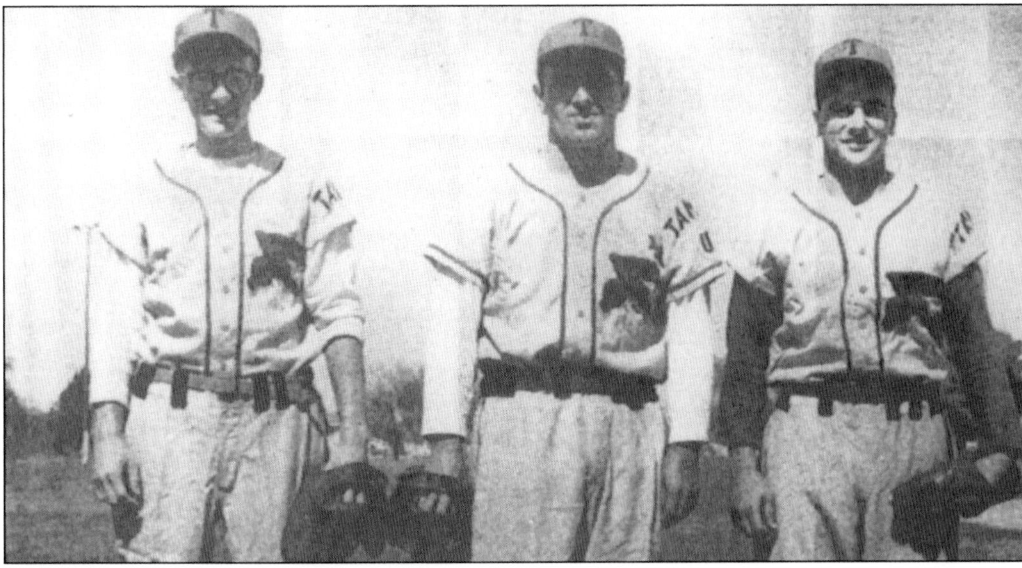

JUDGE RALPH STEINBERG, 1953. In 1949, Steinberg's passion for baseball attracted him to the University of Tampa, with its proximity to the spring training camp of the Cincinnati Reds. Pictured here in the middle, he played as pitcher for UT and the Centro Asturiano Team of Ybor City. After graduation, he played ball in the Army. He was a Tampa lawyer for 18 years and then a judge for 23 years. Gov. Reuben Askew appointed him to the county court in 1977, and in 1981, he was appointed as circuit court judge for the 13th Judicial Court. He retired in 2000 and continues to serve as a senior judge.

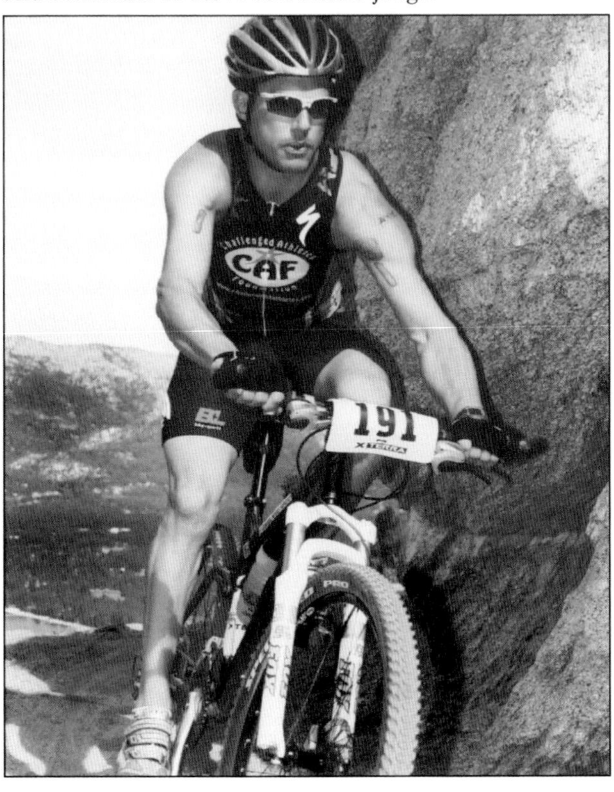

RYAN LEVINSON, NATIONAL LEVEL CYCLIST WITH PHYSICAL DISABILITY, 2006. Levinson was a cyclist in high school in Tampa, winning the Florida State Championships. He planned on turning professional, but was diagnosed with muscular dystrophy. His doctors told him to train for a nonphysical job, but Levinson engaged in a wide range of athletic activities, got back on his bike, and his healthy muscles strengthened. Today, as a competitor and trainer, he inspires others with disabilities.

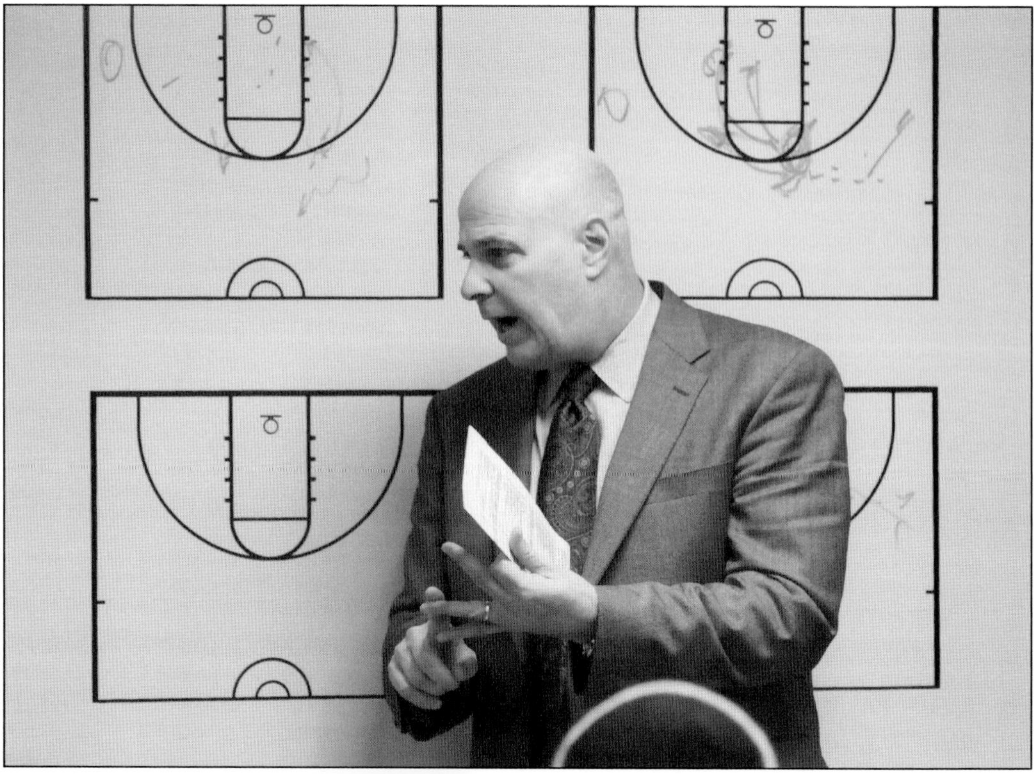

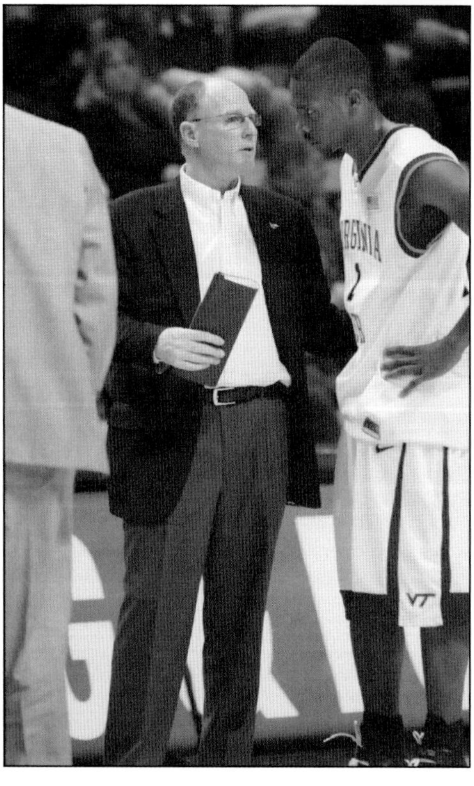

SETH GREENBERG, HEAD BASKETBALL COACH, UNIVERSITY OF SOUTH FLORIDA, 1996–2003. At USF, Greenberg led the Bulls to two National Invitation Tournaments and victories in Conference USA play. He was twice named the Atlantic Coast Conference's Coach of the Year, is often a guest on sports talk shows, and volunteered to coach the USA Men's Basketball team at the 19th Maccabiah Games in Israel in July 2013.

BRAD GREENBERG, BASKETBALL COACH. Brad Greenberg was most recently head coach at Maccabi Haifa. When his brother, Seth, was at USF, Brad was the director of basketball operations. With more than 25 years of successful NBA and NCAA coaching, management, and media experience, Brad went from USF to Virginia Tech as assistant coach (2003–2007) when Seth was appointed head coach there.

Eight

Generation to Generation

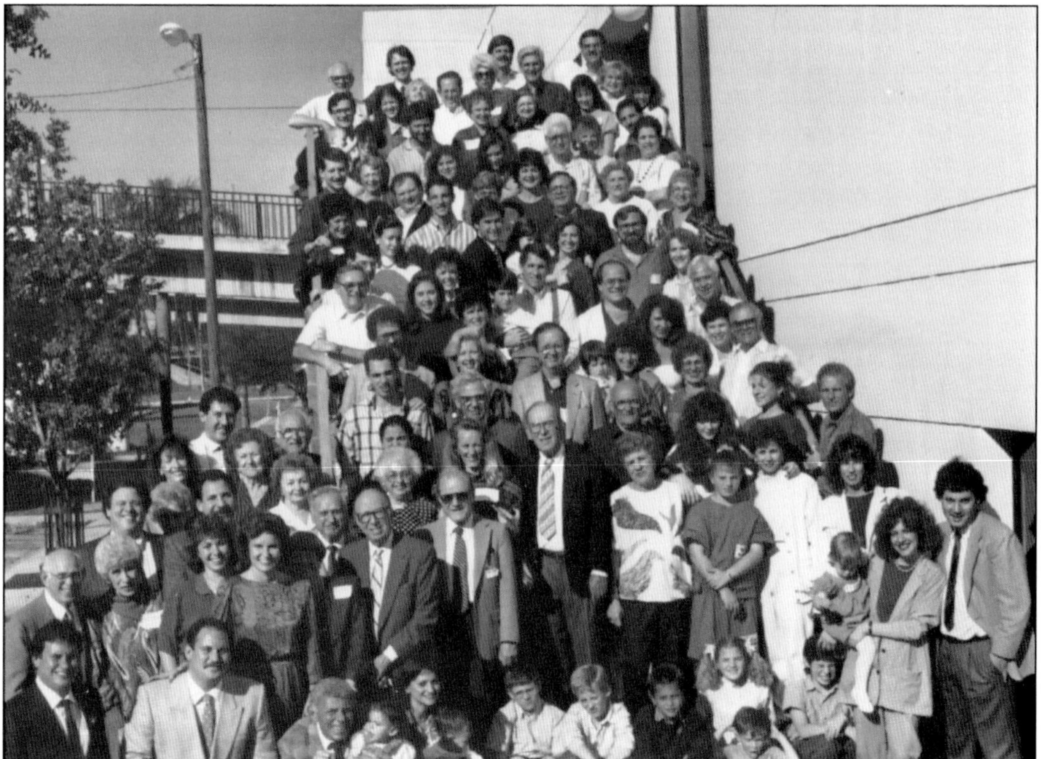

Solomon Family Reunion in Tampa, 1988. This last section of *Jews of Tampa* includes some of the families who have lived in Tampa (or in Florida) for more than 100 years. They demonstrate the strength of the Jewish community and help ensure Jewish continuity into future generations. The Solomons comprise the following families: Haimovitz, Rosenberg, Verkauf, Rippa, Sierkese, Segall, Weber, Kantor, Fyvolent, and Solomon.

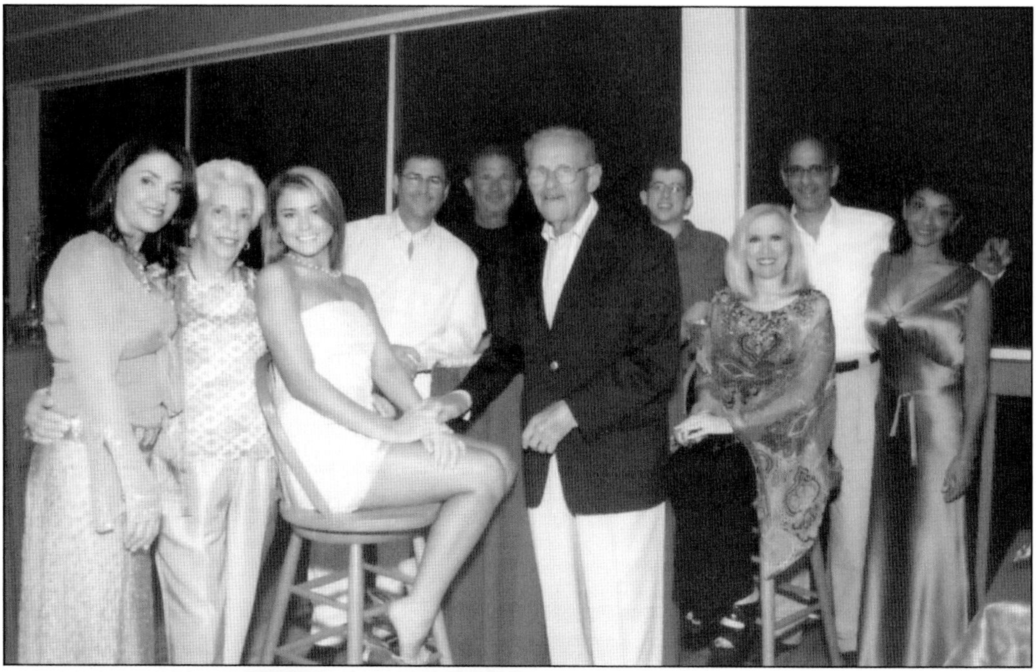

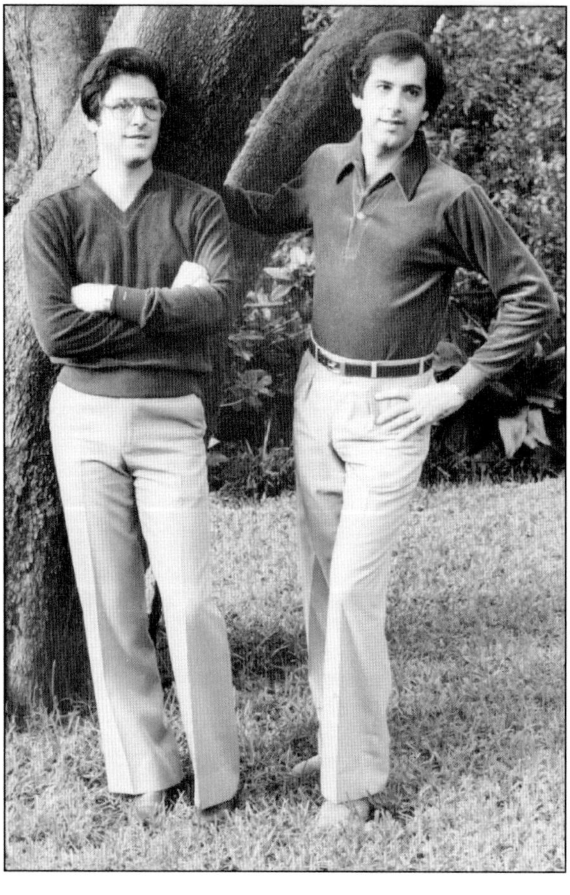

MAAS-SHINE FAMILY, 2005. Austrian immigrant Louis Shine came to Tampa in 1896 and operated The Palace, a small department store with jewelry, appliances, and clothing, in Ybor City, from 1911 to 1958. His son, Mark, married Audrey Maas, daughter of Ernest Maas Sr. Shown here are, from left to right, Charlsie Shine, Audrey Maas Shine, Taylor Shine Jones, Martin Shine, Buck Hicks, Mark Shine, Michael Shine, Susan Shine, Stephen Shine, and Barbara Hicks. (Courtesy of Barbara Shine Hicks.)

MARTIN AND STEPHEN SHINE, KIRBYS MENS WEAR, C. 1977. Martin bought the business from his father, Mark, who started it in 1959. This represents the family's third generation in men's retail, which began with Louis Shine. Their mother, Audrey Maas Shine, continues to work at Kirbys, as does Martin's daughter, Taylor. Martin and Stephen's sister, Barbara Shine Hicks, also works for Kirbys. It is a genuine family business! (Courtesy of Kirbys Mens Wear.)

MAX ARGINTAR'S FAMILY, C. 1926. Max settled in Tampa in 1904, and the family has continuously resided in the area. Shown here are, from left to right, (seated) Lena, Esther, Florence, and Sammie; (standing) Arnold, Max, Annie, and Rachael. (Courtesy of Arnold Argintar.)

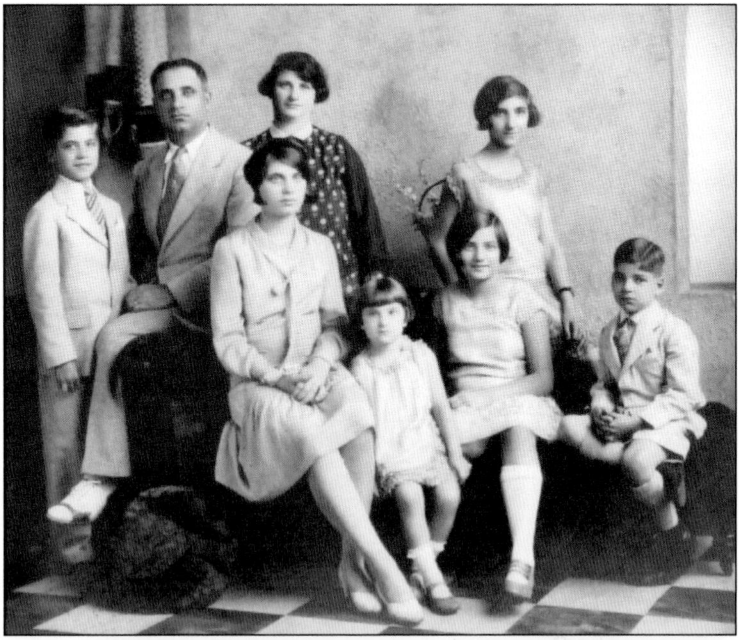

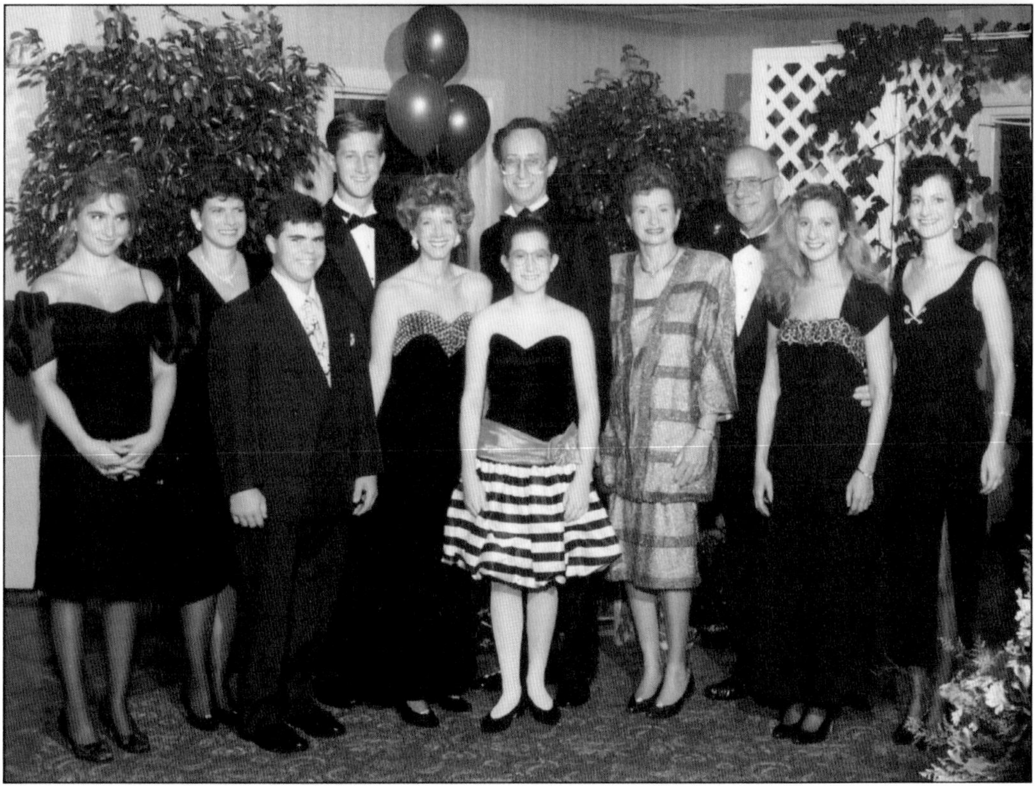

ARNOLD ARGINTAR FAMILY, 1990S. Son of Max Argintar, Arnold proudly shares a family simcha. Shown here are, from left to right, (first row) Kari Neal, Hillary Argintar Conner, J.B. McClellan, Deborah Argintar Rutz, Dori Moss, Ellie Argintar, Arnold Argintar, Patty Tucker, and Abi Tucker; (second row) Randy Moss and Dr. Frank Moss. (Courtesy of Arnold Argintar.)

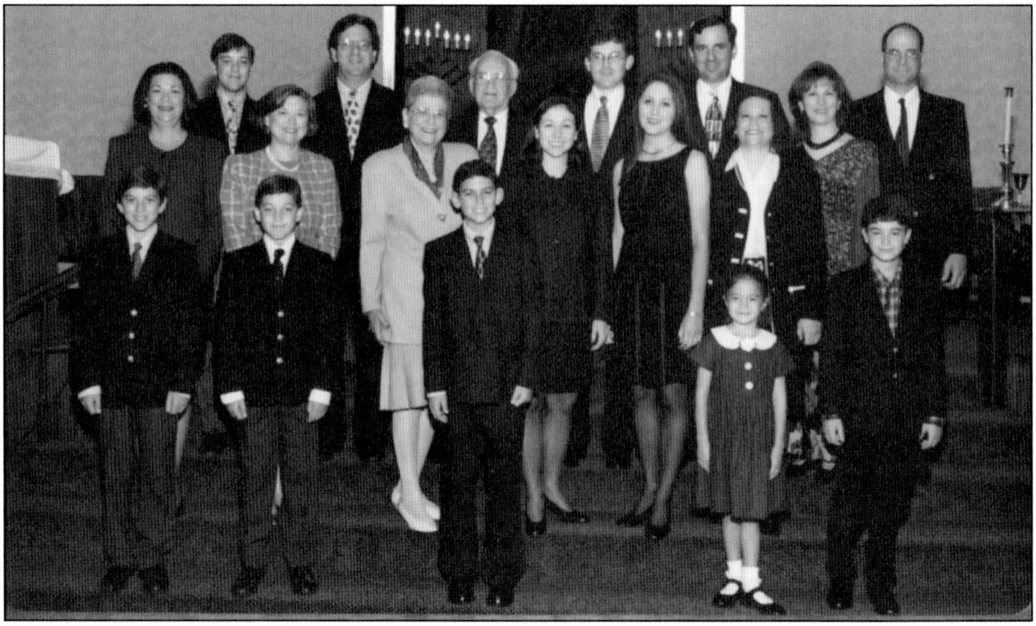

FRIEDMAN-KRAMER FAMILY AT BRUCE KRAMER'S BAR MITZVAH, 1997. Nellye Friedman's maternal grandparents, Julia and Julius Frank, settled in Miami in 1896. Shown here are, from left to right, (first row) Richard and Andrew Friedman, Bruce Kramer, Hannah Friedman, and Marcus Berkowitz; (second row) Frances Williams, Julie Friedman, Nellye Friedman, Becky, Jennifer, and Mary Kramer, and Toni Friedman; (third row) Christopher, Frank, and Herbert Friedman, Bob and Ted Kramer, and Bill Friedman. (Courtesy of Mary Kramer.)

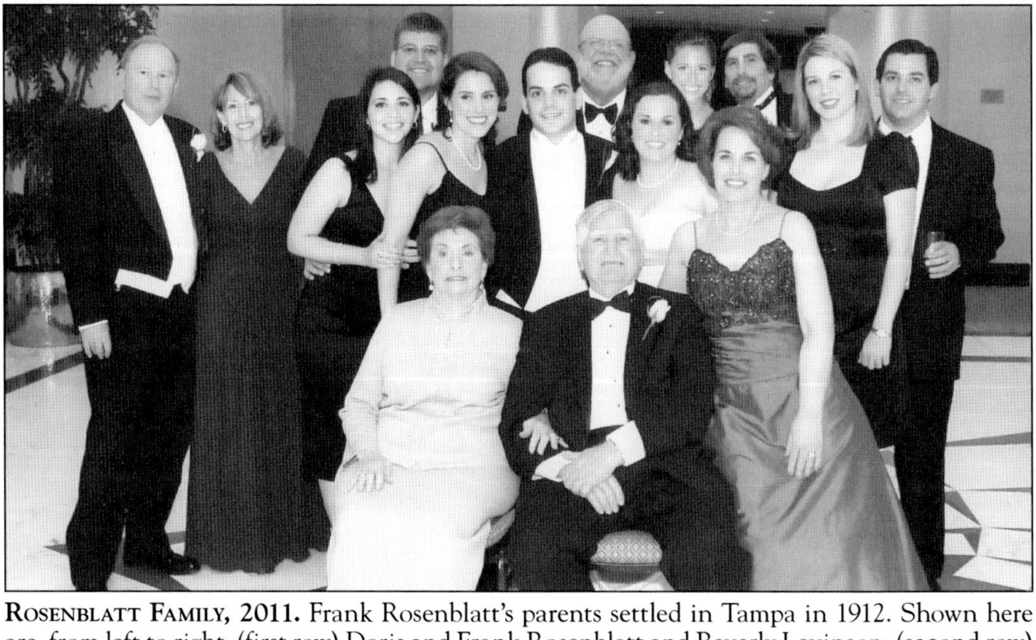

ROSENBLATT FAMILY, 2011. Frank Rosenblatt's parents settled in Tampa in 1912. Shown here are, from left to right, (first row) Doris and Frank Rosenblatt and Beverly Levinson; (second row) Frankie Forer Linsky, Sara Levinson, Jason Kristall, and Andy Levinson Kristall; (third row) Leon Levinson, Nancy Linsky, Ron Linsky, David Linsky, Katie Rosenblatt, Rob Rosenblatt, Stacie Marks Linsky, and Sam Linsky. (Courtesy of Doris Rosenblatt.)

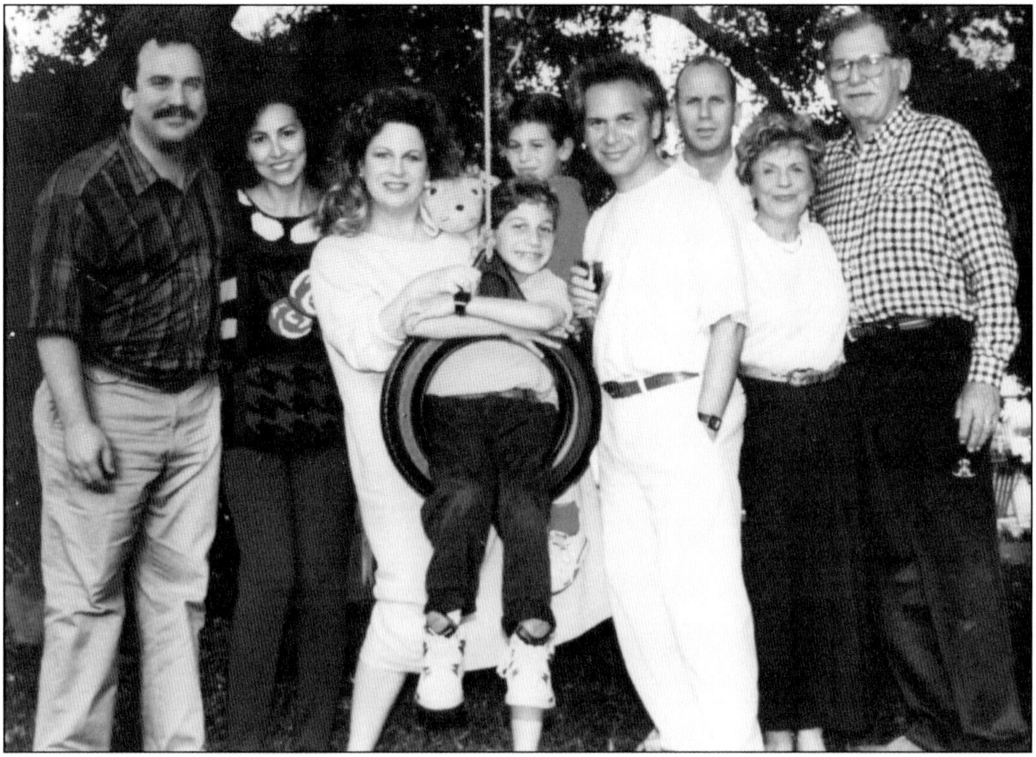

RIPPA-PREISER FAMILY, C. 1990. The Rippa family can be traced to Key West in 1888. Babs Rippa Preiser is a descendant of the Solomon-Rippa families and a granddaughter of Isador and Sarah Rippa. Shown here are, from left to right, Mark and Elsa Rippa, Babs Preiser, Matt Preiser (on tire), Aaron Preiser (behind Matt), Doug Preiser, Gary Rippa, and Arlene and Robert Rippa. Robert, a son of Isador, was a 34-year owner of the Colony Shops of Florida. (Courtesy of Doug Preiser.)

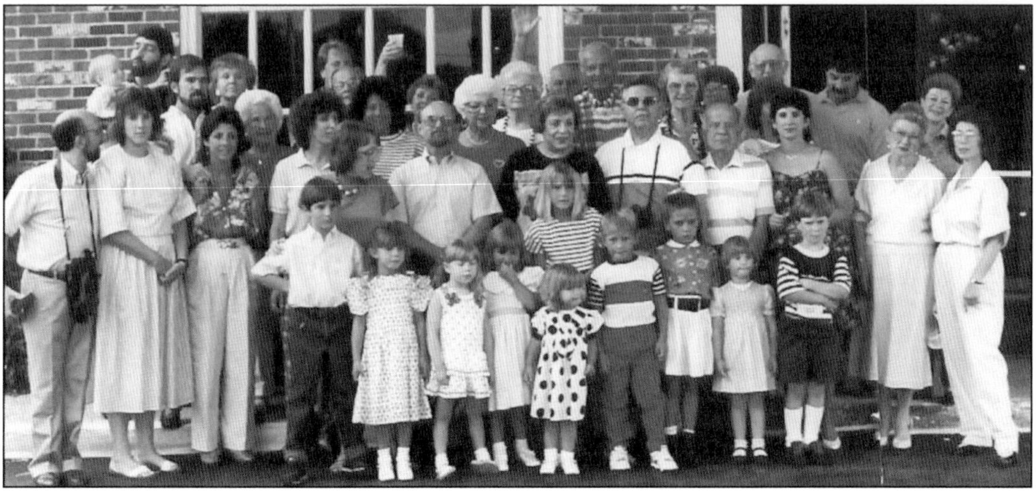

MARKS-MARKOWITZ FAMILY, 1987. Simon Markowitz and his mother, Brana, arrived from Romania around 1908. He changed his name to Marks to get into the Army. Brana ran a Jewish boardinghouse. Roberta Golding was a daughter of Simon and Fannie Marks. This family, which has had reunions for at least 75 years, includes Marks, Markowitz, Golding, Scher, Peckett, Herris, Gettis, Salz, Jenkins, Brenning, and Losner relatives. (Courtesy of Sara Golding Scher.)

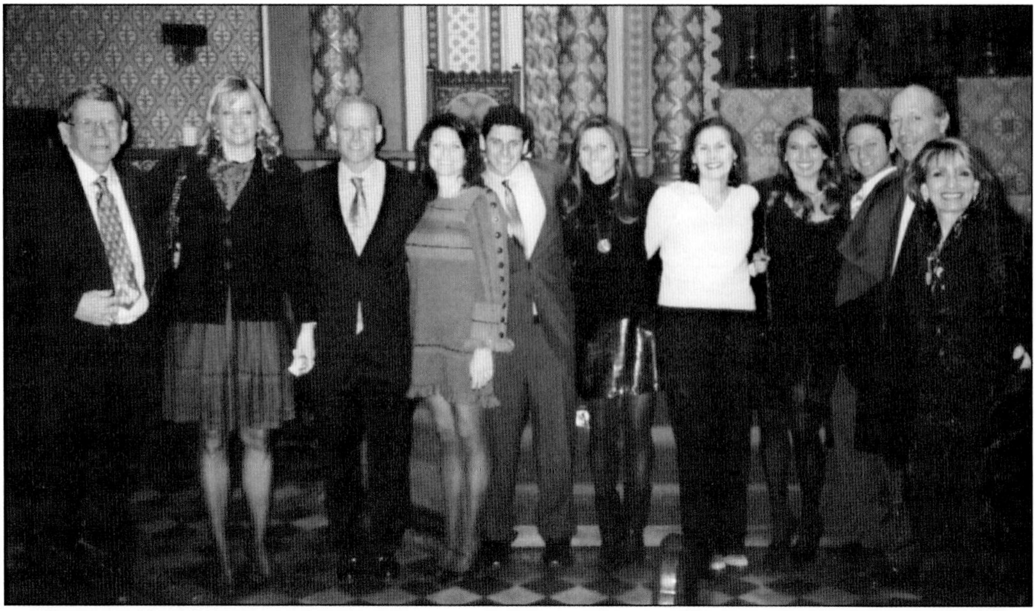

Rosenthal Family, 2011. This family settled in Tampa in 1885. In this photograph are, from left to right, Victor Rosenthal Jr., Lisa Rosenthal, Todd, Debbie, David, and Jaclyn Rosenthal, Barbara Rosenthal, Jennifer, Jason, Mark, and Deborah Rosenthal. (Courtesy of Debbie Rosenthal.)

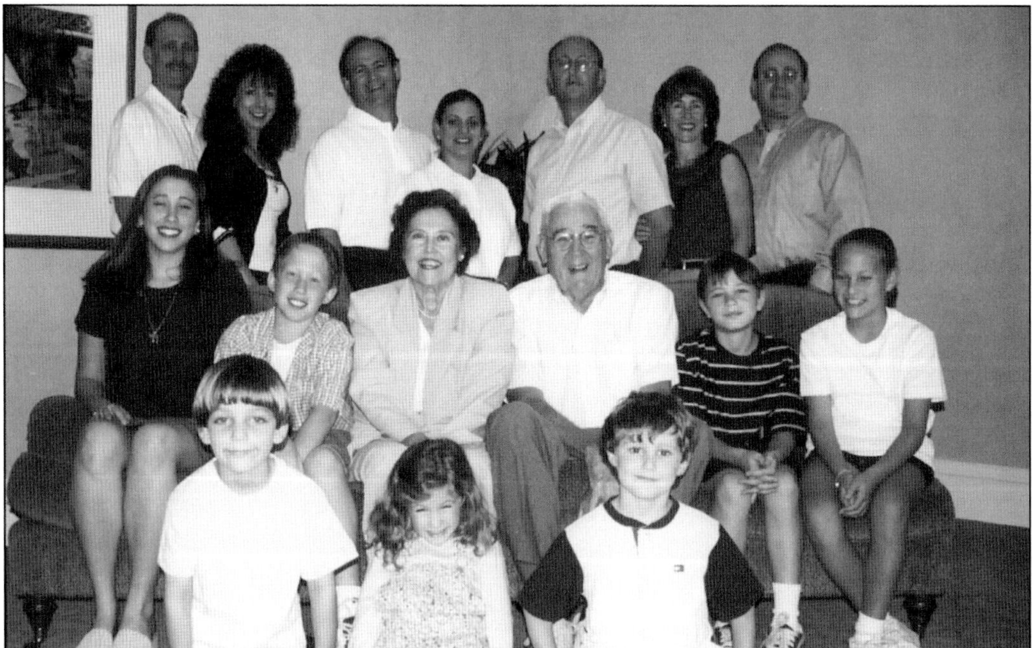

Wolfson Family, c. 2000. These descendants of Adam Wolfson are, from left to right, (first row) Max Wolfson, Monica Wacks, and Adam Wacks; (second row) Alexis Wolfson, Andrew Wolfson, Jacqueline Falis Wolfson, Dr. Sorrell L. Wolfson, Cameron Stempel, and Rachel Wolfson; (third row) Dr. Aaron H. Wolfson, Adrienne Mates Wolfson, Mark J. Wolfson, Myra Schwartz Wolfson, Dr. Israel L. Wacks, Sharon Wolfson Wacks, and Dr. David Wolfson. (Courtesy of Mark Wolfson.)

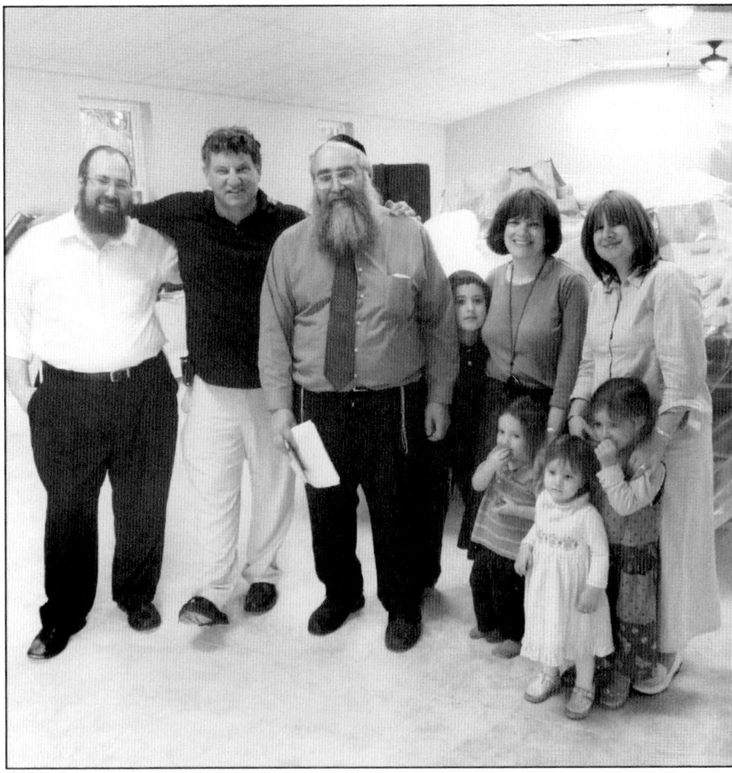

THE NORMAN JEWISH LIBRARY OF TAMPA BAY OPENS, APRIL 18, 2012. The library was built in 2010 near the USF campus and houses more than 2,500 titles of Jewish works, including studies in Torah, Talmud, and Kabbalah. Activities include classes, lectures, Jewish community events, religious services, and celebrations such as challah baking and weddings. The library was constructed with funds from Dr. Robert Norman (second from left), and has been organized by the Rivkin family (pictured) and others.

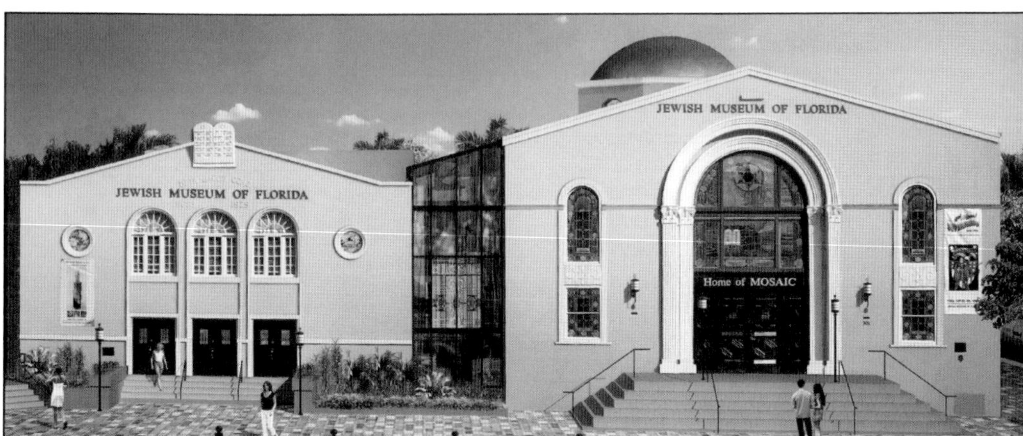

JEWISH MUSEUM OF FLORIDA—FLORIDA INTERNATIONAL UNIVERSITY (JMOF-FIU), MIAMI BEACH. Opened in 1995 and housed in two historic former synagogues, the Jewish Museum of Florida collects, preserves, and interprets the history of Jewish life in Florida since 1763, when Jews were first allowed to settle. The collections, core and changing exhibits, and education and cultural programs present stories that relate achievements trumping discrimination. The memories of how Jews contributed to the development of the Sunshine State while maintaining their traditions are presented in the context of American and world Jewish history and as an example of the ethnic acculturation process of one immigrant group.

Discover Thousands of Local History Books Featuring Millions of Vintage Images

Arcadia Publishing, the leading local history publisher in the United States, is committed to making history accessible and meaningful through publishing books that celebrate and preserve the heritage of America's people and places.

Find more books like this at
www.arcadiapublishing.com

Search for your hometown history, your old stomping grounds, and even your favorite sports team.

Consistent with our mission to preserve history on a local level, this book was printed in South Carolina on American-made paper and manufactured entirely in the United States. Products carrying the accredited Forest Stewardship Council (FSC) label are printed on 100 percent FSC-certified paper.

MADE IN THE USA